你不可不知道的
英语学习背景知识

ESSENTIAL BACKGROUND FOR
ENGLISH LEARNERS

对语言的不解与误解，往往源自背景文化知识的欠缺

【英汉对照】

英国历史
重大事件及著名人物

Major Events and Famous People in the
History of the United Kingdom

郝澎◎编著

南海出版公司

2016·海口

图书在版编目（CIP）数据

英国历史重大事件及著名人物／郝澎编著. —海口：南
海出版公司，2007.2（2016.1重印）
（你不可不知道的英语学习背景知识）
ISBN 978-7-5442-3592-1

Ⅰ.英… Ⅱ.郝… Ⅲ.英国－历史－大事记－
汉、英②名人－生平事迹－英国－汉、英
Ⅳ.K561.05 ② K835.61

中国版本图书馆 CIP 数据核字(2006)第 138854 号

声　明

未经同意，不得转载

YINGGUO LISHI ZHONGDA SHIJIAN JI ZHUMING RENWU

英 国 历 史 重 大 事 件 及 著 名 人 物

编　　著　郝　澎
责任编辑　张建军
装帧设计　动力图文
出版发行　南海出版公司　　　　　　　　　电话(0898)66568511
社　　址　海南省海口市海秀中路 51 号星华大厦五楼　　邮编 570206
电子信箱　nanhaicbgs@yahoo.com.cn
经　　销　新华书店
印　　刷　北京爱思济印刷有限责任公司
开　　本　787×1092毫米　1/16
印　　张　18.375
字　　数　300千字
版　　次　2007年2月第1版　　　2016年1月第3次印刷
书　　号　ISBN 978-7-5442-3592-1
定　　价　33.00元

前　言
PREFACE

在某些人看来，语言仅仅是工具，学习英语，就是掌握其语音、语法和词汇。这些东西掌握了，英语也就学好了。这是对于学习外语的一种颇为流行的错误看法。学者们早已指出，语言不仅是交流的工具，而且是文化的载体。语言从整体上反映一个民族的文化，而该民族的文化又无时无刻地对语言的发展变化起着制约作用。语言与文化二者的关系是你中有我，我中有你，相互渗透、互为因果、互相制约、互相推动。其实，即使是英语的一个单词、一个短语，更不必说一条成语，都可能负载着有关讲英语民族的大量的文化信息。读书时只把单词按字面意义串起来，不考察其文化背景，往往会发生误解。许多人学习英语多年，一接触稍有难度的文章，即使并无词汇或语法方面的障碍，理解往往流于肤浅，不能体味其言外之意或微言大义。其原因无非是背景知识的欠缺。甚至那些貌似武断的语法规则，也可能与文化相关，因为它们往往反映了讲英语民族的独特思维方式。与文化联系更密切的是语用。使用英语时最重要、难度最大的不是正确，而是得体。在特定的时间、特定的地点、对特定的人讲特定的话，这就是得体。得体的背后，有一套文化规则在起作用。人们在进行跨文化交流时产生的隔阂、障碍、误解乃至交流的失败，其根源多在文化差异。所以在学习英语时，有必要系统学习英美民族的历史沿革、政治制度、宗教信仰、价值体系、思维方式、神话寓言、文学艺术、风俗习惯等文化知识。

　　为了使英语学习者在较短时间内全面了解英美文化，我们编写了这套"你不可不知道的英语学习背景知识"丛书。目前该丛书已经出版了五本。《英美民间故事与民俗》介绍脍炙人口的英美民间故事、传说、迷信、动物和植物的象征、社交礼节、身体语言、婚俗及节假日等常识。《古希腊罗马神话与西方民间传说》重点介绍古希腊罗马神话。古希腊罗马神话是西方人文精神的摇篮，现代西方文明的根基之一，西方文学、艺术和音乐的题材宝库，也是英语成语的重要来源之一。现代西方文明的另一根基是基督教。基督教早已渗透到西方文化的各个方面，是西方文学、艺术和音乐的另一重大题材库。不了解基督教，了解英美文化就无从谈起。而《圣经》又是基督教的经典，基督教文化的支柱，英语成语的最大来源。《基督教与圣经》提供了这方面的基本知识。任何一个民族的文化现状，都是其历史发展的结果。英美人目前的政治制度、思想观念、价值体系乃至民族特性，无不可从其历史中找出答案。《英国历史重大事件及著名人物》和《美国历史重大事件及著名人物》是两国历史的概述。

　　编写英文部分时，我们的原则是力求语言简明平实，通俗易懂，词汇量限制在 3000 常用词范围内，使高中生中英语较佳者、普通大学生和广大英语爱好者不必借助字典就可以读懂大部分内容；英语教师在教授英美文化时，只需将书中文字略加改动，便可直接用于教学。为便于学习，尤其是为了使读者了解专有名词所对应的中文，我们还提供了译文。此外，为使丛书更加活泼有趣，我们插入了不少"题外话"，介绍更多相关的语言和文化知识，开阔读者的视野，启发进一步的思考。

　　由于丛书涉及领域较广，编者水平有限，疏漏在所难免，望专家和广大读者不吝赐教。

编 者

2007 年 1 月

目　录
CONTENTS

Contents

目　录

Chapter Four

The Early Plantagenets　早期金雀花王朝

Chapter Five

The 13th Century　十三世纪

Chapter Six

The 14th Century　十四世纪

Contents
目　录

Chapter Seven

Lancaster and York　兰开斯特和约克王朝

Chapter Eight

England Under the Tudors　都铎王朝时期的英格兰

Chapter Nine

The Early Stuarts and the Commonwealth
早期斯图亚特王朝与共和国

Contents

目 录

Chapter Ten

The Later Stuarts　晚期斯图亚特王朝

Chapter Eleven

The 18th Century (1714-1815)　十八世纪（1714-1815）

Chapter Twelve

The 19th Century (1815-1914)　十九世纪（1815-1914）

Chapter Thirteen

From 1914 to the Present　从1914年至今

Appendix　English and British Monarchs Since William I

留 言 板

　　多年以来，本公司出版的英语图书受到全国读者的欢迎，我们非常感谢读者多年的支持与厚爱。

　　我们将陆续推出"趣味故事乐园"、"娱乐英语"、"你不可不知道的英语学习背景知识"、"有问必答"等系列丛书。如果您有任何意见或建议，都可以来信告诉我们。如果您有英语方面的好书稿，也可以跟我们联系。如果您能为我们提供高质量英语图书稿件的线索，本公司将提供奖励。

　　欢迎赐稿。

　　给自己一个机会，给读者一个惊喜。

✳ **联 系 人**：张建军
✳ **电　　话**：010-88596048
✳ **来信请寄**：北京市海淀区世纪城远大园 4-12-1806 室
✳ **电子信箱**：jianjunzhang1806@yahoo.com.cn
✳ **邮　　编**：100097

CHAPTER ONE
Ancient Britain
古 代 不 列 颠

1. Britain Before the Roman Conquest

罗马征服前的不列颠

Scholars do not know when the first people arrived in what is now Britain. But they do know that there were people living on the British Isles about 10,000 years ago. Scientists believe that the sea was lower at that time, and what is now the island of Great Britain was part of the European mainland.

These people of the British Isles built large monuments with stones. Scholars believe they built the monuments for religious purposes or as astronomical calendar. The most famous among the monuments, called Stonehenge, was built more than 3,000 years ago, and now still stands near Salisbury. This huge monument tells us that these people were quite intelligent and skilful, and they knew how to organize themselves to do great work together.

人类究竟是在何时迁移到不列颠的，史学家们也不甚了了。但他们可以确定，在大约一万年前已有人在不列颠群岛居住。科学家认为，当时海平面很低，现在的大不列颠岛曾是欧洲大陆的一部分。

不列颠群岛的居民曾用石块垒起巨大的建筑物。学者们认为这些建筑用于祭祀，或是观测天象以确定时令。这类建筑中最著名的一座，称为巨石圆阵，建于3000多年前，现在仍矗立于索尔兹伯里。这一巨大建筑告诉我们，当时的不列颠人很聪明，而且技艺高超，懂得如何组织起来协力完成一项巨大的工程。

Then about 700 BC, the Celts came across the channel to the British Isles. The Celts were a great people who lived in much of western and central Europe at the time. They defeated the natives of the islands and made them members of their tribes. The Celts worshiped nature gods through priests called Druids. They used iron and knew how to make it.

The Celts also made woolen cloth, which they dyed bright colors. Their language, Celtic, was the earliest known language in what is now Britain. A form of Celtic called Brythonic was spoken throughout the island of Great Britain.

大约在公元 700 年前，克尔特人渡过海峡来到不列颠群岛。克尔特人是个大民族，人口遍及西欧和中欧大部分地区。他们打败了不列颠群岛的土著，同化了他们。克尔特人崇拜自然界的神祇，通过被称为德鲁伊特的祭司与神沟通。他们使用铁器，并掌握了冶铁技术。

克尔特人还会用毛纺成粗呢，染上鲜艳的颜色。他们的语言克尔特语是已知的不列颠最早的语言。一种叫做布立吞语的克尔特方言是大不列颠的通用语。

德鲁伊特在巨石圆阵祭神

巨石圆阵

🔊 题 外 话

- 谈起英国，我们首先需要搞清与这个国家有关的几个英文词。这个国家的正式名称为 The U-nited Kingdom of Great Britain and Northern Ireland（大不列颠及北爱尔兰联合王国），亦可简称为 United Kingdom 或 UK 或 Britain（联合王国或大不列颠）。Great Britain 一词曾经也用以指整个国家，但现在已很少这样使用，而用做地理概念，指不列颠群岛中的大不列颠岛，即不包括北爱尔兰的那部分英国的领土。England 一词不应用以指大不列颠，English 也不应用以指大不列颠的居民，因为英格兰不过是大不列颠的一部分。大不列颠的英格兰人、苏格兰人和威尔士人可统称 British，虽然若细细区分，英格兰人应称为 English，苏格兰人应称为 Scottish，威尔士人应称为 Welsh。严格地说，用 England 和 English 指英国整个国家和人民并不合适，但事实上很多人就是这样用，明明写的是整个联合王国的历史，书名却往往是 History of England；文学史著作里尽管包括了爱尔兰和苏格兰的作家，书名却常常是 History of English Literature。爱尔兰人、苏格兰人和威尔士人会因此感到恼火，认为这种用法反映了英格兰人的傲慢与霸道。但说句公道话，这种用法也反映了英格兰在联合王国中的比重。它的面积最大，它的语言是全国通用语，它在历史上的重要性也是其他地区无法相比的。无怪乎莎士比亚的《理查二世》里有这样的名句："这一个统于一尊的岛屿，……这一个镶嵌在银色的海水之中的宝石，……这一个英格兰……（this scepter'd isle...this precious stone set in the silver sea... this England...）"莎士比亚早就用 England 指不列颠了。
- 关于克尔特语，有几点需要说明。它是印欧语系里的一族，历史上和地理上曾分为两个语支，大陆语支和海岛语支。前者曾在西欧广为流行，高卢语便是其中的一种。但后来失传，其形态已不可考。海岛语支依语言特征可分为两种，布立吞语，包括威尔士语、布列塔尼语和康沃尔语；盖尔语，包括爱尔兰语、苏格兰盖尔语、曼克斯语。
- "不列颠"（Britain）一词源于克尔特语的"布立吞"。布立吞人是克尔特人的一支，曾居住在不列颠南部。

2. The Roman Conquest

罗 马 征 服

In 55 BC, the great Roman general Julius Caesar sailed across the English Channel with 10,000 men after he had conquered Gaul (what is now France). He wanted to see if England would make a good colony. He returned the next year with a larger army and defeated some of the Celts. But he had no intention of staying there,

公元前 55 年，罗马大将朱利斯·恺撒征服高卢后（现在的法国所在区域），率一万将士渡过英吉利海峡。他想考察一下英格兰，看看那里是否适于建立殖民地。次年，他率领一支更强大的军队重返英格兰，打败了一些克尔特人。但

and returned to Rome before long.

About 90 years later, in 43AD, the Roman emperor Claudius invaded Britain again. In the next decades, the Romans defeated the Celtic tribes without great difficulty, and completely conquered the southern part of the island of Great Britain, including present-day England and Wales. But they were never able to completely defeat or control what is now Scotland.

The Romans made the part of the island under their control a province of their huge empire, called Britannia, ruled by Roman governors. They built camps throughout the land. Towns sprang up around the camps. Many of them are now important cities: Gloucester, Worcester, Chester, Winchester and others. All these names are formed from the Roman word *castra*, which means an armed camp. The Romans built roads to connect the camps. The greatest of these roads led mostly to London, which began to develop as a port city. The Romans also built walls and forts across northern England to protect the province from the warlike tribes of Scotland. The most famous of the walls was Hadrian's Wall, named after the Emperor Hadrian. It was built in the 120s AD and ran from Solway Firth to the mouth of the River Tyne, the narrow part of the island of Great

朱利斯·恺撒

他无意久留，不久便返回罗马。

大约 90 年后，在公元 43 年，罗马皇帝克劳狄再次入侵不列颠。在其后的数十年里，罗马人并未遭遇十分顽强的抵抗，便打败了克尔特人的部落，完全征服了大不列颠的南部，包括现在的英格兰和威尔士。但是他们却从未能够彻底打败或控制现在的苏格兰地区。

罗马人将他们控制下的部分大不列颠划为他们庞大帝国的一个行省，称之为布列塔尼亚，由罗马派遣的总督管辖。罗马人在各地建立军营，在军营周围形成了城镇。这些城镇中有不少现在仍是重要城市，如格洛斯特、伍斯特、切斯特、温切斯特等。所有这些地名中的后半部都源于罗马字 castra，即"军营"。罗马人修筑了道路来连接各军营。这些道路中最长的大

哈德良长城遗迹

Britain.

During the Roman period, Christianity came to England. A number of things with Christian symbols on them that date from the 4th century AD have been found in various places in England.

题 外 话

哈德良长城用石材建成，长 117 公里，高约 4.5 米，宽约 2 米。沿墙设有碉堡。墙北侧有壕沟，宽 8.5 米，深 3 米。墙南侧有军用车道。现仅存残段，属世界文化遗产。

多通往伦敦，伦敦当时已开始发展成港口城市。罗马人还在英格兰北部修建了城墙和要塞，以保护他们的行省，使之免遭苏格兰好战部落的袭击。最著名的城墙是哈德良长城，以罗马皇帝哈德良的名字命名。这道城墙建于公元 2 世纪 20 年代，横贯索尔韦湾与泰恩河口之间，这是大不列颠岛的狭窄部分。

在罗马人统治期间，基督教传播到英格兰。在英格兰各地都发现了带有基督教标记的物件，其年代可追溯到公元 4 世纪。

CHAPTER TWO
Anglo-Saxon England
盎格鲁-撒克逊时期的英格兰

1. The Germanic Invasions

日尔曼人入侵

After nearly four centuries of occupation, the Romans left England in the early 5th century to help defend Rome against barbarian invaders. With the Romans gone, Germanic people who lived along the North Sea began to invade Britain in the middle of the 5th century. The invaders were worriers and sailors. They belonged to three main tribes — the Angles, the Saxons and the Jutes. All three tribes spoke their own Germanic dialect, but they probably understood one another. Together, the three tribes are called Anglo-Saxons.

By the end of the 6th century, they had occupied nearly all of southern and eastern Britain. The Celts, though they had brave leaders like King Arthur, were wholly defeated. They were pushed back into the mountains of Wales and Scotland and across the sea to Ireland, where

罗马人占领英格兰近四个世纪后，于5世纪初撤离，以加强罗马的防卫，抵御蛮族的进攻。罗马人一离开，居住在北海沿岸的日尔曼人开始于5世纪中叶入侵不列颠。这些入侵者是武士和水手，属于盎格利、撒克逊和朱特三个部落。他们讲各自的日尔曼方言，但大概能够相互交流。三个部落合在一起被称为盎格鲁-撒克逊人。

到了6世纪末，盎格鲁-撒克逊人几乎征服了不列颠东南地区的全部。克尔特人虽有像亚瑟王那样骁勇的首领，还是彻底战败了。他们被驱赶到威尔士和苏格兰山区，或渡海逃到爱尔兰。在这些地区，至今还能听到他们讲的威尔士语、盖尔语和埃尔斯语。到了7世纪，

their separate languages — Welsh, Gaelic and Erse — can still be heard. By the 7th century the Angles and Saxons established Germanic kingdoms in the areas they had occupied.

The Angles must have been very good-looking people, because there is a story that when Pope Gregory saw some of them in Rome he exclaimed, "Not Angles, but angels!" The Angles settled in central Britain. This area became known as *Angle-Land* and, eventually, as England. The Germanic language the Anglo-Saxons spoke became known as English.

Scholars call the language the Anglo-Saxons spoke during the next few centuries Old English. The Anglo-Saxons left their mark on the English language in its grammar and in thousands of

盎格利和撒克逊人在他们的占领区建立了日尔曼人的王国。

盎格利人一定相貌堂堂,据说教皇格列高利在罗马见到他们,不禁赞叹道:"盎格利人乃天使也!"("Not Angles, but angels!")盎格利人在不列颠中部定居,后来这个地区被称为Angle-Land即"盎格利人的土地",最终被称为England(英格兰)。盎格鲁-撒克逊人讲的日尔曼语则被称为English,即"盎格利人的语言"。

学者们将盎格鲁-撒克逊人在以后几个世纪里使用的语言称为古英语。盎格鲁-撒克逊人在英语中留下了印记。英语的语法和数千个

撒克逊人入侵英格兰

words. Many of the simple words we use today come from this Anglo-Saxon language.

单词反映了他们的影响。我们现今使用的许多简单词汇都源于盎格鲁-撒克逊语。

题 外 话

- 自从盎格鲁－撒克逊人入侵不列颠，引进他们的日耳曼语，英语的历史便开始了。学者们一般将英语的历史分为三大段，即古英语时期，从大约 450 年到 1150 年；中古英语时期，从 1150 年到 1500 年；现代英语时期自 1500 年开始。现代中国人可以读懂老祖宗在两千多年前写的《诗经》及诸子的散文，读一千多年前的唐诗宋词更不在话下。但一千多年前使用的古英语，除了少数语言专家外，现代英美人没有人能读懂。古英语与现代英语大相径庭，倒与德语更接近。例如，名词和形容词都要根据性、数、格发生变化，语法比当代英语复杂得多。用古英语方言写的最著名的文学作品是史诗《贝奥武甫》。
- 英国人，以及他们在美国的后裔，有时会自称盎格鲁－撒克逊人。但这一称呼并不科学。现代英国人的祖先民族成分很复杂，有克尔特人、罗马人、盎格利人、撒克逊人、朱特人、丹麦人和诺曼人。自称盎格鲁－撒克逊人的美国人的血统会更不纯粹。

2. King Arthur

亚 瑟 王

King Arthur is a half-legendary king of Britain. He became the main character in some of the most popular stories in world literature. For almost 1,000 years, writers have told of Arthur's brave deeds and the adventures of his Knights of the Round Table.

A real Arthur probably existed, but historians know little about him. He may have been a military leader of the Celts who fought against the invading Anglo-Saxons. Tales about Arthur may have been based on minor victories he won over German invaders in the early 5th century. But the name of King Arthur is still widely loved

亚瑟王是不列颠国王，他的事迹有一半属于传说。他成为世界文学中一些最流行的故事中的主要人物。近千年以来，作家们不断地讲述着亚瑟王的英勇事迹和圆桌骑士们的冒险故事。

亚瑟王可能确有其人，但历史学家对他知之甚少。他可能是克尔特人的军事首领，率领他们抗击盎格鲁－撒克逊人的入侵。亚瑟王的故事多半是根据他在对日尔曼入侵者作战中取得的几场小胜敷衍而成。但亚瑟王仍广受人们的爱戴，

as that of a national hero and great king.

亚瑟王

被视为民族英雄和伟大国王。

题 外 话

亚瑟王传奇在中世纪的西欧十分流行。若想全面了解亚瑟王的故事，可读 15 世纪后期英国人托马斯·马洛礼的《亚瑟王之死》。

3. The Conversion to Christianity

皈依基督教

Christianity died out in most of England as a result of the Germanic invasions. The Germanic invaders were not Christians. They had worshiped their own northern gods like Woden and Thor, whose names have given us Wednesday and Thursday. They believed that courage, loyalty and rough honesty are the greatest virtues.

It is said that Pope Gregory was attracted by some fair-haired young slaves on sale in Rome. Hearing that these slaves came from England, he decided to send his priests to England to turn these "angel-like" people to Christianity. He told Saint Augustine of Canterbury to lead a group of priests to England. Augustine landed at the

由于日尔曼人的入侵，基督教在英格兰大部分地区失传。日尔曼人侵者是异教徒，信奉他们自己的北欧神祇沃登和索尔。英语中的星期三 (Wednesday) 和星期四 (Thursday)就分别源自这两个神祇的名字。日尔曼人视勇气、忠诚和粗豪耿直为最首要的美德。

据说教皇格列高利在罗马的市场上见到一些金发青年奴隶待出售，不禁为他们的美貌所吸引。他听说这些奴隶来自英格兰，就决定派遣教士到那里去改变那些貌美如"天使"的人们信仰，使他们皈依

mouth of the River Thames in Kent in 597. There Ethelbert, king of the Jutes, received them, listened patiently to Augustine's sermon, and promised to give them a place to live in at Canterbury. Ethelbert was baptized the same year, and after that the new faith spread rapidly among the Anglo-Saxons. Augustine was made archbishop of Canterbury in 601 and given authority over all future English bishops. He built the first cathedral at Canterbury and founded a monastery just outside the city walls. Canterbury eventually became the main religious center in England.

基督教。他命令坎特伯雷的圣奥古斯丁率领一个教士团前往英格兰。奥古斯丁于 597 年在肯特的泰晤士河口登陆。朱特人的国王埃塞伯特接待了他们，耐心聆听奥古斯丁的传道，许诺将坎特伯雷划归他们做他们的驻地。埃塞伯特于同年受洗，此后这一新的信仰在盎格鲁-撒克逊人中迅速传播开来。601 年，奥古斯丁被任命为坎特伯雷大主教，统领英格兰的所有未来的主教。奥古斯丁在坎特伯雷建了第一座大教堂，并在城外建了一座隐修院。坎特伯雷遂成为英格兰的宗教中心。

题外话

奥古斯丁率领的传教团对后来英国文化的发展起了难以估量的作用。此后，日尔曼部族的北欧古文字母表逐渐被罗马字母所取代，而且书面文献均用拉丁文，使英格兰被带入西欧文化的主流。教育与研究通过拉丁文这一媒介在英国的隐修院和教会学校发展起来。

4. Bede

比 德

Bede (673?-735), also known as The Venerable Bede, was an English historian and theologian (one who studies God and religion). Bede was born in England, and studied at monasteries when he was young. Like most educated men of his time, he became a monk. He devoted his life to writing at monasteries. Bede understood Greek and probably some Hebrew, and he was familiar

比德 (673?-735) 是英格兰的历史学家和神学家。他出生于英格兰，年轻时曾在隐修院学习。像那个时代的大多数受过教育的人一样，他成为修士，毕生在隐修院写作。比德懂希腊文，或许还懂得一些希伯来文，而且熟悉早年神学家的著作。使比德名声远播的是他用

with the writings of earlier theologians. Bede is best known for his *Ecclesiastical History of the English People*, which he wrote in Latin. The work is a history of England from the Roman occupation to 731, the year it was completed. It is considered a masterpiece, the finest historical work of the early Middle Ages. It has a simple and direct style, and includes colorful and interesting tales. It is the main source for English history up to that time, and for this he has been called "the Father of English History". Bede also wrote works on science and religion.

拉丁文写成《英吉利教会史》。这部著作记述了从罗马占领直至 731 年，即该著作完成那年的英格兰的历史。它被视为记述中世纪早期的一部史学佳作。其风格朴素简捷，包括许多内容丰富、趣味盎然的故事。这部著作是记载比德以前英格兰历史的主要文献，比德因此获得"英国史学之父"的美称。此外，比德还有科学和宗教方面的著述。

◉ 题 外 话

· 比德的名字前常附有"the Venerable"。这是一个表示敬意的称号。

· 比德提出以传说中的耶稣基督诞生之年为基准，其前为"B.C."（"基督诞生之前"），其后为"A.D."（"我主纪年"）的纪年方法，被后人采用至今。

5. The Danish Invasion

丹麦人的入侵

The Angles and Saxons soon became the most powerful tribes in England. Each tribe was later divided into small kingdoms. A lot of wars were fought between them. By the 8th century, there were only seven kingdoms: East Anglia, Essex, Kent, Mercia, Northumbria, Sussex, and Wessex. They are called the Heptarchy. Northumbria and Mercia each controlled, in turn,

　　盎格利人和撒克逊人不久便成为英格兰最强大的部族。每个部族后来又分裂成若干个小王国，诸王国之间多次发生混战。到了公元 8 世纪，只剩下七个王国：东盎格利亚、艾塞克斯、肯特、麦西亚、诺森伯利亚、苏塞克斯和威塞克斯，史称"七国"。诺森伯利亚和麦西

the other six kingdoms. In the 9th century, under King Egbert, Wessex became the last kingdom to control the Heptarchy.

By the end of the 9th century, England was hit by another foreign invasion. This invasion was made by Danish Vikings and is generally called the Danish Invasion. The Vikings came from Norway and Denmark and had begun to attack England and rob the people in the late 8th century. After they conquered some Anglo-Saxon kingdoms in the 9th century, they met the stubborn resistance of Alfred the Great, the king of Wessex. In 886, Alfred defeated the Danes and divided the country with them, giving them the northeastern part of England. The area ruled by the Danes became known as the Danelaw. In

亚曾先后控制过其余六国。9 世纪，威塞克斯国王艾格伯特最终控制了七国。

到了 9 世纪末，英格兰再次遭受外敌入侵。入侵者是丹麦的维金人，因而此次入侵通称丹麦人入侵。维金人的家乡在挪威和丹麦，早在 8 世纪末就已开始袭击英格兰并洗劫当地居民。他们征服了几个盎格鲁-撒克逊人的王国后，遇到威塞克斯国王阿尔弗雷德大王的顽强抵抗。886 年，阿尔弗雷德打败了丹麦人，与他们分治英格兰。英格兰的东北部归丹麦人统治，称为丹麦区。公元 10 世纪，阿尔弗雷德的子孙征服了丹麦人，统一了全

维金海盗船

维金海盗

维金武士

the 10th century, Alfred's sons and grandsons conquered the Danes and united the country. England first became one single kingdom under Alfred's great-grandson, Edgar, in the year 959.

国。公元 959 年，英格兰在阿尔弗雷德的曾孙爱德加统治下首次成为一个统一的王国。

6. Alfred the Great

Alfred the Great (849-899) was king of the West Saxons in southwestern England. He saved his kingdom, Wessex, from the Danish Vikings and made his kingdom very strong so that his sons and grandsons could unite England under the West Saxon kings. He was such an outstanding leader in war and peace that he is the only English king known as "the Great".

Alfred was the youngest of five sons King Ethelwulf of Wessex. As a boy, he was clever and eager to learn. It is said that Alfred's mother offered a book of Anglo-Saxon poems as a prize to the first of her sons who could read it. Alfred

阿尔弗雷德大王

阿尔弗雷德大王（849-899）是英格兰西南部西撒克逊人的国王。他成功地抵御了丹麦维金人入侵，拯救了他的威塞克斯王国，并使其强大起来，使他的儿孙们得以统一英格兰，将其置于西撒克逊诸国王的统治之下。由于他在战争中及和平时期杰出的领导作用，他是唯一一个名字后加上了"大王"称号的英格兰国王。

阿尔弗雷德是威塞克斯国王爱塞沃尔夫的第五个儿子，自幼聪颖好学。据说他的母亲拿一本盎格

won. In his childhood, Alfred twice went to Rome, where he met the pope. The pope admired the noble qualities of the young man from the royal house of Wessex. The journeys also showed Alfred how backward England was compared with the more advanced parts of Europe.

When his brother Ethelred died, Alfred became king in 871. The Danes invaded his country soon after that. He led his army to fight stubbornly and succeeded in making peace with the Danes. Five years later, the Danes broke the peace and began to attack again, and by early 878 they beat Alfred's army and the king had to hide in a swamp. King Alfred did not give up. He wandered among his people in disguise. Slowly he gathered his scattered army together again. It is said that once he stayed at the home of an old woman who told him to watch some cakes she was baking. When he fell asleep before the fire and let the cakes burn, the old woman, not knowing he was the king, scolded him and called him a good-for-nothing. But finally, in 878, Alfred defeated the Danes in a great battle.

During the following 14 years Alfred was able to devote himself to the internal affairs of his kingdom. He set up a good government, passed wise laws, and brought peace and order to his country. In those days most of the people could not read or write, and the few who could write used only the Latin language. Alfred brought teachers and learned men from all parts of his country and from other lands in Europe, to write books and teach the people. King Alfred

阿尔弗雷德大王

鲁-撒克逊诗集做奖品，奖给最先学会阅读诗集的孩子。结果阿尔弗雷德得了奖。童年时他两度游历罗马，见过教皇。教皇对这个出身威塞克斯王族的年轻人的高尚品质大加赞扬。两次旅行也使他意识到，与欧洲更为先进的地区比较起来，英格兰有多么落后。

在长兄艾特尔雷德去世后，阿尔弗雷德于 871 年即位。丹麦人不久便开始入侵他的王国。他率领军队顽强作战，迫使丹麦人议和。五年后，丹麦人撕毁和约，再次发动进攻。878 年初，丹麦人打败了阿尔弗雷德的军队，阿尔弗雷德不得不逃入沼泽躲起来。但他不肯承认失败。他化装成平民在自己的族人中活动，慢慢地把自己失散的军队重新聚集起来。传说有一次他在一个老妇人家歇息，老妇人叮嘱他

helped to write the books. Instead of Latin he used Old English, the language of his own people. He supported Christianity and encouraged the translation of famous Christian books from Latin into Old English. Under his influence, the *Anglo-Saxon Chronicle* began to be compiled. It is now the main source for Anglo-Saxon history up to 1154. Alfred also built forts and well-protected towns, and reorganized the army to protect his kingdom from the Danes. He also built a fleet of fighting ships as well to protect his shores.

By 886 he had captured the city of London, and soon afterward he was recognized as the king of all England. The old, independent Anglo-Saxon kingdoms began to merge under the rule of Wessex. In 893 the Danes invaded England again and after fighting them for four long years Alfred defeated them again.

阿尔弗雷德大王视察学校

看好火上烤着的饼。但他竟在火炉跟前打起瞌睡，把饼烤焦了。老妇人不知他是国王，把他斥责一通，说他是无能之辈。但是，阿尔弗雷德最终在一场大战中击溃了丹麦人。

在其后的 14 年里，阿尔弗雷德得以将全副精力投入到王国的内部事务中。他建立起一个得力的政府，通过了明达的法律，给他的王国带来了和平与秩序。当时大多数人不识字，而那些会写字的少数人只用拉丁文。阿尔弗雷德从全国各地乃至欧洲其他国家搜罗教师和学者，编写书籍，向人民传授知识。阿尔弗雷德本人参与了书籍的编写。他使用的不是拉丁文，而是古英语，他自己人民的语言。他支持基督教，鼓励将基督教的名著从拉丁文译成英文。在他的推动下，《盎格鲁–撒克逊编年史》开始编写。现在这部书是记载 1154 年前盎格鲁–撒克逊人历史的主要文献。此外，阿尔弗雷德修建了要塞和具有良好城防工事的城市，并组建了军队抵挡丹麦人的进攻。他还建立了一支舰队来加强海防。

到了 866 年，阿尔弗雷德攻陷伦敦，不久后被公认为全英格兰国王。在威塞克斯王国的统治下，那些盎格鲁–撒克逊人的古老的独立王国开始合并。893 年，丹麦人再次入侵英格兰，阿尔弗雷德坚持抗战 4 年之久，再次打败他们。

7. The Anglo-Danish State

Alfred died in 899. During the early 10th century, Alfred's successors again conquered the Danelaw. But in the late 10th century, under the weak King Ethelred II, fresh waves of Danish fighters attacked again. Instead of fighting them, Ethelred collected a tax and paid them to go away, but each year they wanted more. The poor were ruined by this tax and even the rich suffered. So when Ethelred II died in 1016, Canute, the son of the king of Denmark Sweyn I who had conquered most of England, became king of England without difficulty. Canute divided England into military districts ruled by earls. In 1019, he succeeded his brother as king of Denmark. He drove the king of Norway out

盎格鲁-丹麦国

阿尔弗雷德于 899 年去世。10 世纪初，他的后继者们再次征服了丹麦区。但到了 10 世纪末，在软弱无能的国王艾特尔雷德二世的统治时期，丹麦武士掀起新一轮的入侵浪潮。艾特尔雷德没有进行抵抗，却征收赋税，向敌人缴纳赎金，以使其退兵。但丹麦人索取赎金的数额却在逐年增加。沉重的赋税使穷人破产，甚至有钱人也因此遭殃。因而当艾特尔雷德于 1016 年去世后，丹麦国王斯韦恩一世（此前他已征服了大部分英格兰）的儿子克努特没有遇到多大阻力就当上了英格兰国王。克努特把英格兰分成若干军区，由伯爵们统辖。1019 年，他继承了长兄的丹麦王位。1028 年，他把挪威国王赶下台，自己兼任了挪威国王。这样，他创造了一个环北海的庞大帝国。与阿尔弗雷德一样，克努特是个贤明廉正的君王。但当他在 1035 年去世后，他的儿子们未能将这个北海帝国维持下去。盎格鲁-撒克逊人乘虚恢复了他们的盎格鲁-撒克逊王朝。艾特尔雷德二世的

克努特证明王权的有限

of power in 1028, and became the ruler of that country himself. In this way he created a great empire around the North Sea. Like Alfred, Canute ruled as a wise and just king. When he died in 1035, his sons failed to hold the North Sea empire together. The Anglo-Saxons were able to restore the old Anglo-Saxon dynasty. The new king, Edward, was son of Ethelred II. He was called from Normandy, where he had spent his youth as an exile. Edward had been brought up in an abbey and was more like a monk than a king, so that people called him Edward the Confessor. He was formally married to the daughter of God-win, the great lord of Wessex, but he made no attempts to give her a child. Edward spoke Nor-man French, and his tastes and his friends were also Norman.

儿子爱德华登上王位。爱德华是从诺曼底返回英格兰的。诺曼底是他的流亡地，他在那里度过童年。爱德华是在隐修院长大的，他更像修士，而大不像国王。所以人们称他为"虔信者爱德华"。他名义上娶了威塞克斯势力强大的贵族戈德温的女儿为妻，但他无意生子。爱德华讲诺曼法语，他的趣味是诺曼式的，他的朋友都是诺曼人。

题 外 话

人们至今记得克努特，不但因为他是一位伟大的君主，更是因为 12 世纪的一位历史学家杜撰了一则关于他的传说。据说他的朝臣们将他奉为神灵，认为他无所不能。而他却颇有自知之明。他将自己的宝座移在海边，坐在上面，然后命令上涨的潮水不得弄湿他的脚。但潮水不久就浸透了他的鞋子，使他不得不离开岸边。他对朝臣们说，这证明了上帝的威力要比尘世君王的威力强大得多。

8. The Norman Conquest

诺曼人的征服

Edward the Confessor died without a child to succeed him. On his death-bed he chose Harold, Earl of Wessex, to be king in his place. Harold was Godwin's son, brother of Edward's wife. Like Canute, he did not belong to the ro-yal family of England; but he was a Saxon lord. The nobles approved of Edward's choice, and Harold was crowned.

虔信者爱德华死时无嗣。临终时他选择威塞克斯伯爵哈罗德继承王位。哈罗德是戈德温的儿子，爱德华的小舅子。与克努特一样，哈罗德并非英格兰王族成员，但他毕竟是个撒克逊贵族。贵族们同意他的选择，哈罗德登上王位。

然而，有个法国贵族，即诺曼

But a French nobleman, William, Duke of Normandy, claimed that Edward had promised him the throne. Duke of Normandy was the highest ruler of the Normans. The Normans were Vikings who had settled down and adopted the French language and religion. A duke is the highest rank of noble below the king, and the Norman dukes were supposed to be loyal to the kings of France; but in fact they were completely independent.

Probably in 1064, Harold's ship was destroyed in an accident off the coast of Normandy and he was taken prisoner by William. He was released after he had sworn to be loyal to William and support William's claim to the English throne. Now William was very angry to hear the news that Harold had broken his promise and became king of England.

Soon after Harold became king, William

底公爵威廉，此时声称爱德华曾许诺王位由他继承。诺曼底公爵是诺曼人的最高统治者。诺曼人是维金人的一支，他们早已在诺曼底定居下来，采用了法国的语言和宗教。公爵是国王之下最高的贵族爵位，诺曼公爵形式上要效忠法国国王，但事实上他们是完全自主行事的。

大约在 1064 年，哈罗德乘的船在诺曼底海岸附近失事，哈罗德被威廉扣留。他发誓效忠威廉，支持威廉继承英格兰王位后才得以获释。现在，威廉听说哈罗德竟然违约，自己当上了国王，不禁大怒。

哈罗德登基后不久，威廉便入侵英格兰。他率军于 1066 年 9 月在英格兰海岸黑斯廷斯附近登陆。诺曼军有 6000 人，部分是步兵，携带弓箭；其余的是武器完备的骑

黑斯廷斯战役

invaded England. He and his men landed on the English coast near Hastings in September 1066. Among the 6,000 Normans, some were soldiers fighting on foot, armed with bows and arrows, the others were heavily armed cavalry, troops who fought on horseback. The English army under Harold were about 7,000 soldiers on foot, armed with spears, swords, and huge battle-axes.

The armies began to fight on October 14, 1066, in the Battle of Hastings. The English took up a position on a hill outside of Hastings. The Normans first sent showers of arrows a-mong the English troops, and then the horsemen charged them fiercely. But the English stood firm most of the day. Then William used a trick to get some of the English down of the hill to a place where they could be easier to defeat. He had his horsemen pretend to run away. When the English left the hill to run after them, the horsemen turned and attacked. Harold and the best of his men fought on the hill until evening, when all of them were killed. On Christmas Day, William, who became known as William the Conqueror, was crowned king of England.

兵。哈罗德手下有7000步兵，配有长矛、刀剑和大战斧。

两军于1066年10月14日会战于黑斯廷斯战役。英军占据着黑斯廷斯城外的一个山头阵地。诺曼人先向英军发射雨点一般密集的箭，然后骑兵发起猛烈的冲锋。但英军在大半天里坚守住了阵地。这时威廉用计吸引部分英军下山到一个易于被歼灭的地方。他率领骑兵佯装退却，当英军下山追逐时，他的骑兵杀了个回马枪。哈罗德与他的精锐部队在山上奋战到傍晚，直至全部战死。在圣诞节那天，威廉（后人称之为征服者威廉）加冕为英格兰国王。

题外话

诺曼底公爵威廉要求得到英格兰的王位也并非没有理由。哈罗德与盎格鲁撒克逊王族毫无血统关系，但威廉却是虔信者爱德华的表亲。爱德华的母亲埃玛是威廉的姑奶奶。

哈罗德在黑斯廷斯的失败有战略上的原因，但作战方法上的落后也使其失败在所难免。英国人只有老式的步兵，手持盾牌、矛、剑和战斧作战，机动性差；诺曼人却以骑兵为主，配有弓箭手，攻势凌厉。

另外，请注意爱德华在选择继任者时，要争得贵族们的同意这一细节。与秦汉以后的中国古代不同，英国的王权一直受到种种制约：法律的制约、教会的制约和议会的制约。在议会出现之前，则有议会的雏形国王法院（the Curia Regis），更早则有诺曼征服前的贤人会议（the witenage-mot）。参加会议的贤者有高级教士、贵族、国王近臣和地方官员。贤人会议既是国王的助手，又是王权的制约者。它在历史上的意义在于保留了群体表决、多数认可的原则，最终将这一原则演化成民主制。这就是为什么英国历史上难以产生中国式的暴君和暴政的重要原因。

CHAPTER THREE
The Normans
诺 曼 时 期

1. William I

威廉一世

The year 1066 was a turning point in English history. In the year, William (1027?-1087), the Duke of Normandy, invaded and occupied England and made great changes in society of the country. For this, he is regarded as one of the outstanding figures in western European history.

Born in France, William was the illegitimate son of Robert I, duke of Normandy, and Arletta, a tanner's daughter, and is therefore sometimes called William the Bastard. When his father died, the Norman nobles kept their promise to Robert, accepted William as the new duke. Rebellion against the young duke broke out almost immediately, but with the help of Henry I, king of France, he defeated the rebels.

As soon as William had been crowned, he began to establish a strong central government in England on the system that had been so suc-

在英国历史上，1066 年是个转折点。当年诺曼底公爵威廉（1027?-1087）入侵并占领了英格兰，在这个国家的社会中引起重大变化。他因此被视为西欧历史上的一个杰出人物。

威廉出生在法国，是诺曼底公爵罗贝尔一世的私生子。他的母亲阿德拉是个皮匠的女儿。因此他有时被称为"私生子威廉"。父亲死后，诺曼的贵族们信守他们对罗贝尔立下的誓言，接受威廉为新公爵。反对新公爵的叛乱几乎立即爆发了，但靠着法兰西国王亨利一世的帮助，威廉打败了叛乱者。

威廉一登基，马上就着手在英格兰建立一个强有力的中央政府。样板是成功的诺曼底政府形式。这

威廉一世

cessful in Normandy. This is called the feudal system, and it was based on the ownership of land. The life of all classes was controlled by strict rules. William took the land away from its English owners and divided it among a number of great Norman lords and the lords' land was further divided among the 5,000 knights who had fought at Hastings. Knights were small landowners who were also experienced professional soldiers, for they held their lands on condition that they fought for their lords whenever necessary. All the lords and knights should swear loyalty to the King.

William was deeply religious, firm in purpose, and unchanging in gaining his ends. Within a few years, he crushed stubborn resistance of the English and completed the conquest of England. He made the king the real ruler of the country and brought peace and order to England.

During William's rule, many cathedrals and castles were built. The construction of the Tower of London began. Shortly before his death in 1087, William sent out men to make a detailed record of all the wealth of England. The record, known as the Domesday Book, is a rich source of information about England in the Middle Ages. It records how much land and other property there was in England, who held it, and what taxes and services the landholders owed the king for their property.

Although most Anglo-Saxons became serfs under the Normans, they kept their language and

种形式叫做封建制，其基础是土地所有制。社会各阶级的生活都受严格的规则制约。威廉从英格兰土地所有者手中夺取所有的土地，分配给若干诺曼大领主，这些大领主再将得到的土地分配到 5000 名参加黑斯廷斯战役的骑士手中。骑士既是小地主又是职业军人，因为他们占有土地的条件是在必要时要为他们的主人作战。所有的贵族和骑士都要宣誓效忠国王。

威廉笃信基督教，意志坚定，不达目的决不罢休。在短短几年里，他粉碎了英格兰人的顽强反抗，彻底征服了英格兰。他使国王成为国家的真正统治者，给英格兰带来和平与秩序。

威廉在位期间建立了许多大教堂和城堡。伦敦塔也开工了。1087 年，在威廉去世前不久，他派遣官员对英格兰全部财产的占有情况做了详细的普查。这本被称为"末日审判书"的调查清册，为后人了解中世纪英格兰提供了丰富的原始资料。这部书记载了英格兰当时占有多少土地和其他财产，谁拥

many of their customs. While for more than 200 years after the Norman Conquest, members of the royal court and the upper class spoke French. Through the years, however, the differences between the Anglo-Saxons and the Normans gradually decreased, and their languages blended together. By about 1300, English had again become the chief national language. But the English had borrowed thousands of French words and made them part of their own language. The English in an altered form is now called Middle English. In time, the Normans and Anglo-Saxons became a united people.

《末日审判书》

有这些财产，以及他们为了拥有这些财产应向国王缴纳多少税赋，服多少劳役。

虽然盎格鲁-撒克逊人沦为诺曼人的农奴，但他们保持着自己的语言和习俗。在诺曼征服后的200多年里，王室成员和上流社会都讲法语。然而，随着时间的流逝，盎格鲁-撒克逊人和诺曼人之间的差异逐渐缩小，两者的语言也开始混杂在一起。到了1300年左右，英语再次成为主要的国语，但此时英格兰人已吸取了数千法语词汇，将它们当做英语词来使用。这种已发生改变的英语现在称为中古英语。诺曼人和盎格鲁-撒克逊人后来融合成一个统一的民族。

伦敦塔

题外话

- 威廉在英格兰实行了封建制。"封建制"(feudal system, feudalism) 这个术语，指以土地分封为基础的权利与义务关系，是一种经济和社会制度。某人拥有一块领地，同时也就享有了这块土地上独立的政治权、司法权、经济权等各项权力。领地拥有者对上级封主有相对的政治独立性。因此，"封建"意味着分权，而非集权。它造成的是一种多元的权利结构体系。中国自秦始皇统一之后，没有出现过欧洲中世纪式的分封制。大一统有利有弊。其弊端是绝对权力极易走向贪污、腐败和暴政，以及政权的暴力更迭和更迭中造成的极大破坏。我们将会看到，分权式的封建结构深刻影响着英国的历史进程。首先是英国贵族和宗教领袖，他们有一种与国王抗争的强烈意识。
- 诺曼征服的后果之一是中古英语的诞生。英语变化之大，即使是五六百多年前的中古英语，现代英美人若不是专家，也只能靠译文或大量注释的帮助才能读懂。用中古英语写的最著名的文学作品是乔叟的《坎特伯雷故事集》。
- 中古英语在一定意义上，是个古英语、法语、拉丁语的大杂烩。据统计，现代英语中约有 30% 的词汇源自法语，其中大多是在这一时期进入英语的。英语的同义词和近义词很多，掌握起来难度大，就是因为其中包含着数种语言的词汇。
- 现代英语的某些词汇，仍能反映出诺曼征服后语言使用的阶级差异。例如，猪牛羊等家畜由讲英语的下层老百姓饲养，这些牲畜便称为 pig, cattle, calf, sheep。但在餐桌上享用猪牛羊肉的，却是讲法语的上层阶级，所以称作 pork, beef, veal, mutton（现代法文分别为 porc, boeuf, veau, mouton）。这种怪现象在世界语言中是绝无仅有的。
- 诺曼王朝的大多数国王都不能用英语会话，据说只能用几个英语词骂人。威廉一世（1066-1087）43 岁时开始学英语，但半途而废。威廉二世（1087-1100）和亨利一世（1100-1135）在位期间有一半时间待在法国，英语水平恐怕不会太高。亨利二世（1154-1189）在法国待了 20 年，懂英语，但说不好。理查一世（1189-1199）只在英国待了几个月，多半不会说英语。直至 14 世纪末，情况才有了改变。理查二世在农民起义期间（1381 年）用英语对老百姓讲话；亨利四世在把理查二世赶下台时发表的讲话也用的是英语。
- 威廉一世对土地和财产的普查清册被称为《末日审判书》，是强调普查准确、彻底、毫无遗漏。基督教徒相信，在世界末日来临时，无人能逃脱上帝的审判。这本普查清册是英国中世纪最早的经济档案。

2. William II

When William died he left Normandy to his eldest son, Robert, and England to his second son William Rufus (1056?—1100). He was known as Rufus because the natural colour of his hair and

威廉二世

征服者威廉死时把诺曼底留给了长子罗贝尔，把英格兰留给了次子威廉·鲁夫斯（1056?-1100）。鲁夫斯是威廉的绰号，因为他的头

the skin on his face was reddish. He was un-popular, because he was cruel, unfair, wilful and showed no respect to religion. As king of England (1087-1100), he was effective and powerful. The year after he was crowned several powerful Norman barons revolted against him. He put down the revolt and strengthened his position as king. William invaded Normandy several times, trying to rob the territory of his brother Robert, duke of Normandy. Later, he gained control of Normandy by financing Robert who needed money for joining a Crusade. He also invaded Scotland and brought it under his control in 1097.

William was killed in 1100 by an arrow shot by a fellow hunter while on a hunting trip in the New Forest in Hampshire. It is not known whether the killing was accidental or intentional. William never married and had no children. No one was sorry for his death. The clergy refused to give him a church funeral. His younger brother succeeded to the throne as King Henry I.

发和面部略呈红色。威廉不得人心,因为他冷酷、霸道、任性,对宗教毫无敬意。但作为英格兰国王(1087-1100),他统治有方而不乏魄力。他加冕后的那年,几个强大的诺曼贵族掀起反对他的叛乱。他平息了叛乱,巩固了自己的王权。威廉数次入侵诺曼底,试图夺取他哥哥诺曼底公爵罗贝尔的领地。后来罗贝尔需要筹款参加十字军东征,威廉出资赞助,作为回报,他控制了诺曼底。威廉还在 1097 年入侵苏格兰,将其置于自己的控制之下。

1100 年,威廉在汉普郡的新林苑里狩猎,被同行的一个猎手射杀。是误杀还是谋杀,不得而知。威廉尚未娶妻,死后无嗣。没有人为他的死感到遗憾。教士们拒绝为他举行宗教葬礼。他的弟弟即位,成为亨利一世。

🎯 题 外 话

威廉二世实际上是征服者威廉的第三子。他有一个哥哥童年夭折。他的死是个历史之谜。杀死他的人是个名叫瓦尔特·蒂雷尔(Walter Tirel)的诺曼贵族。是误杀还是谋杀,尚无足够的史料下结论。但后者的可能性似乎更大。首先,几乎没有人喜欢威廉;再者,威廉中箭当日,他的弟弟亨利恰巧也在新林苑里。

威廉二世

3. Henry I

Henry I (1068-1135) was the third Norman king of England (1100-1135), youngest son of William the Conqueror. But his father left him no land. When his brother William II died in 1100, another brother Robert had the right to become the next king first. But Robert was absent at the time. Henry took this opportunity to have himself crowned king at Westminster. Henry had already done much to earn the loyalty of his English people. He was born in England and knew the English language and law. He married the daughter of King Malcolm of Scotland and Queen Margaret, a member of the Saxon royal house of England. So Henry became popular with his English subjects and strengthened his position.

When Henry took the crown he was determined to keep the nobles in check and gain a firm control over the country. His first thought was to reunite England and Normandy. Most of his lords owned land in both countries and were glad to support his plan. In 1106, an English army under Henry's command defeated Robert and seized Normandy.

Henry was the last of the true Norman kings, for his only son was drowned at sea. He planned to leave his kingdom to his daughter,

亨利一世

亨利一世（1068-1135）是英格兰的第三位国王（1100-1135）征服者威廉的小儿子。但他父亲没有给他留下领地。当他的哥哥在1100年死去时，他的长兄罗贝尔有权成为王位第一继承人。但罗贝尔当时却不在国内。亨利乘机在威斯敏斯特教堂加冕为王。亨利已经做了不少事来赢得英格兰人民的忠诚。他出生在英格兰，懂英语，熟悉法律。他娶苏格兰国王马尔科姆和王后玛格丽特的女儿为妻，而玛格丽特是英格兰撒克逊王室成员。亨利因此在英格兰的臣民中颇得人心，这一点巩固了他的地位。

亨利取得王位后，决心遏制贵族的势力，牢牢地控制政权。他的头一个计划就是重新统一英格兰与诺曼底。他手下的大多数权贵们在海峡两岸都拥有领地，因而乐于支持他的计划。1106年，亨利率领一支英格兰军队打败了罗贝尔，夺取了诺曼底。

亨利是最后一个纯诺曼家族的国王。他的独子在海难中丧生。他打算将王位传给女儿玛蒂尔达，但

亨利一世

Matilda. But England was not ready to be ruled by a woman. So when Henry died, the lords appointed his nephew Stephen as their king.

英格兰尚无裙下称臣的传统。亨利死后，权贵们任命他的外甥斯蒂芬为国王。

4. Stephen

斯蒂芬

Stephen (1097 – 1154, king of England 1135 –1154) was a son of Adela, daughter of William the Conqueror and the nephew of Henry I. After Henry I died, the lords appointed him as their new king. Stephen was popular and he had an English wife, but he was weak. Henry's daughter Matilda soon persuaded half of the lords to support her, and for eighteen years the two sides fought each other. England was thrown into confusion. Thousands of men and cattle were killed, towns and villages were destroyed and farmland laid waste. In 1148 Matilda left England and gave up her claim in favor of her son, Henry of Anjou, later Henry II. Henry continued the war against Stephen until 1153, when Stephen was forced to name Henry his heir. Stephen died the following year, and Henry became the first Plantagenet king as Henry II.

斯蒂芬（1097-1154, 英格兰国王，1135-1154）是征服者威廉的女儿阿德拉的儿子，亨利一世的外甥。亨利死后，领主们任命他为新国王。斯蒂芬声望不错，娶的妻子又是英格兰人，但他缺少魄力。亨利的女儿玛蒂尔达不久便说服了一半权贵支持她，结果对立双方打了18年的内战，使英格兰陷入混乱。成千上万的人口和牲畜被屠杀，城镇乡村遭破坏，田园一片荒芜。1148年玛蒂尔达离开英格兰，将王位继承权让给儿子安茹的亨利，即日后的亨利二世。亨利继续与斯蒂芬作战，直至1153年。当年斯蒂芬被迫指定亨利为自己的继承人。斯蒂芬次年逝世，亨利成为金雀花王朝的首任国王亨利二世。

斯蒂芬

CHAPTER FOUR
The Early Plantagenets
早 期 金 雀 花 王 朝

1. Henry II

Plantagenet was the family name of a line of kings that ruled England from 1154 to 1399. These kings were descended from the marriage of Matilda, daughter of King Henry I, to Geoffrey, count of Anjou, France. Geoffrey was nicknamed Plantagenet because he wore a sprig of the broom (genet) plant in his cap. Historians also call these kings Angevins, meaning from Anjou.

Henry II (1133 – 1189, king of England 1154 –1189) was the first king of England to come from the Anjou, or Plantagenet, family. Few kings of England have done such lasting work as he. He had a strong will and fierce temper; but he was well educated, especially in the study of the law. He was also one of the most powerful European rulers of his time. At the height of his power, Henry ruled England

亨利二世

金雀花王朝指在 1154~1399 年间统治英格兰的一系国王。这些国王都是亨利一世的女儿玛蒂尔达和法国安茹伯爵杰弗里的后代。杰弗里绰号金雀花，因为他喜欢在帽子上插戴金雀花作装饰。史学家也称金雀花王朝为安茹王朝。

亨利二世 (1133-1189, 英格兰国王，1154-1189) 是出身安茹或金雀花家族的第一位国王。像他

亨利二世

and almost all of what is now western France. He forced Ireland, Scotland, and Wales to accept his authority. He made the English government strong and effective enough to keep peace and order.

Henry is best remembered for his reform of courts and their law. He established one system of justice in England. Before him, each local court had decided cases mainly on the basis of local laws and customs and earlier cases. He sent judges to all parts of England to apply the same laws throughout the land. The judges' decisions became the basis for the English system of common law — that is, law that applied equally anywhere in England. Today, English common law is the basis of the legal system in the United Kingdom, the United States, Canada, and many other countries. Henry also introduced the use of the jury, witnesses sworn to tell the truth. No man could be tried unless a jury of 12 men swore that there was a true case against him. This was real progress, for in the past the usual way to determine facts had been by ordeal, where the accused was bound and thrown into water or invited to pick up a hot stone. If he sank or if his hand soon healed, he was considered innocent. A second way to reach a decision was trial by battle. The victor was considered innocent.

In Henry's later years, his sons rebelled against him. Two of them, Richard the Lion-Hearted and John, became the next two kings of England. Henry quarrels not only with his

那样建立了丰功伟业的英国国王并不多。他意志坚强、脾气暴躁，但受过良好教育，专攻过法律。他也是当时欧洲权势最显赫的君王之一。在亨利权势的鼎盛时期，他统治着英格兰和现在法国西部的几乎全部地盘。他迫使爱尔兰、苏格兰和威尔士承认他的权威。他加强了英格兰的政府的力量，使之有效地维护和平与秩序。

亨利留名后世主要是因为他改革了法庭和法律。他在英格兰建立起统一的司法系统。在他之前，各地方法院断案的依据主要是地方法律、习俗和先前的判例。亨利则派遣法官到英格兰各地推行统一的法律。法官们的判决成为英格兰普通法的基础。之所以称之为普通法，是因为它适用于英格兰所有地区。英格兰的普通法是现今联合王国、美国、加拿大等国司法体系的基础。亨利还采用了陪审团制度，即证人出庭宣誓所述为实的制度。照此制度，任何人不得受审判，除非有一个12人组成的陪审团宣誓罪证确凿。这是真正的进步，因为此前通常的断案法是神明裁判法。依照神明裁判法，被告被捆绑起来抛入水中，或要他们拿起一块烧烫的石头。若被告下沉，或烫伤很快复原，则被认为无罪。另一种神明裁判法是让原告和被告决斗。胜者被认为无罪。

sons, but also with Archbishop Becket of Canterbury, because the church tried to be independent of his control. Thomas Becket was a proud and fierce-tempered man like Henry himself. He defied Henry. Henry finally lost his temper completely, and said, would no one get rid of this troublesome priest? Four knights who heard his words went straight to Canterbury and killed Becket in 1170 while he was at prayer in his cathedral. The people were so angered by the murder that Henry had to give in and granted many special rights to religious leaders.

After his murder Becket was regarded as a holy man. Bottles of Canterbury water were soon sold for high prices, and men claimed that

亨利晚年，儿子们起兵反叛他。有两个儿子，即狮心理查和约翰，后来相继成为英格兰国王。亨利不但与儿子们不和，还与坎特伯雷大主教贝克特相互争斗。托马斯·贝克特跟亨利本人一样桀骜不逊、脾气暴躁。他拒不服从亨利。亨利最终被气得忍无可忍，在火头上说，难道没有人能把这个不安分的教士干掉？四个骑士听到他的话，径直赶往坎特伯雷，于1170年刺死了贝克特。遇刺时贝克特正在祈祷。这一谋杀案使群情激愤，亨利不得不妥协，给教士们许多特权。

贝克特遇刺身亡后被奉为圣

亨利二世与托马斯·贝克特大主教争吵

prayers to Becket had healed their sickness. Two hundred years later the poet Chaucer described in his *Canterbury Tales* how men still travelled there from all England to pray at Becket's grave.

Henry was succeeded by his son Richard I, called Richard the Lion-Hearted.

徒。坎特伯雷的水被装入瓶中,以高价出售;有人声称向贝克特祈祷后医好了自己的疾病。两百年后,诗人乔叟在其《坎特伯雷故事集》里描述了当时人们仍从全英格兰前往坎特伯雷朝圣,在贝克特的墓前祈祷。

亨利死后,他的儿子理查一世即位。理查又称狮心理查。

🔘 题 外 话

- 亨利二世是英国历史上一个有雄才大略的君主,但他长期受到家庭矛盾的拖累。妻子与他作对,儿子们争权夺利,兄弟阋墙,最后竟公然与他为敌。他死得很凄惨。当他得知他最宠爱的小儿子约翰也背叛了他的时候,悲痛欲绝。
- 亨利是个法律改革家。他在位期间,"不成文法"逐渐形成,即司法官所实行的法律都是源于民间的判例和习惯。一般认为,欧洲大陆的法律体系为成文法,以罗马法为基础,以成文法典为基本形式。英国却以不成文的习惯法而自成体系,独立于罗马法体系之外。
- 英国王权之下的改革,无论从次数和频率上看,还是从成功率上看,都远远超过中国王(皇)权之下的改革。在漫长的中国历史中,只有商鞅、王莽、王安石、张居正和康有为等发动了可数的几次改革,而且除商鞅变法外,均以失败告终。

2. Richard I

理查一世

Richard I (1157-1199, king of England 1189-1199) is known in history as Richard the Lion-Hearted, or Richard Coeur de Lion. Richard was born in England, but spent nearly all of his life in France. Richard rebelled against his father several times and finally defeated Henry II in 1189. After he became king, he joined Philip II of France in a crusade to the Holy Land. The crusades were religious wars, in which the Christian kings of Europe tried to win control

理查一世(1157-1199,英格兰国王,1189-1199)史称狮心理查。理查出生在英格兰,但几乎在法国度过一生的时光。理查数次起兵反对父亲,最终于1189年打败了亨利二世。理查登基后,与法王腓力二世联合募集十字军,远征圣地。十字军东征是宗教战争,欧洲的基督教国王们发动战争是为了从穆斯林手中夺回圣城耶路撒冷。理

of the holy city of Jerusalem from the Muslims. Richard was a popular and able soldier who loved adventure. His success in battle won him glory but it annoyed the jealous Duke of Austria, who seized him on his way home and imprisoned him in a castle. He was released in 1194 only after a heavy ransom was paid.

While Richard was in prison, his brother John tried to seize power, but the lords and London's mayor remained loyal. They defeated John and bought Richard's freedom.

As king, Richard was most of the time absent from England, leaving his able ministers in charge of England. Under his rule, however,

理查一世

查是个受人爱戴而又英勇善战的军人，性喜冒险。他的赫赫战功给他带来了荣誉，但同时也遭到奥地利公爵的妒忌。公爵在理查回国的路上扣留了他，把他关押在一座城堡里。1194 年，在交了大笔赎金后他才被释放。

理查被关押期间，他的弟弟约翰想夺权，但权贵们和伦敦市长却忠于理查。他们挫败了约翰的叛乱，赎回了理查。

理查大部分时间都不在英格兰，由那些能干的大臣们来治理。但在他的统治下，英格兰人民不得不为维持他进行的连年不断的战争缴纳沉重的赋税。理查时而冷酷，时而和善而慷慨，但总是无所畏惧，被视为当时骑士道的样板。他同时还是个诗人。

作为金雀花王朝的国王，理查不但继承了英格兰，还继承了法国北部和西部的大部分地区。但在他被监禁时，腓力二世乘机夺取了法

狮心理查

the English people had to pay heavy taxes to support his continual wars. He was sometimes cruel, sometimes kind and generous, and always brave, and was considered a model of chivalry of his age and was also a poet.

As a Plantagenet, Richard had inherited not only England but also most of northern and western France. While he was in prison, Philip II seized some of the Plantagenet lands in France. Richard spent the rest of his life fighting to get the lands back. In 1199, he was fatally wounded by an arrow during a battle and died. His brother John became king.

国属于金雀花家族的部分土地。理查一生中余下的几年都在为夺回土地而战。1199年，在战斗中他中箭身亡。他的弟弟约翰即位。

题外话

英国民间有许多关于狮心理查的传说。理查也是英国小说家瓦尔特·司各特的名作《艾凡赫》里的重要人物。小说描写理查王与他邪恶的兄弟之间的斗争，以及撒克逊英雄艾凡赫和他的女友罗文娜如何在化名洛克斯雷的绿林豪杰罗宾汉的帮助下终成眷属。

3. John

约翰王

John, called John Lackland (1167-1216, king of England 1199-1216), is remembered as one of England's worst kings and as the king who granted Magna Carta, the famous charter of liberties.

John was the youngest and favorite son of King Henry II. He grew up to be cruel, selfish, treacherous and thoroughly unpopular. The legendary Robin Hood supposedly fought against John's officers. John tried but failed to take the crown while Richard was away on the Third Crusade. Upon returning to England, Richard forgave him. When his brother died in 1199, John became king. During his reign, John

约翰（1167-1216，英格兰国王，1199-1216），又称"失地王约翰"，是英格兰历史上的昏君之一。他之所以有名，还因为他是签署了大宪章——著名的自由宪章的国王。

约翰是亨利二世最小也是最宠爱的儿子。他长大后却成了一个冷酷、自私、奸诈的人，极其不得人心。传说中的罗宾汉就是与约翰的贪官们作对的。理查参加第三次十字军远征期间，约翰试图篡位，但没有成功。返回英格兰后，理查原谅了他的不义之举。1199年，理

made enemies among the barons and religious leaders. He quarreled over his French territories with his nephew Arthur and King Philip II of France, which led to a war in 1202 between England and France. But he was defeated and lost much of the land England held in France, including his lands in Normandy and Anjou. He quarreled with Pope Innocent III over who should become archbishop of Canterbury. As a result, the pope punished England by forbidding all church services throughout the country, and punished John by declaring that he was no longer a member of the Church.

To recover those lost lands, John needed more money to continue the war against France. He demanded more taxes and services from his subjects than ever before. In addition, he ruled them with a high hand because he suspected that the English barons were disloyal. But his war to recover his lands in France failed. When John returned to England to collect even more money, many of the English barons revolted. They forced John to agree to a settlement in 1215 that became known as Magna Carta (Great Charter). The Magna Carta stated that every freeman had a right to a trial before being imprisoned or executed; that property could not be taken or destroyed without legal procedure; that justice must not be sold, denied, or delayed. The Magna Carta placed the king under English law rather than above it. Shortly afterward John and the barons were at war. He died in 1216 and was succeeded by his son, Henry III.

查阵亡,约翰登基。在位期间,约翰与贵族和教会领袖结怨甚深。他与侄子亚瑟和法国国王腓力二世为他自己在法国的领土争吵不休,导致 1202 年的英法战争。但他吃了败仗,丢掉了他在法国的大部分领土,包括诺曼底和安茹。他还与教皇英诺森三世就坎特伯雷大主教的人选发生争执。结果,为惩罚约翰,教皇责令英格兰教会停止一切宗教活动,并革除约翰的教籍。

为收复失地,约翰需要更多的资金以维持征讨法国的战争。他向臣民们征收更繁重的赋税和劳役。此外,他疑心贵族不忠实于他,以高压手段控制他们。但他收复法国失地的战争还是失败了。当约翰返回英格兰再次聚敛钱财时,许多贵族起兵反抗他。他们于 1215 年迫使约翰签署了一项协议,这一协议后来被称为《大宪章》。《大宪章》规定,每个自由人在被拘禁和处决之前有权通过法律的审判;未经司法程序,任何自由人的财产不得被剥夺或破坏;公正的审判不得出售、拒绝或拖延。《大宪章》将国王置于英国的法律之下。但此后不久,约翰便与贵族们开战了。约翰于 1216 年逝世,他的儿子亨利三世即位。

4. Magna Carta

《大宪章》

Magna Carta (Latin words, meaning "Great Charter") is a historic document that laid the basis for the development of constitutional government and legal ideas in England. In later centuries, many western countries also benefited from it by following English models in creating their own governments.

Before King John, most of the kings who ruled England had tried to govern justly and respected feudal law. Under feudal law, nobles called barons did military and other services for the king, and in return received land from the king. But there was no actual control over the king's power. When John became king in 1199, he used his power more forcefully than earlier kings. He demanded more military service than they had done. He sold government positions to

《大宪章》(Magna Carta 是拉丁文，"伟大的宪章"之意)是一个具有历史意义的文件，它为日后英国宪政的发展奠定了基础。在以后的几个世纪里，许多西方国家都从《大宪章》中获益，依照英国的模式建立起他们自己的政府。

约翰以前，大多数统治英格兰的国王都试图公正地治理国家，并且遵从封建法律。在封建法律之下，贵族们为国王服兵役并提供其他服务，作为回报，从国王那里接受土地。但当时尚无抑制王权的有效手段。约翰于 1199 年登基后，比先王们更多地使用了自己的权力，强征了更多的兵役。他将政府的官职出售给出价最高的人。他未

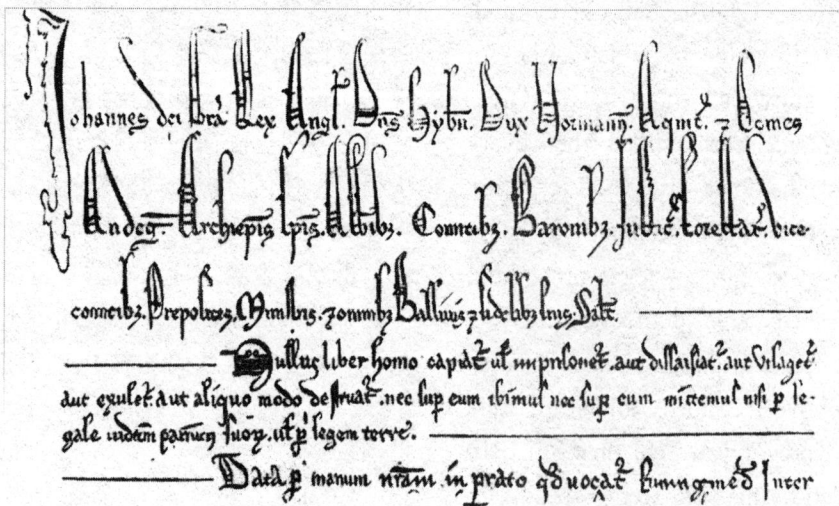

《大宪章》细部

the people who offered to pay the most. He demanded larger amounts of money without asking the barons' consent, which was contrary to feudal custom. He decided cases according to his wishes, and people who lost cases in his court had to pay fines heavy enough to make them bankrupt.

English barons and church leaders began to feel dissatisfied with John's rule. Their dissatisfaction grew when John lost most of the English territories in France. In 1213, a group barons and church leaders met and drew up a list of articles to demand their customary rights. Then they rose in a rebellion to force the king to grant their demands. Under great pressure, John approved the articles on June 15, 1215 at Runnymede, southwest of London. Four days later, these articles were written out in legal form as Magna Carta.

Magna Carta had 63 articles, which made the king promise to give many rights to the nobles and other landowners, but ordinary free people and peasants were hardly mentioned in the charter, even though they made up by far the largest part of England's population. In later centuries, however, Magna Carta became a model for those who demanded democratic government and individual rights for all the people. For example, one article said that the king could make no special demands for money without the consent of the barons. Later, this article was used to support the argument that no tax should be raised without the consent of Par-

经贵族们的认可强征赋税，这违背了封建制的习俗。他随意判案，在他的法庭里输了官司的人须缴纳大笔罚款直至他们破产。

英格兰的贵族和教会领袖开始对约翰的统治感到不满。约翰丧失了英格兰在法国的大部分领土后，不满情绪更为高涨。1213 年，一群贵族和教会领袖举行会议，起草了一系列的条款，要求维护他们向来具有的权利。然后他们起兵迫使国王答应他们的要求。在压力下，约翰于 1215 年 6 月 15 日在伦敦南面的兰尼米德签署了这些条款。4 天后这些条款写成法律文件的形式，称为《大宪章》。

《大宪章》共有 63 条款，迫使国王承诺给予贵族和其他土地所有者许多权利，但普通自由人和农民几乎没有提及，尽管他们构成了英格兰人口的大部分。然而在其后的几个世纪中，《大宪章》提供了一个标准，使那些为全体人民争取民主政府和个人权利而斗争的人有章可循。例如，其中一个条款说，未经贵族同意，国王不得提出特殊的筹款要求。后来，人们援引这一条款来支持未经议会同意不得课税的主张。有些条款成为现代司法公正的基础。一个条款说国王不得出售、拒绝或拖延公正的审判。另一条说自由人未经同等人的合法裁决和本国法律之审判，不得被拘禁、

liament. Some articles became foundations for modern justice. One article said that the king must not sell, deny, or delay justice. Another said that no freeman should be imprisoned, deprived of property, exiled, or executed, except by the lawful judgment of his peers (equals) or by the law of the land. The idea of due process of law, including trial by jury, developed from these articles. In its own time, however, the greatest value of Magna Carta was that it limited royal power and made it clear that no person, not even the king, is above the law.

In the 17th century, members of parliament used Magna Carta in their struggle to win support of the people and to check the power of

剥夺财产、放逐或处决。现代人的通过法律程序解决争端以及陪审团审判的理念，就源自上述条款。但在当时，《大宪章》的最大价值在于它限制了王权，申明了任何人，包括国王本人，均不得凌驾于法律之上这一原则。

在 17 世纪，议员们正是用《大宪章》为武器来赢得人民的支持、限制斯图亚特诸王的权力的。他们援引《大宪章》作法律依据，主张未经议会通过，不得任意立法或课税。他们援引《大宪章》来确保陪审团的审判，免受不公正的拘禁，以及别的权利。革命者们也正

约翰王被迫签署《大宪章》

the Stuart kings. They cited it as a legal support for the argument that there could be no laws or taxation without the consent of Parliament. These lawmakers used the charter to demand guarantees of trial by jury, safeguards against unfair imprisonment, and other rights. It was in the name of the charter that the revolutionists sent King Charles to his death. In the 18th century, the American lawmakers put these English ideals on legal and political rights into the Constitution of the United States.

是以《大宪章》的名义将查理一世处死的。在 18 世纪，美国的立法者们将这些英国人关于法律和政治权利的理念注入了美国宪法。

题 外 话

- 就其内容和性质而言，《大宪章》不过是一个典型的封建法文献。其中所说的人民，主要指贵族和上层教士以及以他们为主体的大会议；所谓自由，亦指封建贵族的自由。尽管如此，《大宪章》仍具有深远的象征意义。首先，它隐含了法律至上和王权有限的宪法精神，使后人对这一精神得以强调和发挥；再则，它规定的一些封建原则，使后人得以根据不同时代的政治需要加以引申，赋予新的内涵。另外，这一文件的产生，为日后英国议会建立奠定了法律基础。无怪乎美国政治理论家塞缪尔·亨廷顿说，西方文明的本质是《大宪章》(Magna Carta)，而不是"大麦克"(Magna Mac)；当前西方通俗文化和消费品流行于全世界，并不意味着西方文明（即民主理念）的胜利。
- 莎士比亚写过历史剧《约翰王》，但剧中竟没有提及大宪章。可见，至少在莎士比亚时代，人们并不看重这一文件。其实，在 17 世纪王权与议会进行过一系列较量之后，英国人才把《大宪章》看做有重大象征意义的历史文献。在这场较量中，《大宪章》是议会的武器。

CHAPTER FIVE
The 13th Century
十三世纪

1. Henry III

亨利三世

Henry III (1207-1272, king of England 1216-1272) was the son of King John. He became the new king at the age of nine, on the death of his father. When he was young, the kingdom was ruled by his ministers, and for a decade, all was peaceful. When he became old enough to rule, however, all the old troubles began again. Henry was not an able king, and he displeased the barons by filling government and church posts with hated foreigner, many of them relatives of his wife. He filled his own household with foreign advisers. He made expensive and useless attempts to win back the French lands that his father lost. In order to get the throne of Sicily for one of his sons, Henry agreed to pay the pope a large sum. When the king asked the barons for money to pay his debt, they refused and in 1258 forced him to agree to the Provisions

亨利三世（1207-1272，英格兰国王，1216-1272）是约翰王的儿子。父亲死后，他9岁便登上王位。他未成年时，王国由大臣们治理。十年间，一切平安无事。当他开始亲政时，早年的老问题又出现了。亨利能力不强，加之在政府和教会中任用那些令人痛恨的外国人，其中不少是外戚，使贵族们大为不满。在宫廷里，他聘用的也是外国顾问。为夺回他父亲失去的法国土地，他耗费了大笔资财，却徒劳无功。为了替自己的儿子争得西西里的王位，亨利答应向教皇支付一大笔钱。当亨利向贵族们筹款付账时，贵族们拒绝了，并在1258年迫使国王签署《牛津条例》，规定国王须与由贵族组成的议事会共

of Oxford, which said that he should share his power with a council of barons. Henry soon broke his oath. Civil war broke out in 1264. The barons, under the leardership of Simon de Montfort, earl of Leicester, defeated Henry and captured him and his son (later Edward I). Simon de Montfort controlled the government for a time. He enlarged the council of barons in 1265, to include elected representatives from towns, shires, and boroughs. This council is considered a forerunner of the later Parliament. In the following year, however, the barons were defeated by Edward's royal troops. Simon de Montfort was killed in the battle, and the barons agreed to a compromise with Edward and his party in 1267. From that time on Edward ruled England, and when Henry died, he succeeded him as king.

Montfort was Henry's brother-in-law, and used to be the king's favorite. But he lost favor because of his desire for political reform. Montfort wished to give more people a voice in political affairs and led a rebellion to limit the king's power by law. Montfort contributed to the growth of parliamentary government in England. For this he has been called "the father of the House of Commons".

同执政。亨利不久便撕毁协议，内战于 1264 年爆发。贵族们在莱斯特伯爵西蒙·孟福尔的领导下打败了亨利，并逮捕了亨利和他的儿子（后来的爱德华一世）。西蒙·孟福尔一度控制了政府。他于 1265 年扩大了贵族的议事会，将城镇、郡和自治市选出的代表也纳入其中。这个议事会被认为是后来议会的雏形。然而，就在第二年，贵族们被爱德华率领的皇家军队击败，西蒙·孟福尔阵亡。1267 年，贵族们同意与爱德华和他的支持者达成妥协。此后爱德华执掌英格兰的政务，亨利死后，他继任为王。

孟福尔是亨利的妹夫，曾是亨利的宠臣。他由于锐意改革而失宠。他希望让更多的人参与政务，他反叛的目的是利用法律限制王权。孟福尔为英国议会的发展做出了贡献。为此，他被称为"议会下院之父"。

题外话

- 一些学者将孟福尔于 1265 年召开的议事会视为英国议会产生的标志。《大宪章》和议会的形成在英国历史上意义重大。没有这两个事件发生，作为一个地理位置偏远的小国，英国后来很可能会像挪威、瑞典、丹麦一样，在世界历史上的影响微乎其微。英国人的自由意识根植于其深厚的传统之中；正是这种意识，使英国人成为世界历史中不可忽视的一个伟大民族。

- 英文 parliament 一词源于法语词 parler，意为"谈话"，自 13 世纪中叶开始在英格兰广泛使用。当时此词并非完全指一种固定机构,而是一种国王与贵族代表进行谈话、交换意见的场合。从英国议会的起源和发展看,英国人似乎有一种偏好,即每当遇到问题或冲突时,首先想到的是组成代表委员会来讨论解决,而不把武力当做首选。其影响所及,在现代任何一个文明国家,社会及政治生活中的一切,都应当由代表委员会用"谈话"的方式解决,而不首先诉诸暴力。

2. Edward I

Edward I (1239-1307, king of England 1272-1307) was the eldest son of King Henry III. He was one of England's best kings. Quite different from his weak father, he was a soldier with great courage and a strong will. In the struggles of the barons against his father for reforms, Edward seemed uncertain what course to take. When war broke out between the crown and the barons, Edward fought on the side of the king, winning a decisive battle in 1265. Five years later he left England to join the Seventh Crusade. While he was still abroad, his father died, and on his return to England, he was crowned.

Edward spent the first years of his reign to strengthen his power. He dismissed dishonest officials, both in his household and in the government. He limited the Church's civil power, and strengthened the royal court system. He also supported proposals for making more new laws than any other kings before him. The English constitution developed under his reign.

Edward I's greatest contribution to the English constitution was the part he played in

爱德华一世

爱德华一世 (1239-1307, 英格兰国王, 1272-1307)是亨利三世的长子。他是英国历史上的最贤明的国王之一。与他软弱无能的父亲完全不同, 爱德华是个果敢刚毅的军人。当贵族们起兵反叛他的父亲、争取改革时, 该如何行事, 爱德华似乎拿不定主意。国王与贵族之间的内战爆发后, 爱德华站在国王一边, 在 1265 年的一场决定性的战役中, 取得了胜利。5 年后, 他离开英格兰, 参加第七次十字军东征。父亲去世后, 他返回英格兰, 立即加冕为王。

爱德华即位后, 用最初几年的时间来巩固自己的权力。当时无论在宫廷里还是政府中, 都有贪官污吏。他撤消了他们的职务。他限制教会的干预政务的权力, 加强了朝廷的力量。比起以前的国王, 爱德华支持更多的立法建议。他在位期间英国的宪法得到了发展。

爱德华一世对英国宪法的最大贡献是他促进了议会的发展。他无

the development of Parliament. He did not intend to share his powers with the Parliament, but he hoped to rule more efficiently by keeping in touch with popular opinion. Earlier kings called meetings of only leading nobles and churchmen to discuss government problems. But Edward adopted many of the changes Montfort had made, and enlarged the meetings to include knights elected from the shires, less important church leaders, and representatives of the towns. A meeting in 1295 became known as the Model Parliament because it set the pattern for later Parliaments. In 1297, Edward agreed not to collect certain taxes without the consent of the Parliament.

Edward I is often remembered for his conquest of Wales and attempted conquest of Scotland. He fought two wars against the Welsh, one in 1277 and another in 1282 and 1283. He conquered Wales in the second war. In 1301, Edward gave the title of Prince of Wales to his son, who had been born in Wales and who later became Edward II. Since then, it has become a custom followed by later English kings and queens to give the title to their eldest son.

Edward I also tried to conquer Scotland. In 1296, he invaded the country and declared himself king of Scotland. Edward then brought the Stone of Scone to England from Scotland. For hundreds of years before that, the kings of Scotland had been crowned on the stone. He placed the stone in Westminster Abbey, where

意与议会分享权力，但他希望能随时了解民意以便更有效地进行统治。先王们召集讨论政务的会议只有贵族和教士首领们参加。但爱德华采取了许多孟福尔的改革，将会议扩大，让各郡选出的骑士、低级教士和城镇代表参与其中。1295年的一次会议史称"模范议会"，因为它为后来的议会确立了一个可供仿效的模式。1297年，爱德华承诺未经议会首肯不擅自征收某些赋税。

爱德华一世之所以扬名后世，还由于他征服了威尔士并试图征服苏格兰。他发动了两次征讨威尔士的战争，一次在1277年，另一次在1282和1283年。在第二次战争中他征服了威尔士。1301年，爱德华将威尔士亲王的称号授予自己出生于威尔士的儿子，这就是后来的爱德华二世。从那以后，英国的国王和女王们依照这一惯例，将威尔士亲王的称号授予长子。

爱德华一世也试图征服苏格兰。1296年他入侵苏格兰，宣告自己为苏格兰国王。爱德华将斯昆石从苏格兰劫往英格兰。此前的数百年间，苏格兰历代国王都在此石上加冕。他将斯昆石放在威斯敏斯特教堂，英国的君主们都在这里加冕登基。但是苏格兰的叛乱仍在继续。1298年他再次入侵苏格兰，试图扑灭威廉·华莱士爵士领导的

English monarchs were crowned. But the Scots rebelled continually. In 1298 he again invaded Scotland to put down the revolt led by Sir William Wallace. He defeated the rebels, but Wallace escaped and carried on the fight in the mountains. In 1303 Edward invaded Scotland once more, and captured Wallace and executed him in 1305. No sooner had Edward established his government in Scotland, however, than a new revolt broke out and Robert Bruce was crowned king of Scotland. In 1307 Edward set out for the third time to subdue the Scots, but he died on his way.

起义。他打败了起义者，但华莱士逃脱了，继续在山区作战。1303年，爱德华再次入侵苏格兰，俘获了华莱士，并于1305年处决了他。但爱德华刚刚在苏格兰建立政府，新的起义再度爆发，罗伯特·布鲁斯加冕为王。1307年，爱德华第三次出征苏格兰，但病死途中。

题外话

布鲁斯

- 斯昆石，亦称命运之石（Stone of Destiny）。斯昆石色淡黄，呈长方形，长26英寸，宽16英寸，高11英寸，重336磅。约在840年移至斯昆的隐修院，嵌在加冕用的宝座下。爱德华一世将此石劫往伦敦后，在威斯敏斯特教堂特制一宝座，将它嵌在座下。苏格兰民族主义分子曾将它取下，试图运回苏格兰，但未成功。
- 华莱士和布鲁斯被苏格兰人视为伟大的民族英雄。14世纪苏格兰诗人巴伯写过一首13000行的史诗描述布鲁斯大败英军的故事；另外，还有很多关于布鲁斯的传说，如布鲁斯和蜘蛛的故事。15世纪有一位名叫亨利的苏格兰盲诗人写过一首12000行的长诗《华莱士》歌颂华莱士的事迹。
- 据说，爱德华制服了威尔士，杀死了威尔士亲王大卫后，威尔士贵族们要求他指派一位新的亲王，但这位亲王必须出生在威尔士，有王族血统，既不会说英语也不会说法语，而且一生清白，没伺候过任何人。爱德华欣然应允。此时爱德华即将临产的妻子埃利诺与他一起住在威尔士的卡纳封城堡里。不久后，爱德华将威尔士贵族们召集在一起，将自己刚刚出生的儿子举起来，说："这就是你们的威尔士亲王，他满足了你们提出的所有条件。"贵族们方知中了圈套，但也只好自认倒霉。再说，他们谁也不服谁，这一结果倒也不错，免得威尔士人之间为夺权相互厮杀。

3. The Development of Oxford and Cambridge Universities

England became an important center of learning during the 13th century. Oxford and Cambridge universities developed and students from many countries flocked to them.

Oxford University, the oldest university in Britain, had its beginning in the 12th century. It gradually developed from a number of schools in the city of Oxford, about 80 kilometers northwest of London. At the time France was considered a more advanced country and English students who wanted to acquire better education went to the University of Paris. However, when the relations between England and France became hostile sometime in the late 12th century, many English students went to Oxford instead, and many English scholars also returned from France and settled in Oxford. Oxford was already an important center of learning by the end of the 12th century. The university received its first official recognition in 1214.

During the 13th century, two of the greatest thinkers of the Middle Ages, Roger Bacon and John Duns Scotus, both studied and taught in Oxford.

Cambridge University, another worldfamous British university, probably had its beginning in 1209, when some scholars left Oxford University after several conflicts there between students

牛津与剑桥大学的发展

英格兰在13世纪成为重要的学术中心。牛津和剑桥大学得到发展，各国的留学生聚集在这两所大学里。

牛津大学是英国最古老的大学，起源于12世纪。它是在位于伦敦西北80公里的牛津镇的几所学校的基础上逐渐发展起来的。当时法国被认为是更先进的国家，想得到更好教育的英国学生都到巴黎大学留学。但在12世纪末，英法关系趋于敌对，许多英国学生不再出国，而去牛津学习。许多英国学者也离开法国到牛津定居任教。到12世纪末，牛津已成为重要学术中心。牛津大学于1214年得到官方的承认。

在13世纪，中世纪的两个伟大的思想家，罗吉尔·培根和约翰·邓·斯各脱，都曾在牛津学习并任教。

剑桥大学是英国另一所世界著名大学，可能成立于1209年。当年牛津学生与市民发生多起冲突，一些学者离开了牛津。其中几位学者来到伦敦北面80公里的剑桥，一所新的大学便在那里发展起来。

在中世纪，大学生学习人文学

and townspeople. A number of these scholars moved to the city of Cambridge, about 80 kilometers north of London, where a new university grew up.

In the Middle Ages, university students studied liberal arts, which then consisted of grammar, rhetoric, logic, music, astronomy, geometry, and mathematics. After completing the liberal arts, some students went on to the professional studies of theology, law, or medicine.

科，包括语法、修辞、逻辑、音乐、天文、几何和数学。学完人文学科后，一些学生继续学习神学、法律和医学等专业。

剑桥大学

牛津大学

题 外 话

- 中国人有重视教育的传统，但从未建立过稳固的教育体系，尤其是官办学校。西方意义上的大学，19 世纪末才在中国出现，竟比西欧历史悠久的大学，如巴黎、牛津、剑桥等晚了 800 年。即使与文艺复兴后现代意义上的西方大学相比，也要晚 400 年。难怪目前中国第一流大学的学术水准与西方著名大学仍相去甚远。

- 英国革命时期，清教徒视牛津与剑桥大学为传播异端邪说、威胁宗教信仰的场所，坚持要将它们关闭。但恰恰是清教徒革命领袖奥立佛·克伦威尔制止了这一愚蠢举动。

- 牛津大学是学术界名人的摇篮。在中世纪，曾在牛津大学学习或从事研究的著名学者有罗吉尔·培根、邓·司各脱、威廉·奥卡姆和宗教改革家约翰·威克里夫。文艺复兴时期，荷兰人文主义学者伊拉斯谟、英国人文主义学者格罗辛、科利特、莫尔都曾为提升牛津大学的学术水准做出过贡献。出身牛津大学的名人还有政治家和枢机主教沃尔西、探险家和作家罗利爵士、天文学家哈雷、物理学家波义耳、诗人雪莱、戏剧家和诗人王尔德等。另外，从老威廉·皮特到玛格丽特·撒切尔，共有 12 位英国首相出自牛津。

- 荷兰人文主义学者伊拉斯谟也曾在剑桥授课。英国的宗教改革家廷德尔、拉蒂默、克兰默都出身剑桥。其他出自剑桥的名人有科学家牛顿、达尔文；诗人密尔顿、华兹华斯、柯尔律治、拜伦、丁尼生；政治家克伦威尔；经济学家凯因斯。在剑桥卡文迪什实验室从事研究的学者中有 20 多人获得诺贝尔物理学奖。到 21 世纪初，出身剑桥的诺贝尔奖获得者已多达 70 多人。

- 但对中世纪的西方大学的水平也不宜估计过高。去大学读书，不一定要有小学和中学的毕业文凭。至少在 16 世纪，不识字者仍可到某些大学读书。例如，十岁的孩子也可以读大学，先只是听课，不读不写；到十七八岁时开始学读写。其间可随意转学。这样看来，中国古代的高等教育机构，还真不算差。秦有博士官，收纳弟子，传播学术；汉武帝建太学，教五经；唐代太学生多达八千余人，其中有不少外国留学生，学习书、算、律各门专科；宋代有太学和书院；明代有国子监，都可说是古代意义上的大学。只可惜这些大学最后堕落到只读孔孟，学写八股而已。

CHAPTER SIX
The 14th Century
十四世纪

1. Edward II

爱德华二世

Edward II (1284-1327, king of England 1307-1327) was one of the most unsuccessful kings in English history. He was weak and lazy, and liked having fun rather than fighting in war and dealing with affairs of state. He left the work of government to his favorites. Edward II had a close friend, a Gascon knight, called Piers Gaveston. His father, Edward I, finding the knight had a bad influence on his son, sent Gaveston into exile. As soon as his father died, however, Edward II asked his favorite to come back. But the powerful English nobles disliked Gaveston. Their dislike became stronger in 1308, when Edward let Gaveston govern the country instead of him during his absence in France, where he went to marry Isabella, daughter of King Philip IV. Soon a group of nobles, led by Thomas, earl of Lancaster, took

爱德华二世（1284-1327, 英格兰国王，1307-1327）是英国历史上最无作为的国王之一。他既无能又懒惰，贪图享乐，不愿领兵作战或操持政务。他把政务交给宠臣办理。爱德华二世有一位密友，是加斯科尼的骑士，名叫皮埃尔·加瓦斯顿。他父亲爱德华一世发现这个骑士对儿子有不良影响，就放逐了加瓦斯顿。可是，父亲刚一死，爱德华二世就把自己的宠臣召回。但有权势的英国贵族都不喜欢加瓦斯顿。1308 年，爱德华去法国迎娶腓力四世的女儿伊莎贝拉，将国务全盘委托加瓦斯顿。此时贵族们对加瓦斯顿的憎恨更为强烈。不久，兰开斯特伯爵托马斯率领一群贵族夺回了统治权。他们迫使国王

back the ruling power by forcing the king to appoint from among them the king's household as well as of the state officials. After they had twice forced the king to send Gaveston into exile, and the king had twice asked him to come back, the nobles finally had the king's favorite kidnapped and executed.

In the meantime, Robert Bruce had gained control of almost all of Scotland. Then he advanced into England, destroying everything as he went. In 1314 Edward II and his barons raised an army of some 100,000 men to crush Bruce. Quite different from his father, Edward II was a poor general. Bruce's forces defeated his army in a battle at Bannockburn. Edward III finally recognized Scotland's independence.

For the following eight years the earl of Lancaster almost ruled the kingdom. In 1322, however, with the advice and help of his new favorites, the baron Hugh le Despenser, and his son, also Hugh le Despenser, Edward defeated Lancaster in battle and had him executed. Then the le Despensers took almost all the power in their hands.

Queen Isabella wanted to drive the le Despensers out of power. In 1325, she visited France. There she got the support of some barons who had been exiled by Edward. From there, she and her lover, Roger de Mortimer, raised an army and invaded England. They defeated the king's army, executed the le Despensers, and imprisoned Edward. In January 1327, Parliament forced Edward to resign and declared the Prince of Wales king as Edward III.

从他们当中选择宫廷和国务官员。他们两次迫使国王放逐加瓦斯顿，国王又两次将他召回。贵族们最终劫持了这位国王的宠臣，将他处决了。

与此同时，罗伯特·布鲁斯已控制了大部分苏格兰。然后他开进英格兰，一路烧杀。1314年爱德华二世和他的贵族们征集了十万大军迎击布鲁斯。与他的父亲完全不同，爱德华二世是个糟糕的统帅。布鲁斯的军队在班诺克本一役中击败爱德华。爱德华三世最终承认苏格兰的独立。

在其后的8年里，兰开斯特伯爵几乎控制了王国。1322年爱德华二世的新宠休·勒·德斯彭瑟父子为爱德华出谋划策，协助他打败了兰开斯特，并处决了他。此后德斯彭瑟父子将几乎全部权利握在手中。

王后伊莎贝拉想把德斯彭瑟父子赶下台。1325年，她回法国探亲，在那里赢得了被爱德华放逐了贵族们的支持。她和情夫莫蒂默在法国募集一支军队，入侵英格兰。他们打败了国王的军队，处决了德斯彭瑟父子，囚禁了爱德华。1327年1月，议会迫使爱德华逊位，宣布威尔士亲王登基为爱德华三世。

爱德华二世当年被杀害。据说伊莎贝拉和她的情夫下令应以极痛苦的方式处死爱德华。于是狱卒们将一根烧红的铁棍刺入国

Edward II was murdered that year. It is said that Isabella and her lover ordered that Edward should be executed in an extremely painful way. Accordingly, the jailors pushed a red-hot iron bar into the anus of the king.

王的肛门。

王被谋杀。剧中马洛将爱德华二世描绘成一个堕落纵欲的君主，但他的惨死又引起人们的恐惧与怜悯。

题外话

• 英国剧作家马洛在其悲剧《爱德华二世》里，描写了爱德华二世即位后发生的一系列事件，直至国

• 爱德华二世在议会的胁迫下将王位让给儿子，虽确保了王位世袭的原则，却否定了王权神圣不可侵犯的理论。这一事件开了一个先例，即议会可以以法律的名义废黜国君。

2. Edward III

Edward III (1312-1377, king of England 1327-1377) became king of England in 1327 after Edward II was forced to hand over the crown to him. When Edward was young, the power was in the hands of his mother and her lover, Roger de Mortimer. In 1330, however, the young king staged a palace coup and took the power into his own hands. He had Mortimer hanged and imprisoned his mother for life.

In the 1330s, Edward invaded Scotland. He defeated the Scots, but failed to establish him permanently as king of Scotland. In 1337 France came to the aid of Scotland. England had already had a series of quarrels with France, and now Edward finally lost his patience and declared war on Philip VI of France. The war between the two countries was fought

爱德华三世

爱德华三世 (1312-1377，英格兰国王，1327-1377)在父亲爱德华二世被迫逊位后于1327年登基。爱德华未成年时，大权握在母亲和她的情夫莫蒂默手中。1330年，年轻的国王发动宫廷政变，夺回权力，将莫蒂默处以绞刑，将母亲终生监禁起来。

14世纪30年代，爱德华入侵苏格兰。他打败了苏格兰人，但未能将自己确立为苏格兰国王。1337年法国开始帮助苏格兰。英格兰本来就与法国有一系列的争端，这时爱德华终于失去耐心，向法国腓力六世宣战。两国间的战争时断时续，打了一百多年，直至1453年。与法国进行的这一系列

on and off for more than 100 years, until 1453. The series of wars with France is called the Hundred Years' War.

While the king was busy with the wars, parliament developed rapidly towards its present form. The elected representatives began to meet separately to discuss their business before they joined the nobles and bishops. The parliament was thus divided into two houses: a House of Commons and a House of Lords. As long as parliament supported his wars, Edward was content to increase its powers. He gave it complete control of taxes. But it still depended on him to see that its wishes were carried out, for the government officials and the armed forces were loyal to the crown and not to parliament.

Edward also made some changes in local government. The Commons had been used for some time as servants of the crown without pay, to keep public order everywhere. Edward now appointed them Justice of the Peace and gave them the local powers of his sheriffs and judges. The English people's great respect for the law is the result of the honest justice that these J.P.s have given them through the centuries.

In the last years of his reign, Edward lost most of his French territory. He was completely in the power of a mistress, Alice Perrers, who, along with his fourth son, John of Gaunt, controlled England. Edward's popularity declined. Even so, he was long remembered as an ideal king and a fine soldier.

Edward died in 1377, and was succeeded by his grandson, Richard II.

战争称为百年战争。

在国王忙于战争时，议会迅速发展，形成其现代的模式。被选出的代表单独开会讨论政务，然后再与贵族和主教们一起讨论。这样议会就分成了两院：下议院和上议院。只要议会支持战争，爱德华就任其扩大权利，不加反对。他给议会以全权控制税收。但议会的愿望依然要靠国王首肯才能得以实现，因为政府官员和武装力量效忠国王而不是议会。

爱德华也在地方政府中做了些变更。下院议员多年来已惯于当国王的仆人，维持各地秩序而不取报酬。爱德华任命他们为治安官，赋予他们地方行政司法长官的权力。英国人十分尊重法律，这是多少个世纪以来这些治安官的公正执法的结果。

爱德华在位末期，失去了他在法国的大部分领土。他完全为情妇阿丽斯·佩雷尔斯所左右。佩雷尔斯与他的第四个儿子冈特的约翰控制了英格兰。爱德华渐失人心。即使如此，他作为理想的君王和善战的军人的形象仍长期留在人们的记忆中。

爱德华于 1377 年逝世，他的孙子理查二世即位。

题外话

英法百年战争的直接导火索是法国国王理查四世 1328 年死后无嗣而引起的王位继承问题。爱德华的母亲是理查四世的姐姐，但作为女性不能继承王位，也不能将王位传给儿子。于是法国贵族拥立瓦卢瓦伯爵之子为法王腓力六世。爱德华作为理查四世的外甥提出了对法国王位的要求。

3. The Hundred Years' War 百年战争

The Hundred Years' War began in 1337, when the French king, Philip VI, declared he would take over lands held by Edward in France. Edward, in turn, formally claimed to be the rightful king of France, since his mother was the sister of three French kings who all died without a son. Edward had good reasons to want to control France. The French were doing their best to spoil his country's wool trade. Their ships threatened the Channel, that narrow strip of water between England and France. They were always supporting the Scots in their rebellion against England. They held the pope as a prisoner and used his influence on the English Church for their own benefit. They broke again and again their promise that they would respect English rights to territories on the mainland.

In 1340 the English fleet destroyed a larger French fleet off Sluis, the Netherlands. The battle was followed by a period of peace that

百年战争于 1337 年爆发，当年法国国王腓力六世宣布他将收复爱德华在法国的领地。而爱德华也正式宣布他是法国的合法国王，因为他的母亲是三位法国国王的姊妹，而这几位国王都死后无嗣。爱德华想控制法国不足为奇。法国在竭力破坏英格兰的羊毛贸易。法国的军舰在英法之间狭窄的水域上游弋，威胁着英吉利海峡的安全。法国人总是支持苏格兰人反抗英格兰的叛乱。他们挟持了教皇，利用他对英格兰教会的影响来为他们自己谋取利益。他们许诺要尊重英格兰在大陆上的领地的所有权，但他们一次又一次地违背自己的诺言。

1340 年英格兰舰队在荷兰斯勒伊斯附近的海战中摧毁了法国舰队。这次战役之后维持了 6 年的停战。

1346 年，战端再起，头一场重

lasted for six years.

War broke out again in 1346, when the first important battle was fought at Crécy, in what is now the Normandy region of France. In the battle English troops defeated an enemy force more than twice their number. Almost half the French force was killed, including more than a thousand knights. French knights on horses never reached the English lines, for the English were using a new weapon in this war, the longbow. It could send an arrow through the best plate armour. The hero of the battle was Edward, the Black Prince (so called because of the colour of his armour) son of Edward III. The prince was only 16 at the time, but won a reputation as an excellent commander of the English army. After Edward III captured Calais in 1347, and a truce was reestablished.

The war with France was renewed in 1355, and the Black Prince won the next great English victory at Poitiers in 1356. Edward conquered much of that country. The Peace of Calais, in 1360, gave England all of Aquitaine, and Edward in return declared to give up his claim to the French throne.

要战役发生在克雷西,现在的法国诺曼底地区。在这次战役中,英格兰军队击败了敌方两倍多的兵力。近一半的法国兵力阵亡,包括一千多名骑士。法国的骑士根本未能接近英格兰军的阵线,因为英格兰军在这场战争中使用了一种新式武器,即长弓。长弓射出的箭可穿透最优良的铁甲。这场战役中的英雄是爱德华三世的儿子黑太子(他身披黑色盔甲,故名)爱德华。王子当年只有 16 岁,但已享有英军杰出统帅的美名。爱德华三世于 1347 年夺取加莱后,双方再次停战。

1355 年,英法战争再起,黑太子于次年的普瓦提埃战役中再次获胜。爱德华征服了法国的许多地区。1360 年的加莱条约将整个阿

加莱义民

In the last few years of his reign, Edward renewed his war with France. This time, however, the English armies were unsuccessful. The English lost most of the French territory they gained before.

基坦割让给英格兰，作为交换，爱德华放弃对法国王位的要求。

爱德华在位末年，他再次发动讨伐法国的战争。但这一次英军未能取胜。英格兰丧失了以前获得的大部分法国领土。

题外话

爱德华在克雷西战役获胜后，北上进攻加莱。英军围困这座城市，使用了火炮，城中居民伤亡惨重。但加莱却顽强抵抗长达 11 个月，直至 1347 年夏才陷落。爱德华对城中居民的顽强怒不可遏，宣称要将全城居民处死。1347 年 8 月 4 日，加莱城的 6 位市民，颈上套着绳索，走向英军，愿意以自己的死，换取对其余居民的赦免。后来由于爱德华的王后的劝说，6 人被免除了死刑。19 世纪法国雕塑家罗丹以这个历史悲剧为主题，为加莱城创作了表彰民族英雄的群雕纪念碑《加莱义民》。

普瓦提埃
战役

爱德华为黑太子授勋

克雷西战役

4. The Black Death

The Black Death was an epidemic of plague that swept across Asia and Europe in the mid-14th century. This epidemic probably began in central Asia early in the 14th century. Trading ships carried the disease west to the Mediterranean. From there, plague spread throughout most of Europe. In Europe it lasted from 1347 to 1352, killing about 40 million Europeans, almost one-quarter of Europe's population.

The Black Death struck England in 1348 and 1349. It killed about one-third of the English population. It struck all classes, and three archbishops died within a year. But the poor suffered most. In some places whole villages disappeared. Landowners everywhere were short of workers. Some landowners stopped growing crops and used all their land for raising sheep. Others let the serfs pay a small rent instead of their feudal service. Serfs demanded higher wages. Parliament passed an Act to keep down wages, but the serfs formed unions and went on strike against fixed wages, and against the whole idea of feudal service or forced labour. Their spirit spread to the towns, where workmen began demanding higher wages from merchants and manufacturers. The struggle between higher and lower classes led to the Peasants' Revolt of 1381.

黑死病

黑死病是一种恶性传染病，14世纪中叶流行于亚洲和欧洲。这场瘟疫可能于世纪初起源于中亚，商船将它传播到地中海西部，再从那里蔓延到欧洲大部分地区。在欧洲，黑死病从1347年持续到1352年，4000万欧洲人病死，几乎占欧洲总人口的四分之一。

黑死病于1348年和1349年袭击了英格兰。三分之一人口殒命。染病者不分贵贱，一年之内，死了三位大主教。但受难最深的还是穷人。有些地方整村的人无一幸免。农业劳力出现短缺，有些地主不再种粮，转而将土地用于牧羊。还有些地主允许农民缴纳少量地租，代替封建劳役。农民们要求更高的工资。议会通过立法试图压低工资，但农民们组织工会，举行罢工，抗议固定工资，反对封建强制劳役。农民的反抗精神蔓延到城市，工人们开始要求商人和厂主付给他们更高的薪酬。上下阶层间的斗争导致了1381年的农民起义。

题外话

黑死病可能是淋巴腺鼠疫和肺病。老鼠和跳蚤是病毒携带者。

5. Richard II

Ri chard II (1367-1400, king of England 1377-1399) became king of England in 1377 when his grandfather King Edward III died. He had been created Prince of Wales in 1376, when his father, Edward, the Black Prince, died. Richard was only 10 years old, and the government was in the hands of his uncle John of Gaunt, duke of Lancaster.

In 1381, English peasants revolted against the government's attempt to raise a tax. A mob led by Wat Tyler invaded London, broke into the Tower and executed the Archbishop of Canterbury. Richard was only 14 at the time, but he dealt with the revolt with great courage, and put it down. For the next few years, Richard tried to increase his control over the government with the help of favorite advisers.

In 1389, Richard declared he was old enough to rule the country by himself, and for a few years he ruled well. But later he began to punish many of his enemies and used his power to get rid of anyone who controlled Parliament and prevented him from doing what he liked. A number of powerful lords were arrested. These included duke of Gloucester, who died in prison. John of Gaunt's son Henry Bolingbroke was sent into exile. Richard often changed his mind suddenly and behaved in an unexpected way. He displeased the English people because

理查二世

理查二世（1367-1400, 英格兰国王，1377-1399）在祖父爱德华三世逝世后于 1377 年加冕登基。他父亲是黑太子爱德华，父亲死后他于 1376 年受封为威尔士亲王。理查当时只有十岁，朝政由他的叔父兰开斯特公爵冈特的约翰掌管。

1381 年，英格兰爆发农民起义，抗议政府试图增加赋税。起义民众由瓦特·泰勒率领进入伦敦，强行进入伦敦塔，处决了坎特伯雷大主教。理查当时只有 14 岁，但他勇敢地应对并平息了暴乱。在其后的几年里，靠亲信为他出谋划策，理查试图加强对政府的控制。

理查于 1389 年宣布自己已成年，从此亲临朝政。头几年里，他

理查二世

he forced them to lend money to him and take the oath of loyalty.

In 1399, Richard left England to conquer Ireland. When he returned from Ireland, he found that Bolingbroke had returned from exile and raised a large army against him. Richard was captured, put into prison and forced to resign his crown. Henry Bolingbroke became King Henry IV, and Richard either died of hunger or was murdered in 1400.

Richard II was the last of the direct line in the House of Plantagenet (Anjou). After he was overthrown, the Plantagenets split into the houses of Lancaster and York. These two houses then ruled England until 1485.

题外话

理查二世富于想象力，精明能干，有指挥才能。他生活奢侈，爱好文学艺术。但他又反复无常，专横独断，放逐、处决权贵们毫不留情。他在位末年，已成为公认的暴君。在他为自己撰写的墓志中，他说自己"打倒了那些侵犯王权的人"。在莎士比亚的历史剧《理查二世》里，理查是个不称职的国君，但他多愁善感，在表达被废黜的痛苦时，他口中流出的那些滔滔不绝的动人诗句催人泪下。

6. The Peasants' Revolt

After the death of Edward III, the English people began to oppose the long war with France. To fight the French, a tax was collected from every male over fifteen years old. The

的统治还算得当。但后来他开始惩罚政敌，利用权力剪除任何操控议会、妨碍他为所欲为的人。几个权贵被逮捕，其中包括格罗斯特公爵。格罗斯特公爵后来死于狱中。冈特的约翰的儿子亨利·博林布鲁克也被放逐。理查反复无常，常做出人意料的事。他在民间强行贷款，迫使人们宣誓效忠，这使他颇不得人心。

1399年，理查离开英格兰去征服爱尔兰。当他从爱尔兰返回时，发现博林布鲁克已从流放地返回，募集了一支大军与他对抗。理查被俘，关入监狱，被迫逊位。亨利·博林布鲁克登基为亨利四世，理查于1400年饿死狱中或被谋杀。

理查二世是金雀花(安茹)王朝直系中最后一位国王。他死后，金雀花家族分裂成兰开斯特和约克两个家族，两家族统治英格兰直至1485年。

农民起义

爱德华三世死后，英格兰人民开始反对与法国进行的漫长的战争。为与法国人作战，每个15岁以上的男人都须缴纳人头税。但人

农民起义

people refused to pay the tax. The Black Death had caused labour shortage and higher wages. Parliament's attempts to keep down wages also made the people angry. In 1381, peasants from many parts of the country rebelled and marched to London under the leadership of an old soldier named Wat Tyler. They demanded an end of feudal service. The workers of London opened their gates in welcome. Some of the peasants became violent. They killed the archbishop and the treasurer who were responsible for collecting taxes. They broke open the prisons, and attacked foreign merchants. After much looting and killing, the peasants forced King Richard II to make promises to accept their demands and abolish the tax. A public meeting was held, and in the middle of it the mayor of London killed Tyler. Richard told the simple countrymen to calm down and persuaded them to go home. Then the revolt in other places of England was put down. The king's promises were not kept, but at least the tax was no longer collected and gradually the landown-

民拒绝纳税。黑死病使劳动力短缺，工资提高。议会抑制工资的企图也激怒了百姓。1381年全国多处爆发农民起义，起义者在老兵瓦特·泰勒的率领下向伦敦进发。他们强烈要求废止封建劳役。伦敦的工人们打开伦敦城门欢迎农民。部分农民诉诸暴力。他们杀死了负责征税的大主教和财务大臣。他们还打开监狱，袭击外国商人。经过一番杀人抢掠，农民迫使国王理查二世答应接受他们的要求并废除人头税。在一场公开的大会上，伦敦市长刺杀了泰勒。理查要求那些朴实的农民镇静下来，劝说他们返回家乡。继而英格兰其他地方的起义也被镇压下去。国王并未履行自己的诺言，但是人头税不再征收，地主

理查二世向农民起义军讲话时，泰勒被杀

ers gave up their claims to feudal service, and accepted rent instead.

们也逐渐放弃了对封建劳役的要求，而接受了地租的形式。

题外话

1381 年的农民起义是英国历史上头一次，也是唯一的一次大规模的农民起义。起义领袖之一约翰·保尔（John Ball）是威克里夫的门徒，一个鼓动家。他的两句诗大大鼓舞了起义者，一直流传至今，常常被人引用：

When Adam delved and Eve span,
Who was then a gentleman?
（人类之初，亚当耕田，夏娃织布，何来贵族?）

7．John Wycliffe and the Lollards

威克里夫与罗拉德派

John Wycliffe, or John Wicliff (1330?-1384) was an English philosopher, theologian, and religious reformer, a chief forerunner of the Protestant Reformation.

Wycliffe was educated at Oxford University, and later he became a Roman Catholic priest, and soon after that he began to attack the Pope for political reasons. He attacked the luxurious life of the upper clergymen, and contrasted it with the poor life of the parish priests. A group of nobles headed by John of Gaunt became his protectors. The nobles hated those upper clergymen, who were too powerful and very difficult to control. They also hated the Pope's powers to interfere in national affairs. Wycliffe then went on to attack some of the most impor-

约翰·威克里夫（1330?-1384)是英国哲学家、神学家和宗教改革家,基督教新教的重要先驱。

威克里夫在牛津受教育，后来成为罗马天主教教士。但此后不久便开始因政治原因抨击教皇。他指责上层教士过着奢侈的生活，与教区神甫的清贫生活形成巨大反差。以冈特的约翰为首的一伙贵族成了他的保护人。这些贵族痛恨那些上层教士，他们权力过大，难以控制。贵族们也对教皇有权干预内政感到愤恨。威克里夫进而攻击罗马天主教的某些重要教条，如在圣餐礼上所用的饼和酒果真变为耶稣的肉和血的教义。他宣传个人与上帝直接

tant doctrines of the Roman Catholic Church, such as the doctrine that the bread and wine taken in Holy Communion become the actual body and blood of Christ. He also preached direct communion between the individual and God, and wanted to translate the Bible into English so that it could be understood by the common people. A translation appeared in 1380s, but probably Wycliffe himself did not do much of the actual translation. It was chiefly the work of his followers. The translation is regarded as one of the foundation works of English prose.

Wycliffe's writings influenced a number of reformers, including Bohemian reformer John

交往的教义,并试图将《圣经》译成英语,使普通人都能读懂。一个译本出现在 14 世纪 80 年代,但可能威克里夫本人没有参与多少实际翻译工作。大部分工作是他的弟子们做的。这个译本被视为英语散文的奠基之作之一。

威克里夫的著作影响了几位宗教改革家,包括波西米亚的约翰·胡斯与德国的马丁·路德。许多早期的英国新教徒将威克里夫的教义视为宗教改革的先声。他们认为他是一位伟大的英国宗教改革家。

威克里夫的追随者们称为罗拉德派。罗拉德派攻击教会的腐败,

威克里夫为冈特的约翰读《圣经》

Hus and German reformer Martin Luther. Many early English Protestants regarded the teachings of Wycliffe as forerunners of those of the Reformation. They considered him the first great English reformer.

Wycliffe's followers were called Lollards. The Lollards attacked the Church for its corruption; they tried to persuade the clergy to return to the simple life of the early church; they rejected the richness of the Mass, most sacraments, and the supremacy of the pope. They opposed confession, and the use of images in worship, and the doctrine that the bread and wine taken in Holy Communion become the actual body and blood of Christ. They denied that an organized church was necessary for salvation. Lollards held the Bible provided the only rule necessary for holy life. Most Lollards were poor priests or people who were not members of the clergy. The Lollards helped to pave the way for the Protestant Reformation.

他们劝说教士们重过早期教徒们的简朴生活。他们抵制奢华的弥撒，大多数圣事以及教皇至高无上的权力。他们反对告解，反对在崇拜中使用圣像，反对圣餐礼上所用的饼和酒果真变为耶稣的肉和血的教条。他们否认参加有组织的教会是获救的必要条件。罗拉德派认为，《圣经》提供了过神圣生活的唯一必要准则。罗拉德派中的大多数人是贫穷的教士或俗人。他们奠定了宗教改革的基础。

题外话

一般认为，宗教改革运动始于德国，以马丁·路德于 1517 年将《九十五条论纲》张贴出去为标志。但实际上，更早的宗教改革家应当是约翰·威克里夫，他对后起的宗教改革家，包括马丁·路德，都有影响。威克里夫死后教会判定他为异端，下令将他的尸体掘出焚烧。

威克里夫的尸体被掘出焚烧

CHAPTER SEVEN
Lancaster and York
兰开斯特和约克王朝

1. Henry IV

亨利四世

Henry IV (1366-1413, king of England 1399-1413) was the first king of England of the House of Lancaster. He was the son of John of Gaunt, Duke of Lancaster. He was often called Henry of Bolingbroke because he was born at his father's castle of Bolingbroke, in Lincolnshire.

Richard II sent Henry into exile for six years in 1398, because Henry had a quarrel with Thomas Mowbray, 1st duke of Norfolk. But Richard promised that Henry would not lose the money and property his father would leave him. When Henry's father died, however, Richard broke his promise and took all Henry's property. Consequently, Henry raised an army, invaded England, and captured Richard, and forced him to give up his throne. In 1399 Henry was elected king by Parliament. Many people questioned

亨利四世（1366-1413，英格兰国王，1399-1413）是兰开斯特王朝的头一个国王。他是兰开斯特公爵冈特的约翰的儿子。他也常被称为亨利·博林布鲁克，因为他出生在父亲在林肯郡的博林布鲁克城堡。

1398年，理查二世以亨利与诺福克公爵一世托马斯·毛伯雷争吵为由，下令放逐他，六年不得返回英格兰。但理查向他许诺，他不会失去父亲遗留给他的资财。但当亨利的父亲死后，理查却食言，没收了亨利的财产。亨利因而募集了一支军队入侵英格兰，俘获了理查，强迫他逊位。1399年亨利被议会推选为国王。不少人对他的继位权提出质疑。但议会支持他，在

Henry's right to be the new king. However, Parliament supported him and established the Lancastrian dynasty in England.

In the rest of his life, Henry was busy fighting his enemies. He first put down a revolt of nobles who supported Richard in 1400. Then he had to fight the Scots and the Welsh, who began a rebellion against him with the help of the French. The Scots were defeated in 1402, but the Welsh continued the rebellion for more years under the leadership of the Welsh chief Owen Glendower. In 1403 the Percy family rebelled against Henry because they were dissatisfied with the rewards for helping Henry come to the throne. But they were defeated in the Battle of Shrewsbury in the same year. In his later years wars and rebellions went on troubling him. He was sick and allowed his son Henry, who would succeed him as King Henry V, to play a major role in government affairs.

Henry IV spent much of his time fighting against English nobles and paid little attention to the war with France. But

英格兰建立了兰开斯特王朝。

在一生中其余的时间里，亨利一直忙于与敌人作战。1400 年他先镇压了一场支持理查的暴乱。接着他又不得不与苏格兰人和威尔士人作战。他们在法国人的帮助下，发动了叛乱。苏格兰人在 1402 年战败，但酋长欧文·格伦道尔的率领下的威尔士人的叛乱又持续了多年。1403 年帕西家族发动叛乱，这个家族曾帮助亨利取得王位，对得到的回报感到不满。但在同年，他们在什鲁斯伯里一役中被打败。亨利在世的最后几年战争和叛乱一直使他不得安宁。他健康恶化，让儿子亨利主持朝政。这个儿子后来继位，即亨利五世。

亨利四世耗费太多的岁月与英格兰的贵族们作战，无暇顾及与法国的战争。但是他的儿子亨利五世得到了普遍

亨利四世与妻子雕像

his son Henry V gained popular support for continuing the Hundred Years' War.

的支持，使之得以将百年战争继续下去。

题 外 话

亨利四世虽然夺得了王冠，但他毕竟是个篡位者，名不正，言不顺。为了维护自己的地位，不得不与各方的反对势力作战，搞的身心憔悴。据说他当上国王后不久，正是三十多岁的壮年，却已经成为一个焦虑不安、面色苍白的老人。莎士比亚在他的著名历史剧《亨利四世（下）》里，有一段亨利四世的独白，绝妙地表达了他在深夜由于焦虑而失眠时内心的痛苦。他妒忌那些睡在茅屋里的穷苦百姓，他们缺少奢华，但不缺睡眠。他说："幸福的卑贱者啊，安睡吧！戴王冠的头是不能安于他的枕席的。"（Then, happy low, lie down! / Uneasy lies the head that wears a crown.）他死时才47岁，想必是让王冠压垮了的。

2. Henry V

Henry V (1387-1422, king of England 1413-1422) was the eldest son of Henry IV. He was a born soldier and a popular military leader. He is best remembered for his great victory over the French at Agincourt during the Hundred Years' War.

In 1403, when he was only 16, Henry led the royal army that defeated the rebellious Percy family, led by Sir Henry Percy, at Shrewsbury. He also commanded the English forces that put down the revolt of the Welsh chief Owen Glendower.

After he came to the throne, Henry renewed the Hundred Years' War. He again declared that he, as king of England, had a right to the French throne. In 1415, Henry won one

亨利五世

亨利五世（1387-1422，英格兰国王，1413-1422）是亨利四世的长子。他是个天生的武士，深得人心的军事统帅。他在百年战争中的阿让库尔战役中大败法军，因而留名后世。

1403年，当时亨利只有16岁，就率领王军在什鲁斯伯里一役中挫败了以亨利·帕西为首的帕西家族叛乱。他还率领英军平息了威尔士人酋长欧文·格伦道尔发动的叛乱。

亨利即位后，重开百年战争。他再次宣告，作为英格兰国王，他有资格继承法国王位。1415年，亨利打了一场胜仗，这是英国历史上最著

of the most famous victories in English history when his small army crushed a large French force at Agincourt. The English army had only about 6,000 soldiers. But its archers, well trained and firmly disciplined and supported by cavalry, defeated a French army that probably had about 20,000 to 30,000 soldiers. The French had not learned a lesson of Crécy, for their army still depended on knights, who wore heavy armour, mounted on horses that also were protected by armour, fighting with swords and lances. The English archers, with their strong longbows, could shoot arrows strong enough to pierce the steel armour of the French knights. The archers did not need to wear armour, because they could shoot the knights down before the knights could get close enough to attack them with their swords and lances. So the archers could get around faster, without armour to weight them down. The victory at Agincourt was the third great English victory in the Hundred Years' War.

After this victory Henry tried to reach agreement with Paris, but in vain. His armies then began to seize northern France. In 1419, Henry completed his conquest of all Normandy with

名的大捷之一。他率领的弱小的军队，在阿让库尔战役中击溃了一支法国大军。英军只有大约6000人，但其训练有素、纪律严明的弓箭手在骑兵的支援下，打败了一支拥有两万到三万兵力的法军。法国人没有接受克雷西的教训，他们的军队仍然依靠骑兵，人马都有重甲防护，用剑和矛作战。而英军的弓箭手用威力强大的长弓，射出的箭足以穿透法国骑士的钢甲。弓箭手无须披甲，因为在骑兵能够接近他们，用剑和矛攻击他们之前，早已把他们射下马了。因而弓箭手没有盔甲的拖累，机动性更强。阿让库尔的胜利是百年战争中英方的第三次重大

亨利五世

the capture of Rouen, and then went on to attack Paris. By 1420 the French had had enough. Henry made a peace treaty with Charles VI of France at Troyes in the year. According to the treaty, Charles VI was to keep his crown for life, Henry was to marry his daughter and become king of France on Charles's death. And meanwhile Henry was to rule for him.

When Henry returned to England in 1421, leaving his brother Thomas, duke of Clarence, as governor of Normandy, the French rose against English rule and defeated the duke. Henry returned to France for a third campaign, but he became ill and died in 1422. He was succeeded by his son Henry VI. Then the French declared that the English king had no right to the French throne, and the war broke out again. By 1428, the English had swept through northern France. But the tide turned

胜利。

取得这次胜利之后，亨利试图与巴黎达成协议，但未能成功。英军开始夺取法国北部。1419年，亨利攻陷鲁昂，征服了整个诺曼底，然后乘势攻打巴黎。1420年法国已无力再战。亨利当年在特鲁瓦与法王查理六世订立和约，规定查理六世终生保有王位，亨利将娶其女儿为妻，待查理去世后继位为法国国王。查理在位期间，亨利代为统治。

亨利1421年返回英格兰，留下弟弟克莱伦斯公爵托马斯做诺曼底总督。此时法国人起兵反抗英国统治，打败了公爵。亨利返回法国

贞德

in 1429, when French forces gathered around an eighteen-year-old peasant girl, Joan of Arc, and defeated the English army in the Battle of Orleans. French successes continued. By the time the war ended in 1453, the English held only the city of Calais.

Henry V was one of the greatest kings in English history. He had not only military talent but also a strong sense of justice. At least in Shakespeare's play *Henry V*, Henry loves his soldiers, keeping his men well clothed and fed, and he walked round his camp at night to encourage his men and to see that the guards were properly at their posts.

发动第三次战役，但于 1422 年病故。他的儿子亨利六世继位。法国此时宣布英格兰国王无权继承法国王位，于是战端再起。1428 年英军横扫法国北部。1429 年局势骤变。法国军队聚集在一位 18 岁的村姑贞德周围，在奥尔良战役中打败了英军。此后法军连连取胜，1453 年百年战争结束时，英格兰在法国仅剩下加莱一个据点。

亨利五世是英国历史上最伟大的君王之一。他不但有杰出的军事才能，也有强烈的正义感。至少在莎士比亚的历史剧《亨利五世》里，亨利爱护士兵，确保他们吃饱穿暖；晚上巡视兵营，鼓舞将士，监督哨兵忠于职守。

题外话

- 莎士比亚在其历史剧里如此赞扬亨利五世，并不奇怪。在他同时代人眼里，除了伊丽莎白女王外，英国的君主没有那一个能够像亨利五世那样完美无缺。19 世纪的英国历史学家威廉·斯塔布斯这样赞美这位理想君王："（他）虔诚、寡欲、谦和、慷慨、谨慎、伟岸、仁慈、诚实、正直。他言语谨慎、深谋远虑、料事精明、朴实无华、豁达大度"。
- 关于贞德，不得不说几句。她的英文名是 Joan of Arc，法文名是 Jeanne d'Arc。其实正确的法文拼法应当是 Jeanne Darc，因为她父亲名叫雅各·达克（Jacques Darc）。她的名字音译成汉语应当是让娜·达克，不知那位将它译成贞德，根据何在。贞德又称奥尔良姑娘。她 1412 年出生于多雷米的一个农家，13 岁时，她相信自己听到天国的圣徒在对她讲话。1429 年，奥尔良即将被英军占领，来自天国的声音要她协助当时尚未加冕的查理七世保卫奥尔良。她使查理相信她负有拯救法国的神圣使命，被许可指挥军队。结果，她率领法军取得决定性的胜利。1430 年，贞德率法军在贡比涅的战斗中被英军的盟军勃艮第军俘获，被勃艮第人出卖给英军。英军指控贞德行巫术，将她交给鲁昂的教会法庭处置。1431 年，法庭以巫术和异端的罪名判处贞德终生监禁。同年，贞德被移交世俗法庭审判，被处以火刑，时年仅 19 岁。1456 年，教皇法庭撤消 1431 年的判决。1920 年，天主教会追谥贞德为圣女。贞德是法国的主保圣徒之一。大量的文学艺术作品都以贞德富有传奇色彩的一生为题材。如德国剧作家席勒的剧作《奥尔良姑娘》、英国剧作家萧伯纳的剧作《圣女贞德》、美国剧作家安德森剧作《洛林的贞德》、伏尔泰的叙事诗《奥尔良姑娘》、马克·吐温的《贞德传》。此外，还有以贞德的事迹为题的音乐作品和大量美术作品。

3. Advances in Literature and Education

Great advances in literature and education occurred in England during the Hundred Years' War. English poetry became important for the first time. William Langland wrote *Piers the Plowman*, one of the first major poems in English. Geoffrey Chaucer helped shape the English language with such works as *The Canterbury Tales*.

After the Norman Conquest the French language was the language of the court and the upper classes. Most Normans learned some English, but they were too proud to speak it openly. But the wars of Edward III made French the language of the enemy. Then the king ordered that only English should be spoken in the courts and schools and other public places, and the nobles began to use it among themselves. So the difference between Normans and the English disappeared; from then on, all were Englishmen. Books in English became fashionable. The English writer who made the greatest contribution to the English language was Chaucer.

Chaucer had enough pride and confidence in his native language to use it in his work. With his *Canterbury Tales* he greatly increased the prestige of English as a literary language. At

文学与教育的成就

在百年战争期间，英格兰的文学和教育都取得很大成就。英国诗歌确立了重要地位。威廉·朗兰写下最早的英语诗作之一《农夫皮尔斯》。杰弗里·乔叟写下《坎特伯雷故事集》，对英语的形成做出重要贡献。

诺曼征服之后，法语是宫廷和上流社会的语言。大多数诺曼人也学会了一些英语，但不在公开场合讲，怕有失身份。但爱德华三世发动的战争使法语成为敌国语言。国王下令在法庭、学校和其他公共场所只允许讲英语，贵族们之间也开始用英语交流。于是，诺曼人和英格兰人的差异消失了，从那以后，所有的人都是英格兰人。用英文写的作品开始流行。对英语的发展贡献最大的作家是乔叟。

乔叟在用英语写作时，他为自己的母语感到自豪，对其表达力充满信心。他的《坎特伯雷故事集》大大提高了英语作为文学语言的声誉。在他那个时代，英语有多种方言，很不一致。但乔叟讲的是牛津、剑桥和伦敦的方言，《坎特伯雷故事集》便用这一方言写成。由

his time, there were differences between the various kinds of English spoken in the north, south, east and west, but Chaucer spoke the English of Oxford, Cambridge and London, and wrote his *Canterbury Tales* in this dialect. Since his work was very popular and widely read, it helped to make the London dialect the standard of the educated classes. With his *Canterbury Tales*, Chaucer proved that the English language was a beautiful language and can be easily handled to express different ideas and feelings. Chaucer introduced a rhythmic pattern called iambic pentameter into English poetry. This pattern, or meter, consists of 10 syllables alternately unaccented and accented in each line. Iambic pentameter became a widely used meter in English poetry.

During the Hundred Years' War, many rich men gave their money to build schools. New grammar schools were opened in big towns. Often they were built by guilds or by private merchants, who were proud of their towns and wanted to give local boys a chance. They gave free education to the "poor"; but everyone was considered poor who could not afford a private teacher for the children. So the grammar schools were filled with the sons of traders, farmers and skilled workers. These students gradually formed a valuable new force in society — well informed public opinion.

于这部作品大受欢迎并被广泛阅读，促使伦敦方言成为有教养阶层的标准。乔叟用《坎特伯雷故事集》证明，英语是一种美丽的语言，易于表达种种不同的思想感情。此外乔叟将抑扬格五音步这一节奏模式引入英语诗歌。按照这一模式，每一诗行有 10 个音节，轻音与重音交替出现。抑扬格五音步后来被广泛用于英诗中。

百年战争期间，许多有钱人出资办学。大城市里开办了文法学校。这些学校常常是商会或个体商户开办的，他们为自己的城镇感到自豪，因而希望给当地的男孩子们出人头地的机会。他们的免费教育是针对"穷人"的，然而凡是雇不起私家教师的都算穷人。因此，文法学校里学生很多是商人、农夫和

乔叟

In 1382 William of Wykeham followed the example of King Alfred and opened a public school in Winchester. The school, called Winchester College, is the oldest and one of the most famous public schools in the country. The name of "public schools" is misleading. They are not free schools. They are privately supported institutions for secondary education. William was a bishop, and he realized the importance of training those who were likely to fill important positions when they grew up. So his school was planned for "the sons of noble and powerful persons" as well as for clever boys from ordinary homes, who did not have to pay. He also opened New College at Oxford, and encouraged boys to go and study there.

King Henry VI saw the value of Wykeham's work. In 1440 he opened his own school at Eton, and his own King's College at Cambridge.

技术工人的儿子。这些学生逐渐形成了社会中一种宝贵的新势力——建立在广见博识基础上的舆论。

1382 年，威克姆的威廉按照阿尔弗雷德大王创建的模式在温切斯特建立一所公学。这所被称为温切斯特学院的公学，是英国最古老的公学，也是最著名的公学之一。"公学"这一名称常使人误解。它们并非免费学校。它们的办学资金来源于私人对中等教育的赞助。威廉是个主教，他意识到训练那些长大后有可能担任重要职位的孩子是极其重要的。所以他的学校旨在招收那些付不起学费的普通人家聪慧的男孩，以及"贵族和大户人家的子弟"。他还创办了牛津大学的新学院，鼓励男孩子们到那里学习。

亨利六世认识到威克姆的事业很有价值。于是在 1440 年开办他自己的伊顿公学，并在剑桥创立国王学院。

题外话

- 在中世纪，隐修院为年龄较大的孩子开办的各种学校通称文法学校（grammar school），因为拉丁文法是主修科目。16 世纪，文法学校脱离教会，改为公办，或转移到市政当局手中后，拉丁文法仍是主修科目。随着时间的推移，文法学校的课程发生了很大变化，拉丁文法的地位下降为"七艺"（文法、修辞、逻辑、音乐、天文、数学、几何）之一，但为高校入学打基础的中等学校仍保留了文法学校的旧称。

- 英国在中世纪就开始了教育的普及。这对日后民主制度的发展提供了必要条件。教育投入不足，受过良好教育的人在总人口中的比例过低，是实行民主的最大障碍。

- 英国的公学（public school）实际上是高收费的私立学校。之所以称为"公学"，是因为它们最初是针对中产阶级的子弟建立的。教学的目的是为了训练未来的政府、教会、军队及法律界的领导人才。入学考试难度大，入学后寄宿学校，纪律严格，生活艰苦。

4. Henry VI

亨利六世

Henry VI (1421-1471, king of England 1422-1461, 1470-1471) was the last English king of the House of Lancaster. He succeeded his father, Henry V, when he was less than a year old. According to a peace agreement made between England and France, Henry VI should also succeed Charles VI of France, who died the same year Henry became king of England, as the new king of France. But the French declared that the English king had no right to the French throne, and so England never controlled all of France in Henry's reign. Henry was educated, gentle, and had strong religious beliefs, but he was a weak ruler and had mental illness, and occasionally became quite mad.

Throughout his life Henry's court was controlled by different groups of English nobles who struggled against one another for power and took advantage of Henry's weakness to further their own interests. And since Henry VI was very weak, his queen, Margaret of Anjou, actually had more power than he. France took this opportunity and gradually freed itself from English control between 1430 and 1453. The vast territory Henry V won in France was gradually lost. By the end of 1453, the French had taken back all the land they had lost to England except Calais. Now the English people were

亨利六世（1421-1471，英格兰国王，1422-1461，1470-1471）是兰开斯特王朝的最后一任国王。他继承父亲亨利五世的王位时，还不满一岁。按照英法订立的条约，亨利六世将继承法国国王查理六世的王位。查理在亨利继位为英格兰国王当年去世。但法国宣告英格兰国王无权继承法国王位，所以亨利在位期间，英格兰从未控制过整个法国。亨利有知识，性情温和，笃信宗教，但作为统治者却软弱无能，而且患有精神病，时而完全失去理智。

在亨利一生中，朝政由不同的英国贵族集团控制，各集团争权夺势，利用亨利的软弱谋私利。而且由于亨利软弱，王后安茹的玛格丽特实际上比他的权力更大。法国利用这一机会，在1430年至1453年间逐渐摆脱了英格兰的控制。亨利五世在法国夺取的大片领土逐渐丢掉了。1453年末，除去加莱，法国夺回了所有被英格兰占领的国土。这时，英格兰人开始对亨利的政府表示不满。

15世纪50年代，野心勃勃的约克公爵理查挑动人们支持他的家

displeased with Henry's government.

During the 1450s, Richard, the ambitious duke of York, stirred up people to support his family's claim to the English throne. A series of wars, called the Wars of the Roses, were fought between the houses of Lancaster and York. The two houses were both descended from Edward III. This struggle went on for thirty years. In 1461, the nobles of the House of York and their supporters forced Henry from the throne and made Edward IV king. Henry regained the crown in 1470. But in 1471, Edward captured Henry and had him imprisoned in the Tower of London, where he soon died. Edward probably had Henry murdered.

族夺取英格兰王位。于是在兰开斯特和约克家族之间爆发了一连串的战争，史称玫瑰战争。两个家族都是爱德华三世的后代。战争持续了30年。1461年，约克家族的贵族和他们的支持者迫使亨利逊位，拥立爱德华四世为王。亨利于1470年夺回王位，但在第二年爱德华俘获亨利，将他囚禁在伦敦塔，不久亨利在塔中死去。有可能爱德华下令杀死了他。

亨利六世

题外话

在中世纪，一旦国王被废黜，往往必死无疑。即使他真心想当平民也不成。因为只要他活着，必然会有人打着他的旗号，对当权者构成威胁。爱德华二世、理查二世、亨利六世都是例子。此外，还得把那个无辜的孩子爱德华五世包括在内。

5. The Wars of the Roses

玫瑰战争

The Wars of the Roses (1455-1485) was a struggle between two branches of the royal family for the throne. It began to develop near the end of the Hundred Years' War. Since Hen-

玫瑰战争（1455-1485）是两个王族争夺王位的战争。百年战争接近尾声时冲突已见端倪。从亨利四世开始，兰开斯特家族的国王已

ry IV, kings of the House of Lancaster had ruled England for more than fifty years. Henry VI was a weak ruler, and the nobles of the House of York decided to overthrow him. Then Richard, 3rd duke of York, brought forward a claim to the throne. Richard was the richest nobleman in England. He was descended through his mother from the third son of King Edward III. Henry VI was descended in a line of males from Edward III's fourth son, John of Gaunt, Duke of Lancaster. Because the Duke of York was descended from an older son, he claimed that he had a better right to the throne than Henry VI. Parliament considered Richard's claim just, and it was agreed that the house of York should inherit the throne on Henry's death. Henry consented to this proposed arrangement. Henry's wife, Margaret of Anjou, however, wanted her son Edward to succeed his father, and in 1455 she raised an army to defend his claim. A series of wars began between the two houses and their supporters. The wars came to be called the Wars of the Roses, for the badge of the House of Lancaster was a red rose and that of the House of York a white rose.

With the support of the powerful nobleman Earl of the Warwick, Richard defeated the king's forces during the first years of the war, and captured King Henry VI in 1459. Henry was forced to promise to give the throne to Richard after his death. But Margaret would not give up. She again raised an army and in a bat-

统治英格兰50余年。亨利六世是个软弱无能的君主，约克家族的贵族们决定推翻他。约克公爵三世理查提出王位要求。理查是最富有的贵族，他的母亲是爱德华三世的第三个儿子的后代。亨利六世则是爱德华三世的第四个儿子兰开斯特公爵冈特的约翰的直系后代。由于约克公爵的祖先比亨利的祖先年龄较大，他自称比亨利有优先继承王位的权力。议会认为理查的要求合理，于是达成协议，约克家族在亨利去世后继位。亨利同意了这一安排。但亨利的妻子，安茹的玛格丽特却希望儿子爱德华继承父亲的王位，便于1455年征集了一支军队捍卫儿子的权利。两个家族和各自的支持者之间爆发了一连串的战争，史称玫瑰战争，因为兰开斯特家族以红玫瑰为族徽，约克家族的族徽是白玫瑰。

由于得到一位势力强大的贵族沃里克伯爵的支持，理查在战争初年打败了国王的军队，并于1459年俘获亨利六世。亨利被迫许诺死后王位由理查继承。但玛格丽特不肯罢休。她重整旗鼓，在1460年的一场战斗中打败理查，杀死了他。1461年，沃里克宣布理查的长子为英格兰国王爱德华四世，约克家族的头一个英格兰国王。当年晚些时候，爱德华和沃里克在一场恶战中打败了兰开斯特军，亨利和

tle in 1460 defeated Richard and killed him. In 1461, Warwick declared Richard's his eldest son as Edward IV king of England, the first of the Yorkist line of English kings. Later in the year, Edward and Warwick defeated the Lancaster army in a fierce battle, and Henry and Margaret escaped to Scotland. In 1464 Henry returned to take part in a rebellion against Edward but was captured again in the following year and imprisoned in the Tower of London.

But Edward and Warwick soon quarreled. In 1470, an army led by Warwick invaded England from France and drove King Edward into exile. Warwick then brought back Queen Margaret and Henry VI to the throne. But in 1471, Warwick met Edward in battle again and was killed. Edward sent Henry back to the tower, where Henry died in the same year, probably murdered on Edward's order. Henry's only son, Edward, was also killed, so that the direct line of the House of Lancaster came to an end.

Edward IV ruled until 1483. He was succeeded by his 12-year-old son, Edward V. Shortly afterward, the boy king's uncle, Richard, Duke of Gloucester, imprisoned boy and his younger brother in the Tower of London and declared himself King Richard III. The boys were never heard of again.

Soon after Richard became king, Henry Tudor, Earl of Richmond, claimed the throne on the grounds that he was relative of the House of Lancaster. Henry defeated and killed Richard III at Bosworth Field in 1485. He as-

玛格丽特逃往苏格兰。1464 年，亨利重返英格兰参加推翻爱德华的叛乱，于次年再次被捕，囚禁在伦敦塔。

但不久爱德华与沃里克发生争吵。1470 年沃里克率领一支军队从法国入侵英格兰，迫使爱德华流亡到国外。然后沃里克请王后玛格丽特和亨利六世复位。但在 1471 年，沃里克与爱德华再次交战，沃里克战死。爱德华把亨利送回伦敦塔，亨利于当年死去，可能是爱德华下令杀死的。亨利的儿子爱德华也被杀死，兰开斯特家族的直系到此断绝。

爱德华统治到 1483 年。他的 12 岁的儿子爱德华五世继位。不久，幼王的叔父格罗斯特公爵理查将幼王和他的弟弟监禁在伦敦塔，宣布自己为国王理查三世。两个孩子从此音信全无。

理查登基后不久，里士满伯爵亨利·都铎以自己为兰开斯特家族亲戚为理由提出王位要求。亨利在 1485 年博斯沃斯原野一役中打败并杀死理查三世。亨利登基为亨利七世，都铎王朝的首位国王。亨利娶了爱德华四世的女儿伊丽莎白，将兰开斯特和约克两个对立的家族联合起来。

在玫瑰战争中，大批贵族战死或失去土地。亨利在议会的支持下，一劳永逸地摧毁了贵族的势

cended the throne as King Henry VII and was the first English king of the House of Tudor. Henry married Edward IV's daughter, Elizabeth, and so at last united the rival houses of Lancaster and York.

So many nobles had been killed in the Wars of the Roses, or had lost their lands, that with Parliament's support Henry was able to destroy their power for ever. Their feudal rights and duties came to an end. Now they were forbidden by law to keep any armed forces. The most important result of the war was the weakening of the power of great nobles and the increase of the Crown's power.

力。贵族的封建权利和义务已告终结。现在，贵族们被禁止拥有武装力量。玫瑰战争的最重要后果是削弱了大贵族的势力，增强了王权。

下和《理查三世》取材于玫瑰战争。这几部剧作反映出伊丽莎白一世时期英国人对内战的担忧。伊丽莎白没有结婚，英国人担心王位继承问题会引起另一场旷日持久的内战。

- 百年战争和玫瑰战争看似英国的不幸，但从另一个角度看，这两场战争又是英国的大幸。百年战争彻底将英法两个民族分离开，使英国人产生了民族感和爱国心，奠定了民族国家的基础。这场战争也提高了英语的地位，促进了英语的发展。而玫瑰战争则恰恰发生在中世纪即将结束，文艺复兴已初露曙光的时候。这场战争无意中破坏了封建制度的基础，为新制度的建立清扫了障碍。

题 外 话

- 都铎王朝徽章上的玫瑰是红白两色的，象征兰开斯特和约克两个家族的联姻。
- 莎士比亚的历史剧四部曲《亨利六世》上、中、

6. Edward IV

Edward IV (1442-1483, king of England 1461-1470; 1471-1483) became king of England in 1461, during the Wars of the Roses. He was the first king of England from the House of York. Edward was the eldest son of Richard Plantagenet, Duke of York. During the war he was defeated in 1459, and driven from England

爱德华四世

爱德华四世（1442-1483，英格兰国王，1461-1470；1471-1483）在玫瑰战争中于1461年登基。他是约克王朝的首位国王。爱德华是约克公爵金雀花的理查的长子。战争期间他于1459年败北，被亨利六世逐出英格兰。他不久返

by Henry VI. He returned to England, and when his father died in 1460, became head of the house of York. With the support of the powerful nobleman Earl of the Warwick, he defeated the Lancaster army in 1461 and was declared king by his supporters. He then won a major victory against the forces of Henry VI and imprisoned Henry in the Tower of London. But in 1470, Edward had a quarrel with the Earl of Warwick, because Warwick arranged political marriage for him with the French royal house, but Edward refused the plan, and married a commoner instead. Warwick then changed sides and began to support the House of Lancaster. Edward then fled to Holland. But he returned the next year with an army and got back the throne. He then ruled England until his death in 1483.

During his reign, printing and silk manufacturing were introduced in England.

回英格兰。他父亲理查于 1460 年战死后，爱德华成为约克家族的首领。依靠势力强大的贵族沃里克伯爵的支持，他于 1461 年打败了兰开斯特军，被支持者拥立为王。他接着又取得一次重大胜利，把亨利六世俘获，关进伦敦塔。1470 年，爱德华与沃里克伯爵失和，因为沃里克为他安排了与法国王室的政治联姻，但爱德华拒绝接受这桩婚事，娶了一个平民女为妻。沃里克然后倒戈，转而支持兰开斯特家族。爱德华被迫逃往荷兰。但在第二年他率领一支军队返回，夺回王位。此后他统治英格兰直至 1483 年逝世。

爱德华在位期间，印刷术和丝织业引入英格兰。

爱德华四世

7. Edward V

爱德华五世

Edward V (1470-1483) succeeded his father, Edward IV, as king of England in 1483 at the age of 12. But before he was crowned, he and his brother were shut up in the Tower of London by his father's brother, Richard, Duke of Gloucester. Gloucester had himself crowned as Richard III. Edward and his brother were last seen playing in the Tower's garden in 1483, and they were never seen again outside the tower. Some historians believe Richard had the boys murdered. But there is no proof of such a crime, and no one knows what happened to the boys.

爱德华五世 (1470-1483) 于 1483 年继承父亲爱德华四世的王位，当时只有 12 岁。还未加冕，就被父亲的弟弟、格罗斯特公爵理查关进伦敦塔。格罗斯特令人为自己加冕为理查三世。有人最后一次见到爱德华和他的弟弟在伦敦塔花园中玩耍是在 1483 年，此后再没有人在塔外见过他们。有些历史学家认定理查杀害了他们，但罪证不足。没有人知道两个孩子的下落。

🎯 题 外 话

- 爱德华五世之死，是个难以破解的历史之谜。亨利七世宣布是理查杀死了两个少年，都铎时代的历史学家也这么说，但不足为凭。不能指望他们为敌人说公道话。更可怀疑的倒是亨利七世，他同样有谋杀爱德华的动机，因为爱德华是他成为国王的障碍。也有人怀疑凶手可能是白金汉公爵斯塔福德，但也没有确切证据。1674 年伦敦塔内发现两具儿童的骸骨，疑为爱德华和他弟弟的遗骸，但无法断定死亡的确切时间。

- 莎士比亚在历史剧《理查三世》里，把爱德华描绘成一个天真烂漫的少年，与他老谋深算、阴险狠毒的叔父理查形成鲜明对比。而且，在剧里，是理查下令谋杀爱德华的。

爱德华五世和弟弟

8. Richard III

Richard III (1452-1485, king of England 1483-1485) was a son of Richard, Duke of York. Richard fought for his brother, later King Edward IV, during the Wars of the Roses. When Edward was crowned in 1461, Richard was made Duke of Gloucester the same year.

When Edward IV died in 1483, his elder son became King Edward V at the age of 12. The government was put in the care of Richard. The relatives of the queen, young king's mother, plotted to seize power. Richard removed this group of unpopular people from power. Parliament then declared that Richard was the rightful king, on the grounds that the marriage of Edward IV with Elizabeth had been illegal because he had contracted earlier to marry another woman. Richard was crowned as Richard III, and put Edward V and his younger brother in the Tower of London. Some historians believe that King Richard had the boys killed. But no proof of such a crime has been found.

Richard was an able ruler, and tried to govern well. But few people really liked him, especially when it began to be rumoured that he had had his nephews murdered. Powerful nobles of both the houses of York and Lancaster plotted against him. With their help, Henry Tudor, Earl of Richmond, a relative of the House

理查三世

理查三世 (1452-1485, 英格兰国王, 1483-1485) 是约克公爵理查的儿子。在玫瑰战争中, 理查为哥哥即后来的爱德华四世作战。爱德华于 1461 年加冕, 理查同年受封为格罗斯特公爵。

爱德华于 1483 年去世, 长子继位为爱德华五世, 时年 12 岁, 由理查摄政。太后(小国王的母亲)的亲属们策划夺权, 理查将这群不得人心的人从政府里清除了出去。议会然后宣布理查为合法国王, 理由是爱德华四世与伊丽莎白的婚姻不合法, 因为此前他与另一女人立有婚约。理查加冕为理查三世, 将

理查三世

of Lancaster, invaded England from his exile in France. Richard hastened to meet him, and the hostile armies faced each other on Bosworth Field. Richard fought bravely but was defeated and killed, and the Earl of Richmond became Henry VII, the first Tudor king of England.

理查三世的末日

爱德华五世和他的弟弟关进伦敦塔。有些历史学家认为理查下令杀害了他们，但证据不足。

理查是个能干的统治者，也有心治理好国家。但很少有人真正喜欢他，特别因为人们听到传闻说他下令杀害了自己的侄子们。约克和兰开斯特家族的权贵们都阴谋反对他。借助他们的力量，兰开斯特家族的一个亲戚，流亡于法国的里士满伯爵亨利·都铎率军入侵英格兰。理查仓促迎敌，两军在博斯沃斯原野对阵。理查浴血奋战，最终战败被杀。里士满伯爵登基为亨利七世，成为都铎王朝的首位国王。

题 外 话

- 若想了解百年战争和玫瑰战争这段纷杂而有趣的历史，莫如阅读莎士比亚的历史剧理查二世、亨利四世(上、下)、亨利五世、亨利六世(上、中、下)和理查三世。莎剧为我们提供了生动形象的历史，虽然不够精确。读过这些历史剧，你对英国的中世纪史就了解了大半，这些君王们的事迹和他们的在位顺序可脱口而出。理查、亨利、爱德华，就不再是绞尽脑汁也记不住的苍白空洞符号。

- 读过莎士比亚的历史剧《理查三世》的，都知道理查三世集人间几乎一切丑陋邪恶于一身。他外貌畸形、奸诈凶残、口蜜腹剑、寡廉鲜耻。莎士比亚显然受到都铎王历史学家的影响。这些历史学家出于本朝利益的考虑，往理查三世身上抹黑并不奇怪。其实，理查在短暂的在位期间，曾大力促进贸易，实行财政改革，做过一些好事。从他的画像看，也并不像莎士比亚描写的那样丑陋不堪。

CHAPTER EIGHT
England Under the Tudors
都铎王朝时期的英格兰

1. Henry VII

亨利七世

Henry VII (1457-1509, king of England 1485-1509) ended the civil war and brought back peace to England. Henry was a relative of the House of Lancaster. He claimed the throne on the grounds that his mother was a descendant of Edward III. He came to the throne in 1485 after his forces killed King Richard III of the House of York in the Battle of Bosworth Field. To win the support of the House of York and to strengthen his claim to the throne, Henry married Elizabeth, daughter of Edward IV, of the House of York. This marriage ended the struggle between the houses of Lancaster and York for the English throne and united the country.

Henry was serious, thrifty, good at judging people and situation and careful in taking actions. He only appointed people who were able

亨利七世（1457-1509，英格兰国王，1485-1509）结束了内战，给英格兰带来了和平。亨利是兰开斯特家族的亲戚，他要求王位的理由是自己的母亲是爱德华三世的后裔。1485 年，他的军队在博斯沃斯原野一役中杀死理查三世后，他登上王位。为得到约克家族的支持以巩固王权，亨利娶爱德华四世的女儿伊丽莎白为妻。这桩婚事结束了兰开斯特和约克两个家族的争斗，统一了国家。

亨利严肃、节俭，对人对事判断准确，行动谨慎。他只任命那些既能干又忠实的人担任高级职务。他以有力的手段控制了贵族，成功地平息了数起约克家族的叛乱。他愿意与议会合作，尊重英格兰日益

and loyal to him to high offices. He held strong control over the nobles, and put down successfully several Yorkist rebellions against him. He cooperated with Parliament, and respected the interests of England's growing middle class.

Henry VII had no ambition to seize foreign territory by conquest, for he realized that after so many years of war, England needed peace and good trade with foreign countries to increase its wealth. Instead of fighting, he tried to establish good relationship with other royal families. He arranged a marriage between his son Arthur and Catherine of Aragon, daughter of Ferdinand II and Isabella of Spain. After Arthur died, the king arranged Catherine's marriage to his second son, Henry (later King Henry VIII). He also arranged a marriage between his daughter Margaret and James IV of Scotland. In 1494 Henry sent the English statesman Sir Edward Poynings to Ireland to reestablish English control in that country. Henry managed to maintain peaceful relations with Austria, Spain, and France throughout most of his years as king. Henry kept England out of European wars and gathered enormous wealth. England had stronger position among other nations and a greater influence in Europe during his reign.

强大的中产阶级的利益。

亨利七世没有征服外国领土的野心，因为他意识到，在多年的战乱之后，英格兰需要和平，需要发展对外贸易以增加财富。他不再与外国的王族为敌，而是试图与他们建立友好关系。他为儿子亚瑟安排了与西班牙斐迪南二世和伊撒贝拉的女儿阿拉贡的凯瑟琳的婚事。亚瑟死后，他又安排凯瑟琳与二儿子亨利(即后来的亨利八世)结亲。他又将女儿玛格丽特许配给苏格兰国王詹姆斯四世。1494 年，亨利派遣政治家爱德华·波伊宁斯到爱尔兰恢复英格兰对爱尔兰的控制。他在位的大部分时间里，都成功地与奥地利、西班牙和法国保持了良好关系。亨利使英格兰置身于欧陆的

亨利七世

题外话

亨利七世的王冠可说是捡来的，因为兰开斯特和约克两个王族的成员在玫瑰战争中已消耗殆尽。他与王族的血统关系相当远。他父亲是威尔士贵族埃德蒙·都铎，母亲是爱德华三世的儿子约翰的冈特的曾孙女玛格丽特·博福特。

战争之外，积聚了大量财富。在他统治期间，英格兰提高了在各国中的威望，扩大了影响。

2. The Renaissance and Humanism

Renaissance, a French word that means "rebirth", was a series of literary and cultural movements in the 14th, 15th, and 16th centuries. The arts and sciences of ancient Greece and Rome were born again after they had been neglected for hundreds of years. The country where this rebirth began was Italy. Englishmen who studied in Italy brought the new learning back with them to Oxford and Cambridge, and from there it spread to schools all over the land. William Caxton made a contribution to the movement. He set up the first printing press in England in 1476. Before that time, books had to be slowly and painfully copied by hand. Printing made it possible to produce far more books and at far lower cost. Now since books became cheaper and were easily got, more and more people learned how to read.

The most significant intellectual movement of the Renaissance was humanism. Humanism

文艺复兴与人文主义

文艺复兴（英文字 Renaissance 源于法语，意为"重生"，"再生"）是 14~16 世纪的一系列文学和文化运动。古希腊罗马的艺术与科学湮没了数百年之后获得了新生。文艺复兴始于意大利。到意大利学习的英国人将新学问带回牛津和剑桥，再从这两所大学传播到全国各地的学校。威廉·卡克斯顿对这一运动做出了贡献。他于 1476 年在英格兰建立了第一个印刷所。此前，书籍都是手工抄写的，既费时又费力。印刷术使人们能够以低得多的成本印制数量大得多的书籍。由于书籍便宜了，而且容易搞到，越来越多的人开始学习阅读。

文艺复兴时期意义最重大的思想运动是人文主义。人文主义的思想基础是人类是理性动物。人文主

was based on the idea that people are rational beings. It emphasized the dignity and worth of the individual. The humanists believed it was possible to improve human life and society through classical education. This education emphasized teaching and studying a number of subjects that ancient Greeks and Romans were good at, including poetry, history, rhetoric (rules for writing influential prose or speeches), and moral philosophy.

In the first years of the 16th century, scholars like William Grocyn, Thomas Linacre, John Colet and Dutch scholar Desiderius Erasmus, spread their new ideas in Oxford and Cambridge Universities and promoted basic educational and religious reforms in England. The best known of early English Humanists was Thomas More. More told the people in his day that many things they accepted as normal were evils, cruelties and inequalities, and should be eliminated. More's best-known work is *Utopia* (1516). Utopia is a name for a perfect imaginary country, where there are justice and equality for all citizens, freedom of religion, and a national system of education for both boys and girls.

义强调个人的尊严和价值。人文主义者认为，可以通过古典文化的教育改善人的生活和人类社会。古典文化教育强调教授和学习古希腊罗马人所擅长的几门学问，包括诗歌、历史、修辞（写作感人散文和雄辩演说辞的规则）和伦理学。

16 世纪初，威廉·格罗辛、托马斯·利纳克尔、约翰·科利特、荷兰人伊拉斯谟等学者将新思想传入牛津和剑桥大学，促进了教育和宗教的大改革。早期英国人文主义者中最著名的是托马斯·莫尔。莫尔告诉同时代的人们，他们自认为合乎道德的许多行为都是残酷的、不公平的，应当彻底铲除。莫尔的名著是《乌托邦》，写于 1516 年。乌托邦是想象中的完美国家，在这个国家里，所有公民都享有公正平等的待遇，有信仰自由，有男女儿童都能受益的国民教育体系。

伊拉斯谟

From 1485 to 1603, the royal House of Tudor ruled England. Queen Elizabeth I, the last Tudor monarch, reigned from 1558 to 1603. During this period, called the Elizabethan Age, English writers produced some of the greatest poetry and drama in world literature.

从1485~1603年，都铎王朝统治英格兰。都铎王朝的最后一位君主，伊丽莎白一世女王统治时期(1558-1603)称为伊丽莎白时代。在这一时代，英国作家写下世界文学史上最伟大的诗歌和戏剧。

题外话

- 常有人把文艺复兴前的中世纪视为"黑暗时代"，但这种看法并不符合事实。毋宁说，中世纪是文艺复兴的基础，文艺复兴是中世纪文化发展的结果。就英国而言，中世纪的成就有《大宪章》、议会政治和习惯法，有牛津和剑桥大学这样世界一流的教育机构，同时，民族的语言、文学、宗教观念等也在这一时期形成。
- 荷兰学者伊拉斯谟对英国的人文主义者影响很大。他的名著是《愚神颂赞》。在这部书里，他攻击教会的贪污腐化、荒诞的教条、繁文缛节和表面文章。他厌恶经院哲学，认为真的信仰不出于知而发于情，精心打造的神学完全是多余的。

3. Thomas More

托马斯·莫尔

Thomas More (1477?-1535) was a great English author, statesman, and scholar. More was born in London and studied at Oxford University. He studied law after leaving Oxford, but his interests were in science, theology, and literature. During his early manhood, he wrote comedies and spent much time in the study of Greek and Latin literature.

More began his legal career in 1494, and became a government official in 1510. Soon More attracted the attention of King Henry VIII, and was appointed to more and more important

托马斯·莫尔 (1477?-1535) 是英国伟大的作家、政治家和学者。莫尔出生于伦敦，就读于牛津大学。毕业后研究法律，但兴趣在于科学、神学和文学。他青年时写过喜剧，并利用大量时间研究希腊罗马文学。

1494年，莫尔开始从事律师业，1510年开始在政府中任职。不久他引起亨利八世的关注，担任越来越高的职务。莫尔于1521年受封为骑士，两年后成为议会下院

positions. More was knighted in 1521, and two years later, he was made Speaker of the House of Commons. In 1529, he became lord chancellor. During this period Henry VIII made More one of his favorites and often asked More to stay with him, discussing philosophy.

But soon More's fortunes changed. Henry VIII wanted to cancel his marriage to Catherine of Aragon so he could marry Anne Boleyn. He had a bitter quarrel with the pope, who refused to grant his divorce. More resigned his office in 1532 because he could not support the king's policy against the pope. The king hated the attitude of his former friend and had him imprisoned in 1534. More was tried and was beheaded the following year for refusing to accept the king as head of the English church. The Roman Catholic Church declared him a saint in 1935.

More's most important work is *Utopia*, written in Latin in 1516. *Utopia* is an account of an ideal society, with justice and equality for all citizens. In this country the interests of the individual are subordinate to those of society at large, all people must do some work, universal education and religious

议长。1529 年又担任大法官。这一时期，亨利八世视莫尔为宠臣，常常要莫尔作陪，与他讨论哲学。

但不久莫尔的命运发生了改变。亨利八世希望解除他与阿拉贡的凯瑟琳的婚姻，以便娶安妮·博林为妻。由于教皇拒绝允许他离婚，他与教皇发生激烈争吵。莫尔不愿支持国王反对教皇的政策，于 1532 年辞去大法官职务。国王对自己朋友的态度感到愤怒，于 1534 年将莫尔投入监狱。1535 年，因为拒绝承认国王为英格兰教会的首脑，莫尔受审后被砍头。罗马天主教于 1935 年追谥莫尔为圣徒。

莫尔的最重要著作是《乌托邦》，于 1516 年用拉丁文写成。《乌托邦》描写了一个理想中的完美社会，在这个社会里，所有公民都享有公正

托马斯·莫尔

toleration are practiced, and all land is owned in common. This masterpiece gave the word *utopia* to many languages.

More was a patron of the arts. His friends included the humanist Erasmus and the artist Hans Holbein.

平等的待遇。个人利益要服从全社会的利益，所有人都必须工作，所有人能受教育，各教派相互宽容，所有土地归公。这部著作创造了"乌托邦"一词，现已在世界多种语言中使用。

莫尔还是文学艺术的赞助人。他的朋友包括人文主义者伊拉斯谟和画家霍尔拜因。

题外话

· 莫尔是个耿直的人。亨利八世多次召他进宫，但他总是不去。最后国王只得亲自到他家里，与他一同进餐。莫尔对亨利八世不抱幻想。有人祝贺他受到国王的恩宠，他答道："倘若我莫尔的人头能让他换取一座法国城池，这颗头定会落地。"

· 莫尔走上断头台时仍对刽子手开玩笑。他说："帮帮忙，扶我上去；下来的时候就不必劳驾了，我自己能凑合。"

· 《乌托邦》的真正价值不在于共产制度的说教，而在于其开明进步的精神。乌托邦人轻视战功、怜恤敌军中的普通士兵、提倡宗教宽容、反对滥杀动物、主张刑法宽大。这在当时是极其难能可贵的。即使在 21 世纪，人们未必能做到这些。

《乌托邦》模型

4. The Reformation

宗教改革

In England, the Reformation began from an act of state. But its success relied in part on the people's demand for changes in the Catholic Church. The immediate cause for England's break with the Catholic Church was a quarrel between King Henry VIII and Pope Clement VII over Henry's marriage. Henry's first wife, Catherine of Aragon, had not borne Henry a son, and the king wanted to marry Anne Boleyn in the hope that the marriage would produce a male heir to the throne. But the pope refused to cancel his first marriage. In 1534, Henry VIII influenced Parliament to pass an act, which made the monarch the head of the church in England, and in the way, the Church of England became a church independent of the pope.

Thomas Cromwell, chief minister of the king, began to take away all the wealth of the Catholic Church. A survey showed that the buildings, lands, and possessions of the English monasteries were about three times that of the crown. Parliament passed laws, making the monks and nuns leave the monasteries and paying small pensions to them. The crown then took possession of all their property.

Henry VIII broke with the Catholic Church because he wanted more political power and solved his personal problems. However, his actions received general support. More and more

在英格兰，宗教改革开始于一次政府行为，但它的成功却有赖于来自民间的改革天主教的要求。英格兰脱离天主教的直接原因是英王亨利八世就其婚事与教皇克雷芒七世的争吵。亨利的头一个妻子阿拉贡的凯瑟琳未能为他生下子嗣，他因此想娶安妮·博林，希望这次婚姻能为他生下男性继承人。但教皇拒绝宣布他的第一次婚姻无效。1534年，亨利八世说服议会通过一项法案，宣布君主为英格兰教会的首领，英格兰教会就此成为独立于教皇的教会。

国王的首席大臣托马斯·克伦威尔开始没收天主教的所有财产。评估表明，英格兰隐修院的建筑、土地和财产的总价值大约三倍于王室的财产。议会通过法律，规定修士和修女离开隐修院，只给他们一小笔生活补助。王室攫取了他们所有的财产。

亨利八世与天主教会决裂是因为他想获取更多的政治权力，并解决个人婚姻问题。但是，他采取的行动得到了广泛的支持。越来越多

Catholics felt angry about the activities of the pope, the wealth of the clergymen, and the corruption of the monks and nuns. They wanted the Catholic Church to be reformed. Henry also received support from people who were adopting the new religious ideas of German reformer Martin Luther. Luther's ideas had spread into England and had begun to have followers, especially in cities. These Protestant religious views were also becoming popular at both Oxford and Cambridge universities.

During Henry's rule, the Bible was translated into English, priests were allowed to marry, and the shrines of saints were destroyed.

The Reformation in England was not accomplished without opposition. Throughout the 1530s and into the 1540s more than 300 people were executed for rebelling against the Reformation. Sir Thomas More refused to recognize the king as supreme head of the church and was executed for his Catholic beliefs, along with a number of bishops and famous nobles.

Henry VIII remained basically a Catholic, however. Queen Elizabeth I, who ruled from 1558 to 1603, established a moderate form of Protestantism that became known as Anglicanism. But English people who followed John Calvin wanted further reform. They were dissatisfied with the Church of England because it was governed by bishops. These Calvinists in England were called Puritans. Catholicism was officially banned.

的天主教徒对教皇的行径、教士们的财富、修士和修女的腐败感到愤懑。他们希望天主教进行改革。亨利也得到接受了德国宗教改革家马丁·路德的新宗教思想的人的支持。路德的思想已传入英格兰，并开始有信奉者，特别在城市里。这些新教观点也开始流行于牛津和剑桥大学。

在亨利统治期间，《圣经》译成了英语，神甫可以结婚，圣徒们的神龛遭到破坏。

英国的宗教改革并非没有遇到阻力。16世纪30年代和40年代，有300多人由于反抗宗教改革而被处决。托马斯·莫尔爵士拒绝承认国王为教会的最高首领，并为坚持自己的天主教信仰而被处决。同他一起被处决的还有一批主教和著名贵族。

但亨利八世基本上还是个天主教徒。女王伊丽莎白一世统治期间（1558-1603），建立起一种温和的新教，称为安立甘宗。但追随加尔文的英国人要求进一步改革。他们对英格兰教会不满，因为教会仍受主教的控制。这些英格兰的加尔文主义者被称为清教徒。天主教则正式被禁止。

5. Henry VIII

亨利八世

Henry VIII (1491-1547, king of England 1509-1547) greatly influenced English history by separating the Church of England from the Roman Catholic Church. Henry was a powerful and talented man, and is often remembered for having had six wives, two of them he executed and two divorced.

Henry was the second son of Henry VII and Elizabeth of York. Although a willful child, Henry proved a capable student and studied languages, philosophy, mathematics, astronomy, and writing and speaking under his first tutor, English poet John Skelton. Tall and strong, he was an excellent horseman and wrestler. Henry loved music and could play, sing, and dance. He spoke three foreign languages. Henry was a clever politician who trusted Parliament and made full use of it. Most important of all, he thoroughly understood the hearts and minds of his people. When he was 11, Henry's elder brother Arthur died. He became now heir to the throne and was made

亨利八世 （1491-1547, 英格兰国王,1509-1547) 由于使英格兰教会与罗马天主教分离而大大影响了英国的历史进程。亨利是个权势显赫而又多才多艺的君主，人们忘不了他，多是因为他娶了6个妻子，处决了其中两个，休掉了另外两个。

亨利是亨利七世和约克的伊丽莎白的次子。他儿时任性，但善于学习。在首任师傅英国诗人斯克尔顿的教导下，他学习语言、哲学、数学、天文学、写作和演讲。亨利身材高大强壮,善于骑术和角力。他爱好音乐,会奏乐、唱歌和跳舞。他会讲三种外语。亨利是个精明的政治家，信任议会，善于充分利用它达到自己的目的。最重要的是，他透彻了解人民的思想感情。他11岁时,哥哥亚瑟去世。亨利成了王储,于1503年受封为威尔士亲王。

亨利八世

Prince of Wales in 1503.

Henry was 17 years old when he was crowned as Henry VIII in 1509. One of his first acts as king was to marry his brother's widow, Catherine of Aragon. The pope had given special permission for this marriage, as it was against the laws of the Church for a man to marry his brother's widow. Catherine gave Henry a daughter, who later became Queen Mary I, but all her sons died at birth. People at the time believed it unnatural for women to rule over men; such a rule could not be stable. So Henry wanted a son to succeed him to make sure that the Tudor family would continue to control the throne and to prevent any fighting over who would succeed him. Henry began to feel that God had not approved of his marriage and that the pope had been wrong to allow it.

Henry had affairs with ladies of his court until he fell in love with Anne Boleyn, a maid of honor at court. He wanted to marry Anne. There was only one possible way to solve the problem. The pope must declare that his first marriage had been allowed by mistake and was unlawful; Henry would then be free to marry again. Cardinal Wolsey, Henry's chief minister, was sent to persuade Pope Clement VII to cancel the king's marriage. But Catherine's nephew was Charles V, the Holy Roman Emperor and the most powerful ruler in Europe, and the pope was under his influence. It was not surprising that Wolsey could not be successful, though he was a capable diplomat. Wolsey was dismissed

阿拉贡的凯瑟琳

亨利于 1509 年加冕为亨利八世，当时只有 17 岁。登基后做的头几件事之一是娶哥哥的遗孀阿拉贡的凯瑟琳为妻。这件婚事是经教皇特批的，因为娶兄弟的遗孀为妻是违反教规的。凯瑟琳为亨利生了个女儿，这就是后来的玛丽女王一世；但她生下的所有儿子都在出生时死去。当时人们认为女人统治男人是反常的，这样的统治不会长久。所以亨利想要一个儿子继承他的王位，以确保都铎家族稳坐江山，防止因继承人问题出现争斗。亨利开始感到上帝不赞同他的婚姻，教皇特批此事是犯了错误。

亨利与宫廷里的侍女们有染，最终爱上了宫中女官安妮·博林。他想明媒正娶安妮。解决这一问题只有一种途径，即教皇必须宣布他的头一件婚事批准错了，因而不合法。这样就扫除了再婚的障碍。亨利的首席大臣红衣主教沃尔西受命去劝说教皇克雷芒七世取消国王的

for his failure. After that Thomas Cranmer and Thomas Cromwell became the king's closest advisers. They were both sympathetic to Martin Luther, the German religious reformer. They suggested that Parliament pass an act to declare Henry head of the church in England, which would allow the king himself to settle the king's affair.

Beginning in 1529, Henry caused Parliament to pass a series of acts by which he gained the power to appoint his own bishops. In 1531, the English Church recognized him as head of the Church. In 1533, after Anne Boleyn was pregnant, Henry married her in secret. Then Parliament passed an act, making the king the highest court of appeal for all English subject. Soon Henry appointed Thomas Cranmer as archbishop of Canterbury, who declared Henry's marriage to Catherine was unlawful and cancelled it. Henry officially married Anne and made her queen.

In the following year, Parliament passed the Act of Supremacy, which made the monarch head of the Church in England. This act marked the English Church completely broke with the Roman Catholic Church. Following Henry's actions, English church leaders made changes in Roman Catholic services that gradually led to the formation of the Church of England. A number of Henry's subjects who opposed him were imprisoned or executed for treason.

Henry's family troubles did not end with his marriage to Anne. In 1533, Anne bore him

婚姻。但是凯瑟琳的侄子是罗马帝国的皇帝查理五世，欧洲最强大的统治者，连教皇也在他的控制之下。沃尔西无功而返毫不足怪，尽管他是个能干的外交家。沃尔西因此被解职。此后，托马斯·克兰默和托马斯·克伦威尔成为国王最信任的顾问。此二人同情德国宗教改革家马丁·路德。他们建议议会通过立法宣布亨利为英格兰教会的首脑，这样国王本人就可以解决自己的个人问题。

从1529年开始，亨利促使议会通过一系列的法案，使他获得任命主教的权力。1531年，英格兰教会承认他为教会首脑。1533年，安妮·博林有了身孕，亨利与她

安妮·博林

秘密成婚。议会通过一项法案,使国王成为全体英格兰臣民的最高上诉法庭。不久,亨利任命托马斯·克兰默为坎特伯雷大主教,克兰默宣布亨利与凯瑟琳的婚姻不合法,予以

a daughter who later became Queen Elizabeth I. But the king quickly lost interest in Anne, because she did not give him a son, and besides, she was suspected to be unfaithful to her husband. Then in 1536, Anne was imprisoned in the Tower of London on charges of adultery with her brother, three advisors of the king, and a musician of the court and of making secret plans to murder the king. The queen and the five men were tried, and all were declared to be guilty of treason. The musician was hanged, and the other four men beheaded. Two days later, Anne was also beheaded. Whether Anne was guilty of these crimes has never been determined. It is known that Henry wanted to marry again.

Then Henry immediately married another woman Jane Seymour, but Jane died shortly after the birth of a son who later became King Edward VI.

His chief minister Thomas Cromwell then persuaded Henry to marry a German princess, Anne of Cleves. Unfortunately the German girl was neither clever nor beautiful. Within a few months Henry divorced her, cut off Cromwell's head, and married a beautiful girl called Catherine Howard. But soon she too was declared unfaithful and beheaded with her two accused lovers. Henry's sixth and last wife, the wise and gentle Catherine Parr, had the good luck to outlive her husband, but she had no children.

Following the break with Rome, Henry, with the help of Cromwell, began to take away

取消。亨利正式与安妮结婚,使她成为王后。

翌年,议会通过至尊法案,使君主成为英格兰教会的首脑。这一法案标志着英格兰教会彻底脱离罗马天主教。紧随亨利采取的行动,英格兰教会领袖们也改动了罗马天主教的礼仪,逐步导致英国国教的形成。一些反对亨利的人以叛国罪被监禁或处决。

亨利终于与安妮的成婚,但其家庭生活的烦恼并没有就此告终。1533年,安妮为他生了个女儿,这就是后来的女王伊丽莎白一世。但是国王很快对安妮失去兴趣,因为她未能给他生儿子,而且她还有对丈夫不忠的嫌疑。1536年,安妮被囚入伦敦塔,罪名是与自己的兄弟、国王的三个顾问以及一个宫廷乐师通奸,并阴谋策划刺杀国王。王后和5个男人受到审判,被宣布犯有欺君之罪。乐师被处以绞刑,另外几人被砍了头。两天后,安妮也被砍了头。安妮是否真的犯有这几桩罪行至今无法确定。可以确定的是,亨利想再婚了。

亨利马上娶了另一个女人简·西摩,但是简在产下一子后不久去世。这个儿子,后来成为爱德华六世。

首席大臣托马斯·克伦威尔劝说亨利迎娶一位德国公主克利夫斯的安妮。很不幸,这位德国公主既

all the land and buildings of the monasteries. To pay for his continued wars, Henry sold the property to nobles and country gentlemen, who, as new owners of the Catholic Church property, became supporters of the Reformation. Henry's own religious beliefs remained Catholic, but growing number of people at court and in the nation adopted Protestant religious beliefs.

During his rule, Henry reorganized his government to make it more powerful and effective. He built up a strong fleet of fighting ships to expand England's power in Europe. Henry involved England in several expensive wars with France and Scotland and defeated them. In acts of 1536 and 1543, Henry united

无才又无貌。几个月后，亨利就休了她，砍掉克伦威尔的脑袋，又娶了一个名叫凯瑟琳·霍华德的姑娘。但不久后，凯瑟琳被宣布有不贞行为，与她那两个受到指控的情人一同被砍了头。亨利的第六任，即最后一任妻子，聪明温顺的凯瑟琳·帕尔有幸比丈夫活得长久，但她没有孩子。

与罗马决裂后，亨利以克伦威尔为得力助手，开始没收隐修院的土地和房产。为了支付连年战争所需要的开支，亨利将没收的财产出售给贵族和乡绅。这些人，由于成了天主教财产的所有人，也就成为宗教改革的支持者。亨利本人的宗教信仰仍是天主教的，但越来越多的朝臣和百姓开始信奉新教。

亨利在其统治时期，将政府组织得更为强大和高效。他组建了一支强大的舰队以扩大英格兰在欧洲的势力。他将英格兰拖入几场与法国和苏格兰的战争，耗费大量资财后打败了对手。通过

亨利八世将教皇踩在脚下

England and Wales and put them under one system of government.

1536 年和 1543 年的两个法案，亨利将英格兰和威尔士统一起来，置于一个政府之下。

🔘 题外话

- 基督徒主张一夫一妻，不像中国皇帝，可以妻妾成群，所以亨利八世才遇到那么多的麻烦。想再婚，必须先离婚，想离婚，须有教皇的特批。《旧约·利未记》里禁止娶嫂子或弟媳为妻，说如果娶了，则不会有儿女。这条戒律为亨利提供了休妻的借口。
- 亨利八世的主要事业，都是通过他的两个重臣沃尔西和克伦威尔成就的。但伴君如伴虎。两人都没有好下场。沃尔西最终被剥夺了所有的财产，还被控叛国，但在受审之前幸而病死。克伦威尔则不那么走运，他被控叛国，未经审判就被砍了头。
- 亨利八世恐怕是英国历史上最有趣的君主。不但多才多艺，还多欲。娶过六个妻子不说，据说食量和酒量也很大。看来他年轻时气力也不小。现存他的一副铠甲，其重量非常人所能承受。
- 关于亨利八世的功过，历史学家们无法达成一致意见。有人认为尽管亨利自私自利，性情冷酷，生活奢靡，他仍算得上一个伟大的国王。他的勇气和政治智慧使英国强大起来。也有人认为他根本算不上伟大，他死后留下的是个民穷财尽的烂摊子。
- 宗教改革后，为防止罗马教廷利用爱尔兰遏止英格兰，亨利八世于 1541 年加冕为爱尔兰国王。

6. Edward VI

爱德华六世

Edward VI (1537–1553, king of England and Ireland 1547–1553) was the only son of Henry VIII. His mother was Jane Seymour, Henry's third wife.

Edward was only 9 years old when he became king, so his maternal uncle Edward Seymour, who soon became the Duke of Somerset, governed for him. Both Edward and Somerset stuck to the principle of the Reforma-

爱德华六世 (1537-1553, 英格兰与爱尔兰国王，1547-1553) 是亨利八世唯一的儿子。他母亲是亨利的第三任妻子简·西摩。

爱德华即位时仅9岁，他的舅舅

爱德华六世

英国历史重大事件及著名人物 • 93

tion and tried to establish Protestantism in England. A new service book, the first Book of Common Prayer, appeared in 1549 and its use was made compulsory by Parliament. The book was strongly opposed by Roman Catholics, but gradually came into general use in England, making English Reformation more protestant in doctrine. In 1549 Somerset attempted to help poor peasants by forbidding enclosure. His policy caused a serious conflict between peasants and rich landowners. John Dudley, earl of Warwick and later duke of Northumberland, took this opportunity to remove Somerset from power. After that Dudley controlled the government.

When Edward was 15 years old, he became seriously ill with tuberculosis. Before he died, the Duke of Northumberland proposed that Edward should give Lady Jane Grey the right to succeed him as ruler. Lady Jane was the great-granddaughter of King Henry VII, Edward's cousin, and Northumberland's daughter-in-law. She was a protestant. Edward agreed to the proposal because he feared that if his half sister Mary, who was a Roman Catholic, should come to the throne, England would no longer be a Protestant nation. But Lady Jane ruled as queen for only nine days before she was deposed by Mary.

爱德华·西摩不久受封为萨莫塞特公爵，代理朝政。爱德华和萨莫塞特坚持宗教改革的原则，试图在英格兰建立新教。一部新的宗教礼仪书，《公祷书》第一版于 1549 年出版，议会宣布为法定礼仪书。这部书遭到罗马天主教的强烈反对，但逐渐在英国普及开来，使英国的宗教改革在教义上更接近新教。1549 年萨莫塞特试图禁止圈地以保护贫穷农民的利益。他的政策引起农民与地主的激烈冲突。沃里克伯爵（后来封为诺森伯兰公爵）约翰·达德利乘机剥夺了萨莫塞特的权力。此后达德利控制了政府。

爱德华 15 岁时患肺病，病情严重。临终时，诺森伯兰公爵向爱德华建议将王位继承权授予简·格雷郡主。简·格雷郡主是亨利七世的曾孙女，爱德华的表妹，诺森伯兰公爵的儿媳。她是个新教徒。爱德华同意了这一建议，因为他的同父异母姐姐玛丽是天主教徒，他担心如果玛丽继位，英格兰就不再是新教国家了。但简·格雷只在位 9 天就被玛丽废黜了。

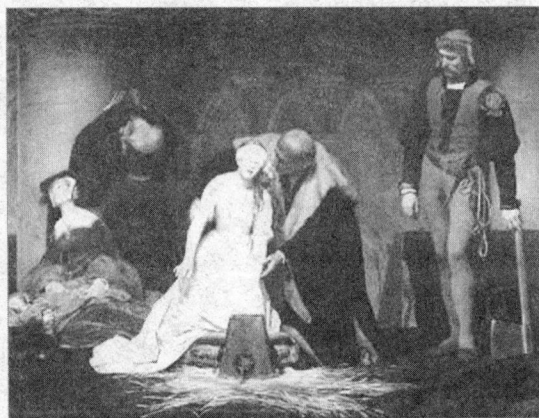

处决简·格雷

7. Mary I

Mary I (1516-1558, queen of England 1553-1558) was the daughter of King Henry VIII and Catherine of Aragon. When her half brother Edward was king, she was next in line for the throne. But since she was a Roman Catholic, Protestants planned to make her cousin Lady Jane Grey queen instead of her. Lady Jane was on the throne for only nine days before Mary, supported by most English people, removed her from power. The English people welcomed Mary because they considered her the rightful queen. But their joy did not last for long.

As soon as she came to the throne, Mary began to sweep away all the changes her father and half brother had made in the Church. First she put the Church back under the power of Rome and brought back the old Catholic beliefs and ceremonies. She made severe laws against Protestant beliefs. She even tried to restore the church lands taken away under Henry VIII. Her

玛丽一世

玛丽一世（1516-1558，英格兰女王，1553-1558）是亨利八世与阿拉贡的凯瑟琳的女儿。她的同父异母弟弟爱德华在位时，她在王位继承人中名列首位。但由于她是天主教徒，新教徒策划立他的表妹简·格雷郡主为女王。简·格雷在位仅9天，玛丽便在大多数英格兰人的支持下将她废黜。英格兰人欢迎玛丽继位，认为她才是合法女王。但他们高兴得太早了。

玛丽一登基，便着手废除父亲和异母兄弟在教会里所进行的一切

玛丽一世

actions displeased the English people. In 1554, Mary married King Philip II of Spain, against the wishes of Parliament. Their marriage made her even more unpopular because many English people considered Spain to be England's greatest enemy and disliked Philip, who had extremely strong Catholic beliefs. To please Spain, Mary joined in a war against France. From the war she gained nothing, but she lost Calais in 1558, the last English territory in the mainland of Europe. It was a serious blow to national pride.

During her short rule, Mary had about 300 English Protestants burned alive. The victims included four bishops and the former Archbishop of Canterbury, Thomas Cranmer. Cranmer was forced at first to sign a confession, but he changed his mind. As the fire rose around him he put out his right hand, which had signed the confession, and held it in the flames, crying: "That unworthy hand! That unworthy hand!" For her cruel treatment of the Protestants, she became known as "Bloody Mary".

Mary died without children and was succeeded by her Protestant half sister, Elizabeth.

改革。首先她将教会重新置于罗马的控制之下，并恢复了往昔的天主教的信仰和仪式。她制定严厉的法规惩治新教信仰。她甚至试图归还亨利八世时没收的教会地产。她采取的措施令英格兰人感到不快。1554 年，玛丽辜负议会的期望，嫁给了西班牙国王腓力二世。他们的联姻使她更不得人心，因为许多英格兰人视西班牙为英格兰的死敌，而且不喜欢腓力，因为他坚持极端的天主教信仰。为讨好西班

西班牙腓力二世

题外话

- 处于政治斗争旋涡中心的皇室成员，很少有一生幸福的。玛丽就是如此。亨利八世与她母亲离婚后，安妮·博林成了王后，剥夺了她的公主封号，叫她给自己的女儿伊丽莎白当侍女。她早年的不幸以及她狂热的天主教信仰使她充满复仇心理，在复杂的政治斗争中缺乏理性，犯下两项重大政治错误。其一是用血腥的暴力恢复不得人心的天主教。其二是与比自己小 11 岁的腓力二世，英国人的死敌结婚。难怪她病死时，整个伦敦响起欢庆的钟声。我们将会看到，伊丽莎白要比她聪明老练得多。

- 关于腓力结婚时的年龄，有一谬说。上海社会科学院出版社出版的《英国通史》称腓力结婚时年仅 11 岁。事实上，腓力出生于 1527 年，玛丽出生于 1516 年，二人于 1554 年结婚，当时腓力 27 岁，玛丽 38 岁。应当是腓力比玛丽小 11 岁。汉译《简明不列颠百科全书》玛丽条亦说腓力结婚时年仅 11 岁，无疑是误译。这部百科全书大概是谬说出处。

牙，玛丽参与了反对法国的战争。从这场战争中她不但一无所获，而且于 1558 年失去加莱，欧洲大陆上英格兰的最后一块领土。这对民族自豪感是个沉重打击。

在她短暂的统治期间，玛丽下令将大约 300 名新教徒处以火刑。被烧死的人包括四位主教和前任坎特伯雷大主教托马斯·克兰默。克兰默此前被迫签署悔罪书，但后来又翻悔。当火焰在他周围升起时，他伸出签署悔罪书右手，放在火里，叫道："这只不争气的手！这只不争气的手！"由于玛丽残酷处置新教徒，被称为"血腥的玛丽"。

玛丽死时无嗣，由信奉新教的异母妹妹伊丽莎白继位。

克兰默的火刑

8. Elizabeth I

伊丽莎白一世

Elizabeth I (1533–1603, queen of England and Ireland 1558–1603) was the daughter of Henry VIII and his second wife, Anne Boleyn. Elizabeth was the first woman to successfully occupy the English throne and ruled as long as nearly half a century. Elizabeth enjoyed enormous popularity during her life and became an even greater legend after her death. Her reign is often called the Golden Age or the Elizabethan Age because it was a time of great achievement in England.

When Elizabeth came to the throne, the English had suffered so much under the rule of Mary that they did not expect anything better than her sister. They soon found that they were wrong. Elizabeth shared many qualities with her father. Like him, she was brave, intelligent, and had strength of character. And like him, she loved hunting and dancing and gay entertainment. She also shared her father's gifts for music and other arts. Her subject loved and admired

伊丽莎白一世（1533–1603，英格兰和爱尔兰女王，1558–1603）是亨利八世和他第二个妻子安妮·博林的女儿。伊丽莎白是成功保持英国王位并统治长达近半个世纪的头一个女人。伊丽莎白在世时大得人心，死后她的事迹传为佳话，其形象更伟大。由于她在位时期英格兰取得伟大成就，这一时期常被称为黄金时代或伊丽莎白时代。

伊丽莎白即位时，英格兰人在玛丽统治下已吃过很大苦头，没有指望伊丽莎白会比她姐姐好多少。他们不久就发现自己错了。伊丽莎白与她的父亲有不少共同点。跟父亲一样，她勇敢、聪慧、有个性。也像父亲一样，

伊丽莎白一世

her. With her red hair and pale eyes she reminded them of her popular father, King Henry VIII.

Elizabeth had a hard childhood. Her mother was beheaded for unfaithfulness to the king when she was two years old. Parliament declared that she was not the daughter of Henry VIII. When Edward VI was king, politicians tried to involve her in plots to prevent Mary becoming the next ruler. In her adolescent years, Elizabeth learned a lot from these experiences and became very shrewd, sensible and careful, and knew how to avoid unnecessary risks. At the same time she received an excellent humanist education. She spoke not only English but Latin, Greek, French, and Italian.

During Mary's rule, Elizabeth cautiously avoided any involvement in politics. She was next in line to the throne and Queen Mary distrusted her. However, Elizabeth came under suspicion in 1554, following an unsuccessful uprising against Mary. Elizabeth was imprisoned for a time, though no evidence was found that linked her to the rebellion. Mary died in 1558, and Elizabeth became queen.

Elizabeth knew that people at the time had little faith in a woman's rule, so she always tried to work together with powerful men in order to rule effectively. She made good use of the Privy Council and had good relations with Parliament. The House of Lords and the House of Commons both grew in size during her rule. She used Parliament to raise taxes and to approve

她爱好狩猎、舞蹈和娱乐。她与父亲同样在音乐和其他艺术方面有天资。她的臣民爱戴她，景仰她。她棕红色的头发和浅色的眼睛使人想起她大得人心的父亲亨利八世。

伊丽莎白的童年多灾多难。她两岁时母亲就以对国王不忠的罪名被砍了头。议会宣布她不是亨利八世的女儿。爱德华六世在位时，政客们曾将她卷入阻止玛丽继位的阴谋活动。伊丽莎白的这些经历使她在少年时期就大长见识，变得十分精明、谨慎、通情达理，知道如何避免不必要的冒险。同时，她也受到良好的人文主义教育。她不但讲英语，而且讲拉丁语、希腊语、法语和意大利语。

玛丽统治时期，伊丽莎白小心翼翼地避免卷入政治活动。在王位继承人的排位中她是下一个，因而玛丽不信任她。然而，1554 年，一场反对玛丽的起义失败后，伊丽莎白还是受到猜疑。虽然没有找到任何证据证明她与叛乱有牵连，她还是被监禁了一段时间。1558 年，玛丽去世，伊丽莎白继位，成为女王。

伊丽莎白知道当时的人们对女人的统治缺乏信任，所以她总是尽力与有权有势的男人们合作，以有效地进行统治。她充分利用枢密院，与议会也保持良好关系。在她统治期间，上院和下院都扩大了。

her policies, but also allowed its members to suggest laws regarding local issues.

At the center of her government, Elizabeth was fortunate in having a number of capable ministers. The ablest of all her ministers was William Cecil, 1st Baron Burghley. Burghley was an honest and far-seeing man, and served the queen faithfully for 40 years. With his help Elizabeth quickly solved her first problem, the Church. Mary's cruelty had excited strong Protestant feelings, but most people wanted what her father had given them: a reformed Catholic Church that used the English language and was free from foreign interference.

Elizabeth faced a dangerous religious situation when she came to the throne. But she handled it with great skill. As a Protestant, she broke Mary's ties with the pope and restored her father's independent Church of England. But under her rule, the Church of England tried to follow a middle course and make its Protestantism moderate and conservative, and so acceptable to both reasonable Catholics and Protestants. But at the same time Elizabeth had also to struggle continuously against both conservative Catholics, who clung to the old faith and plotted to overthrow her, and Puritans, radical Protestants who wanted to remove all the traditional things of the Roman Catholic Church. On the whole, Elizabeth's religious policies successfully held the vast majority of the people together.

Elizabeth never married, though she had

她利用议会征收赋税、批准她的政策，但也允许议员们就地方事务提出立法建议。

伊丽莎白有一批能干的大臣在政府的关键部门任职，这是她的幸运之处。大臣中能力最强的是威廉·塞西尔，伯利男爵第一。伯利是个诚实而有远见的人，为女王忠心耿耿服务 40 年。在他的协助下，伊丽莎白迅速解决了即位后的第一个问题，即教会问题。玛丽的残酷激起了强烈的新教情绪，但大多数人所要的仍是亨利八世带给他们的，即一个使用英语，不受外国的干预的改良了的天主教会。

伊丽莎白即位后面对一个危险的宗教局势。但她很巧妙地处理了它。作为一名新教徒，她中断了与教皇的关系，恢复了父亲在位时独立的英格兰教会。但在她的统治下，英格兰教会试图走一条中间路线，使其新教倾向温和而保守，因而通情达理的天主教徒和新教徒都可以接受。但与此同时，伊丽莎白还须不断与保守的天主教徒做斗争，因为他们固守传统信仰，并阴谋策划推翻她。她也必须与清教徒做斗争，这些激进的新教徒要求彻底清除罗马天主教的一切传统。总的来说，伊丽莎白的宗教政策成功地将大多数人团结在一起。

伊丽莎白终身未嫁，虽然她有不少求婚者。她似乎不想与一个丈

many suitors. She seemed to have no desire to share power with a husband. But she made use of offers of marriage from Philip II of Spain and others as a foreign policy tool to play off the Catholic powers of Europe against one another. Elizabeth seemed to prefer to remain single, if her marriage could not bring her political benefit.

In her last years, Elizabeth was troubled with political and economic problems. The Irish Catholics rebelled, and an army was sent to fight them, but was defeated. The queen's favorite, the Earl of Essex led a rebellion against the government in 1601 and was executed as a traitor. His treachery caused Elizabeth much sorrow. The continued population growth put a heavy burden on the economy. Prices for food and clothing increased very quickly. The 1590s were the worst years of the century. Many people lost their jobs and suffered from hunger and epidemic disease.

Elizabeth I died in 1603 leaving no heir. Her cousin James VI of Scotland became King James I of England.

夫分享权力。但她利用西班牙国王腓力二世和其他人的求婚作推行外交政策的工具，使欧洲的天主教强国相互敌对。看来，如果婚姻不能带给她政治利益，伊丽莎白宁可独身。

到了晚年，伊丽莎白遇到很多政治和经济问题。爱尔兰的天主教徒掀起叛乱，派了一支军队去镇压，却被打败了。女王的宠臣埃塞克斯伯爵于1601年领导一场反政府叛乱，以叛国罪被处决。他的背叛使伊丽莎白感到痛心。持续的人口增长给经济带来很大压力。食品和衣物的价格飞涨。16世纪90年代是这个世纪中最糟糕的几年。许多人失去工作，忍受饥饿和流行病的折磨。

伊丽莎白一世于1603年逝世，死后无嗣。她的孙辈表亲苏格兰的詹姆斯六世继位，成为英格兰国王詹姆斯一世。

伊丽莎白一世67岁时画

伊丽莎白的宠臣埃塞克斯伯爵

伊丽莎白的宠臣瓦尔特·罗利爵士

题 外 话

- 伊丽莎白一世虽然一生独身，却多情善感，与许多男人有浪漫关系。莱斯特伯爵罗伯特·达德利最受她的宠爱。达德利的妻子神秘死去，人们疑心是达德利杀死了她，以便娶女王为妻。但这桩婚事因受众大臣的反对而受阻。后来，达德利娶孀居的埃塞克斯伯爵夫人为妻，使女王大为恼火。达德利死于 1588 年，女王听到他的死讯，足不出户，悲痛欲绝。女王晚年的宠臣是莱斯特伯爵的养子埃塞克斯伯爵。此人聪颖俊美，风度翩翩，但狂妄自大。但终因反叛女王被处决。

- 伊丽莎白虚荣心强，拥有 500 件镶有珍珠的高肩长裙，喜欢盛装在臣民前招摇，接受他们的跪拜。埃塞克斯伯爵曾未经许可闯入她的私室，其时她尚未化妆，使她大为震怒。但她的招摇，也不无政治目的在内，即为了使她的臣民爱戴她，团结在她的周围，以稳定政局。她的一位朝臣说："女王捕捞男人们的魂魄，所用的诱饵又是那么香甜，没有人能逃离她的罗网。"

- 伊丽莎白吝啬，不肯轻易花钱或赐予臣下礼物，喜欢到众臣的府邸宴乐，接受贡品。此外，她也有冷酷、喜怒无常的一面。瓦尔特·罗利爵士是她的宠臣之一。一次，女王出行，在一滩泥水前止步。罗利立即脱下外套，铺在泥水上，为女王垫脚。女王大悦，从此垂青罗利，给他封地，并封他为骑士。罗利爱好探险，两次前往北美，建立殖民地，为了光耀女王命名该地为"弗吉尼亚"，意为"童贞女王之地"。但当他暗中娶了伊丽莎白的一位宫女后，女王大怒，竟将他投入伦敦塔。

9. Mary Queen of Scots

During the Elizabeth's rule, one of the greatest threats to the English government was Mary Queen of Scots. Mary was a great grand-daughter of Henry VII, and Elizabeth nearest cousin and, if Elizabeth died without children, she could claim the English crown.

Mary became Queen of Scotland in 1542, the year of her birth. Although she grew to be a Catholic, she did not oppose the spread of the Protestant faith in her country at first. But in 1565, she married her cousin Henry Stuart, Lord Darnley, father of the future James I of England. Darnley was a Catholic, stupid and ambitious. His rise to power caused leading Protestant noblemen to rebel. The rebellion was quickly put down. Soon after that Mary and her husband began to quarrel for power. And a rumor began to develop that Mary was having

苏格兰玛丽女王

苏格兰的玛丽女王

伊丽莎白统治时期，对英格兰政府的最大威胁是苏格兰女王玛丽。玛丽是亨利七世的曾孙女，伊丽莎白最近的表亲，如果伊丽莎白死时无嗣，她可能会要求得到英格兰王位。

玛丽于1542年，她出生当年即位成为苏格兰女王。虽然她从儿时起就是天主教徒，但起初并未反对新教信仰在苏格兰的传播。但在1565年，她嫁给表弟达恩利勋爵亨利·斯图亚特，即未来的英格兰国王詹姆斯一世的父亲。达恩利是个天主教徒，愚蠢而又野心勃勃。他掌权后引起信奉新教的贵族们的反叛。叛乱很快被镇压下去。不久后，玛丽和丈

an affair with her private secretary, an Italian musician named David Rizzio. A band of Protestant nobles, with Darnley as one of the leaders, dragged Rizzio from Mary's presence and stabbed him to death.

Early in 1567 Darnley was murdered by the Scottish nobleman James Hepburn, 4th Earl of Bothwell, a new favourite of the queen. It was suspected that Mary herself was not wholly ignorant of the plot. Soon afterward Bothwell divorced his wife and married Mary.

This marriage was Mary's fatal mistake. The Scots nobles got angry and forced her to give up the throne to her son in 1567 and put her into prison. She escaped in 1568 and raised a small army, but most people in Scotland opposed her. Her forces were defeated, and she fled to England.

In England, Mary's presence caused uneasiness. Mary was a Catholic and many English people feared she would try to replace Elizabeth. Over a period of almost 20 years Catholic noblemen made several unsuccessful attempts to make Mary Queen by murdering Elizabeth. Mary was believed to be involved in these plots. Parliament demanded that Mary should be executed, but Elizabeth was unwilling to kill her cousin. In 1586, Mary became involved in another plot against Elizabeth. The English government seized Mary's private letters, which proved her guilt. Elizabeth finally, though reluctantly, agreed to Mary's execution in 1587.

夫开始为权力而争吵。此时有谣言流传开来，说玛丽与她的私人秘书，一个名叫大卫·里齐欧的意大利乐师有私情。一群信奉新教的贵族，由达恩利等人的带领，将里齐欧从玛丽身边拉走，刺死了他。

1567 年初，达恩利被女王的新宠，苏格兰贵族詹姆斯·赫伯恩，博思韦尔伯爵第四谋杀。人们怀疑玛丽本人并非对这场阴谋浑然不知。事后不久，博思韦尔与妻子离婚，娶了玛丽。

这桩婚事是玛丽的致命错误。苏格兰贵族愤怒了，迫使她将王位于 1567 年交给儿子，并把她囚禁起来。1568 年她逃离监狱，募集一支兵力不大的军队。但由于苏格兰的大多数人反对她，她的军队败北，她自己逃往英格兰。

玛丽出现在英格兰使人们感到不安。她是个天主教徒，人们担心她会取代伊丽莎白。在将近 20 年的时间里，信奉天主教的贵族们多次尝试谋杀伊丽莎白，拥立玛丽为女王，但均未成功。玛丽本人据信卷入了这些阴谋活动。议会要求处决玛丽，但伊丽莎白不愿杀死自己的外甥女。1586 年玛丽卷入了另一次推翻伊丽莎白的阴谋。英格兰政府截获了玛丽的私信，证明了她的罪行。伊丽莎白虽有些不情愿，但最终在 1587 年同意处决玛丽。

处决苏格兰玛丽女王

🎯 题 外 话

　　在英国古代，卷入最高权力争夺战的女性，下场大多很悲惨。英格兰的玛丽一世由于母亲被父亲抛弃，即位之前一直过着屈辱的生活。即位后与比自己小 11 岁的腓力二世结婚，恐怕是出于政治原因，谈不上爱情。苏格兰的玛丽女王倒把爱情放到首位，但却因此丢了王位，成了伊丽莎白的阶下囚。后来又成了教派斗争的工具，最终被砍了头。伊丽莎白女王又如何？为了保障国家的统一，民族的独立，她不得已的选择就是独身。她是个多情的女人，她的痛苦只有她自己知道。此外，不应忘记那个 "九日女王" 简·格雷。她听说枢密院宣布自己为女王时，吓得昏了过去。但还是在男人们的阴谋中被迫登上政治舞台，结果 17 岁便丢了性命。

10. The Clash with Spain

与西班牙的冲突

King Philip II of Spain had supported all the secret plans to murder Elizabeth and make Mary Queen of England. When Mary's head was cut off in 1587, he at once made preparations to invade England.

Philip had long hated England because Elizabeth sent an army in 1585 to help Protestants in the Dutch Netherlands rebel against Spanish rule. Besides, the Queen encouraged Francis Drake, Sir Walter Raleigh, and other English seamen to attack Spanish ships and towns, even though the countries were officially at peace. In 1587, Drake destroyed 30 Spanish ships and seized a great amount of supplies in the Spanish port of Cadiz. These events and the execution of Mary Stuart led Philip II to decide

西班牙国王腓力二世曾支持所有谋杀伊丽莎白，拥立玛丽为英格兰女王的阴谋活动。玛丽于1587年被处决后，腓力立即准备入侵英格兰。

腓力很久以来就痛恨英格兰，因为伊丽莎白于1585年曾援助荷兰起义反抗西班牙人的统治。此外，女王怂恿弗朗西斯·德雷克、瓦尔特·罗利爵士和英格兰水手袭击西班牙的船只和城市，尽管在形式上，两国相安无事。1587年，德雷克在西班牙港口加的斯摧毁了30艘西班牙船只，攫取了大量物资。这些事件，再加上玛丽·斯图亚特被处决，使腓力二世决定入侵

西班牙无敌舰队的惨败

to invade England. He hoped to destroy the English navy, force Elizabeth out of the war in the Netherlands, and make England a Catholic country.

In 1588 Philip gathered Spain's warships into a fleet called the "Invincible Armada". The Spaniards gave their fleet this name because they thought it could not be defeated. The Armada consisted of 130 ships carrying 8,000 sailors and almost 20,000 soldiers. The English gathered 180 ships, not as large as the Spanish warships but faster and better armed. Their ships had nearly 16,000 men, most of them experienced sailors rather than soldiers.

In the summer of that year, in the English Channel, the English and Spanish fleets fought one of history's greatest naval battles. The English first sent fire ships (vessels filled with gunpowder and set on fire) toward the Armada. The Spanish ships sailed out to sea to escape the flames in confusion. The English sank or captured many Spanish ships. The badly damaged remaining ships were forced to sail north around the British Isles. Fierce storms then wrecked many of the fleeing Spanish ships off the coasts of Ireland and Scotland. Only 67 of the original 130 ships reached Spain, and most of these were in poor condition.

The defeat of the Armada was a heavy blow to the prestige of Spain, then the world's most powerful country. It did not end the war between England and Spain, but it roused a sense of national pride in the English people,

弗朗西斯·德雷克

英格兰。他企图摧毁英格兰舰队，迫使伊丽莎白退出荷兰的战争，使英格兰成为天主教国家。

1588 年，腓力将西班牙的军舰组建成一支舰队，号称"无敌舰队"。西班牙人认为，这支舰队无敌于天下。无敌舰队拥有 130 艘战船，8000 名水手和 20000 名士兵。英格兰方面征集了 180 艘船，不如西班牙战船大，但航行速度更快，火力更强。他们的船上有将近16000 人，大多数是有经验的水手，而不是士兵。

当年夏天，在英吉利海峡上，英格兰和西班牙舰队打了一场海战。这场海战是世界史上最大规模的海战之一。英格兰方面先向无敌舰队放出火攻船（装满火药并点燃了的船只）。西班牙船只慌忙在海面上散开，以躲避火船，一时陷入混乱。英军击沉或俘获许多西班牙舰只。余下的损坏严重的船只被迫向北航行绕过不列颠群岛。猛烈的风暴使许多逃跑的西班牙船只在爱

strengthened the position of Protestantism as England's state religion, helped unite the nation, and bring about the decline of the Spanish Empire.

⊚ 题 外 话

当时英国方面有多少艘军舰，其说不一。比较可靠的数字是 180 至 200 艘，总量大于西班牙。但实际参战的英格兰舰只不足 100。

11. The Age of Elizabeth

The period under the rule of Elizabeth I is often called the Golden Age of English history. During this age, England made advances in many areas. Elizabeth firmly established moderate Protestantism in England, and avoided a religious war. In 1600 merchants formed a great company, the East India Company, to control the trade in Asia, Africa, and America. To expand overseas trade Sir Francis Drake, Sir Walter Raleigh, and other daring English adventurers explored the West Indies and the coasts of North and South America. Already Sir Walter Raleigh had sent settlers to America, opening the way for a great colonial empire. The victory over the Spanish Armada saved the Protestant faith in England, and at the same time united all Englishmen and roused a sense of national pride in the English people. It also

尔兰和苏格兰海岸附近遇难。130 艘战船中只有 67 艘返回西班牙，其中大部分已被损坏。

西班牙当时是世界上最强大的国家，无敌舰队的惨败对它的声望是个严重的打击。虽然这场海战未能结束两国的战争，但它激发了英国人的民族自豪感，增强了新教作为英格兰国教的地位，促成了国家的统一和西班牙帝国的衰落。

伊丽莎白时代

伊丽莎白一世统治时期常被称为英国历史上的黄金时代。在这个时代英格兰在众多领域取得很大成就。伊丽莎白在英格兰确立了温和的新教，避免了宗教战争。1600 年商人们建立了一个庞大的公司，即东印度公司，以控制亚洲、非洲和美洲的贸易。为扩张海外贸易，弗朗西斯·德雷克爵士、瓦尔特·罗利爵士和其他大胆的英国冒险家探察了西印度群岛和南北美洲的海岸。瓦尔特·罗利爵士已将殖民者送往美洲，打开了通向大殖民帝国的道路。战胜无敌舰队拯救了英格兰的新教，同时团结了英国人民，激发了英国人的民族自豪感。这一胜利鼓励商人和探险家到一个更广阔的世界去开拓殖民地。英格兰的经济繁荣了，

established the glory of the English navy and inspired merchants and explorers toward colonization of a wider world. England's economy prospered. Wealth from the colonies poured into England.

English literature thrived during the rule of Elizabeth. William Shakespeare wrote his sonnet sequences and narrative poems *Venus and Adonis* and *The Rape of Lucrece*. Edmund Spenser wrote his unfinished masterpiece, *The Faerie Queene*. In prose, Francis Bacon began to write his famous *Essays*. The greatest achievement during this period, however, was English drama. Christopher Marlowe, the greatest English dramatist before William Shakespeare, greatly advanced tragedy as an English dramatic form. Marlowe was also the first English playwright to write in blank verse. Marlowe's great tragedies include *Tamburlaine the Great* and *The Tragical History of Doctor Faustus*. But the greatest Elizabethan playwright was William Shakespeare.

大量殖民地的财富流入英格兰。

伊丽莎白时代是英国文学的繁荣时代。威廉·莎士比亚写了他的系列十四行诗和叙事诗《维纳斯和阿多尼斯》、《鲁克丽丝受辱记》；埃德蒙·斯宾塞写了他的未完成长诗《仙后》。弗朗西斯·培根开始写他的著名的《散文集》。但这一时期的最大的成就是英国的戏剧。克里斯托弗·马洛是莎士比亚以前最伟大的英国剧作家。他大大提高了悲剧在英国戏剧中的地位。他还是首先使用素体诗的英国剧作家。马洛的伟大悲剧包括《帖木儿大帝》、《浮士德博士的悲剧》。然而，伊丽莎白时期最伟大的剧作家是威廉·莎士比亚。

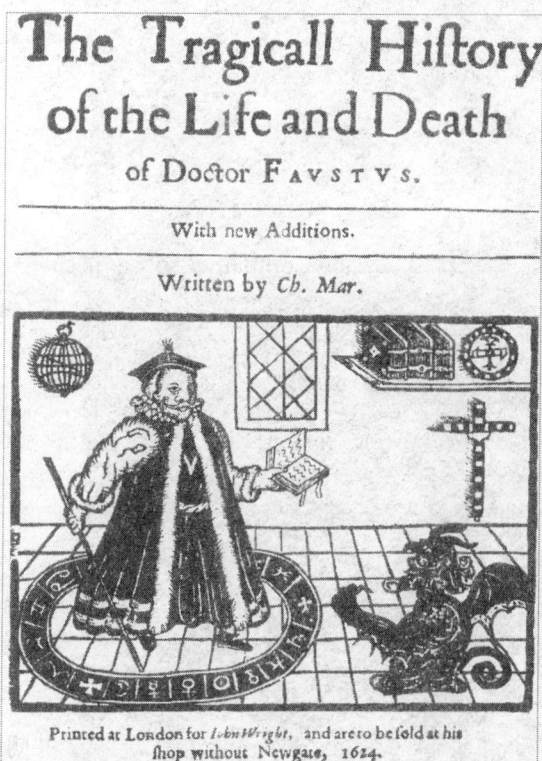

The Tragicall History of the Life and Death of Doctor FAVSTVS.

With new Additions.

Written by Ch. Mar.

Printed at London for *John Wright*, and are to be sold at his shop without Newgate, 1624.

马洛的《浮士德博士的悲剧》的扉页

克里斯托弗·马洛

弗朗西斯·培根

12. William Shakesperare

威廉·莎士比亚

William Shakespeare (1564-1616) is generally considered the greatest dramatist the world has ever known. No other dramatist has equaled him in his rich style, complex plots, brilliant characterizations and deep understanding of human nature.

Very little is known of Shakespeare's life. He was born in 1564 in the small town of Stratford-upon-Avon. His father was a glove-maker and respected citizen of the town. Shakespeare probably attended the Stratford grammar school at about the age of 7, but there is no record of how long he went to school or whether he went to a university afterwards. He probably did not, because when he was 18 years old he married a woman named Anne Hathaway. They had three children.

Then Shakespeare apparently left Stratford to seek his fortune in the theatrical world of London. Within a few years, he had become a successful actor and playwright.

Shakespeare wrote at least 37 plays, which have traditionally been divided

威廉·莎士比亚（1564-1616）是世界公认的最伟大剧作家。他的戏剧风格多样，情节复杂，人物刻画出色，对人性理解深刻，没有其他戏剧家可与之比肩。

对莎士比亚的生平，人们知之甚少。他于1564年出生在埃文河上的斯特拉福德镇。他父亲是手套制作商，一位受人尊敬的市民。莎士比亚7岁时可能上了斯特拉福德的文法学校，但没有记录能够证明他读了几年书，是否上过大学。他多半没上大学，因为他18岁就跟一个名叫安·哈瑟维的女人结了婚。他们一共生了三个孩子。

此后，莎士比亚似乎离开了斯特拉福德，到伦敦的戏剧界去碰运气。没过几年他就成了一个成功的演员和剧作家。

威廉·莎士比亚

into comedies, histories, tragedies, and romances. His best comedies are perhaps *As You Like It*, *The Merchant of Venice*, *A Midsummer's Night Dream*, and *Twelfth Night*. They describe the lovable as well as the ridiculous sides of human nature. His histories tell the stories of kings of England. The most popular ones are *Henry IV* (Parts I and II), *Henry V*, and *Richard III*. His great tragedies are *Hamlet*, *Othello*, *King Lear*, *Macbeth*, and *Antony and Cleopatra*. These plays look deeply into the human soul. Shakespeare's best romance is perhaps his last play, *The Tempest*. Shakespeare's poetic power reached great heights in this beautiful, lyrical play.

Even if Shakespeare had never written any of his great dramas, he would still have been considered to be a great poet, since he also wrote two long narrative poems *Venus and Adonis* and *The Rape of Lucrece*, and a series of 154 sonnets.

莎士比亚写了至少 37 部剧，这些剧一般分为四类，即喜剧、历史剧、悲剧和传奇剧。他最好的喜剧可能要算《皆大欢喜》、《威尼斯商人》、《仲夏夜之梦》和《第十二夜》。这些戏剧既刻画了人性荒唐的一面，也描绘了其可爱的一面。他的历史剧讲的是英国帝王的故事。其中最受欢迎的是《亨利四世》（上、下）、《亨利五世》和《理查三世》。莎士比亚的伟大悲剧有《哈姆雷特》、《奥赛罗》、《李尔王》、《麦克白》和《安东尼与克莉奥佩特拉》。这些悲剧探索了人类灵魂的深处。莎士比亚最好的传奇剧也许是他写的最后一部剧《暴风雨》。在这部美妙而抒情的剧里，莎士比亚的诗才发挥到了极致。

即使莎士比亚从未写过任何一部伟大的戏剧，他仍算得上是大诗人。因为他写过两首叙事诗《维纳斯和阿多尼斯》和《鲁克丽丝受辱记》以及 154 首十四行诗。

题 外 话

一直有人认为记在莎士比亚名下的这三十多部戏剧不可能是那个从斯特拉福德镇走出来，没有受过大学教育，没有见过大世面，名叫莎士比亚的村夫写的。他们推断，这些剧作的作者一定是个受过良好教育的学者或贵族。他们提出一系列"真实"作者的名字，其中有弗朗西斯·培根、克里斯托弗·马洛、牛津伯爵爱德华·德·维尔、瓦尔特·罗利，甚至伊丽莎白一世本人。这些争论和猜测，都是因为莎士比亚不肯写下只言片语来介绍一下自己的生平。在现代，任何一个凡夫俗子都有写一本自传、或刻下"到此一游"来扬名的冲动。但莎士比亚连做梦都梦不到数百年后，自己会被公认为世界最伟大的剧作家之一。跟中国的关汉卿、王实甫差不多，他只知道自己在为"戏子"们写写台词，娱乐大众、养家糊口而已。莎士比亚更看重自己的诗名，所以对他那两篇并不见得出色的长诗精雕细刻。早知自己会因为写剧本成为世界名人，他一定会细心去掉剧本中那些明显的败笔、疏漏和荒唐的时代错误，并监督出版一部标准版的《莎士比亚戏剧全集》。

MR. WILLIAM
SHAKESPEARES
COMEDIES,
HISTORIES, &
TRAGEDIES.
Published according to the True Originall Copies.

LONDON
Printed by Isaac Iaggard, and Ed. Blount. 1623.

《莎士比亚戏剧集》第一对开本扉页

CHAPTER NINE
The Early Stuarts and the Commonwealth
早期斯图亚特王朝与共和国

1. James I

詹姆斯一世

After Elizabeth I died in 1603, her cousin James VI of Scotland became king of England (1603-25). As king of England he took the title of James I. James was a member of the House of Stuart, which had ruled Scotland since 1371. He was the son of Mary Queen of Scots, who was forced to give up the throne to him. Although now England and Scotland came under one ruler, they remained two separate kingdoms.

James was very unpopular in England because he believed in the divine right of kings—that is, that a king's power came from God and not from the people, and so he could do whatever he liked. He increased royal spending, went into debt, and raised taxes. He could not understand it when the House of Commons re-

伊丽莎白一世于1603年逝世，她的孙辈表亲苏格兰的詹姆斯六世继位，成为英格兰国王(1603-1625)。作为英格兰国王，他的称号是詹姆斯一世。詹姆斯是斯图亚特家族的成员，这个家族从1371年开始统治苏格兰。他是苏格兰女王玛丽的儿子，玛丽被迫将王位让给了儿子。虽然英格兰和苏格兰共在一个国王的统治之下，它们仍是两个独立的王国。

詹姆斯在英格兰不得人心，因为他相信君权神授，即国王的权利来自上帝，而非人民，因而他可以为所欲为。他增加了王室的开支，于是欠下债务，继而增加赋税。当议会下院拒绝他提出的增税要求，

fused his demands for tax and talked of laws. In his view, the king's will was the only law. So he quarreled frequently with Parliament.

James was an unwise king, and did not know how to keep the balance of religion. A group of extreme Catholics felt angry about the English government's attitude towards Roman Catholicism and decided to take violent action. They planned to blow up all the members of Parliament, and the king with it, on November 5th, 1605. At the last moment one of the group told their secret plan in order to save the lives of his Catholic cousins in the House of Lords. A search was made under the Parliament building, and a man called Guy Fawkes was found with matches in his hand and a barrel of gunpowder at his side. After this event, which later became as known as the Gunpowder Plot, public's hatred towards Catholics became strong in England and remained so for more than a century.

James supported the Church of England. In 1604, he organized a group of about 50 scholars to prepare a new English translation of the Bible. The new version appeared in 1611 and became known as the King James, or Authorized, Version. This version was widely used in the

并谈论尊重法律时，他感到不可理解。在他看来，国王的意志是唯一的法律。所以他与议会发生多次争吵。

詹姆斯不是一个明智的国王，他不懂如何保持不同教派的平衡。一群极端的天主教徒为英国政府对罗马天主教的态度所激怒，决定采取暴力行动。他们计划在1605年11月5日炸死所有的议员，包括国王在内。在最后一刻，阴谋集团的一个成员向上院里信奉天主教的表亲泄露了这个秘密计划，以挽救他们的性命。官方立即对议会大厦的地下室进行搜查，结果发现一个名叫盖伊·福克斯的人手里拿着火柴，身边有一桶火药。这一事件（后来称为"火药阴谋"）发生后，英格兰公众对天主教的憎恨加强了，这种憎恨保持了一个多世纪。

詹姆斯支持英格兰教会。1604年，他组织起一班

詹姆斯一世

English-speaking world for more than 200 years and is regarded as one of the great treasures of the English language. But James also persecuted certain Protestant groups such as the Puritans. Some Puritans migrated to America in 1620 and founded Plymouth Colony. Jamestown, the first permanent English settlement in America, was named in his honor.

大约 50 名学者重新翻译《圣经》。新版《圣经》于 1611 年问世，称为詹姆斯国王本，或钦定本《圣经》。这个版本在英语世界中广为使用 200 余年，被视为英语语言的宝库之一。但詹姆斯也迫害新教中的某些派别，如清教徒。有些清教徒于 1620 年移居美洲，建立了普利茅斯殖民地。英国在美洲建立的头一个永久殖民地，詹姆斯敦，就是以詹姆斯的名字命名的。

题外话

- 英国人每年 11 月 5 日举行庆祝活动，焚烧盖伊·福克斯的模拟像。为纪念这一事件，在议会召开大会之前，议会大厦的地下室要照例搜查一番，这已成为一种仪式。
- 钦定本《圣经》在英语语言的宝库中首屈一指，为英语提供了大量词语，特别是成语。在题材和风格上，对后世英国作家也有很大影响。仅次于钦定本《圣经》的英语语言的宝库就是莎士比亚的戏剧。

公开处决火药阴谋案的参与者

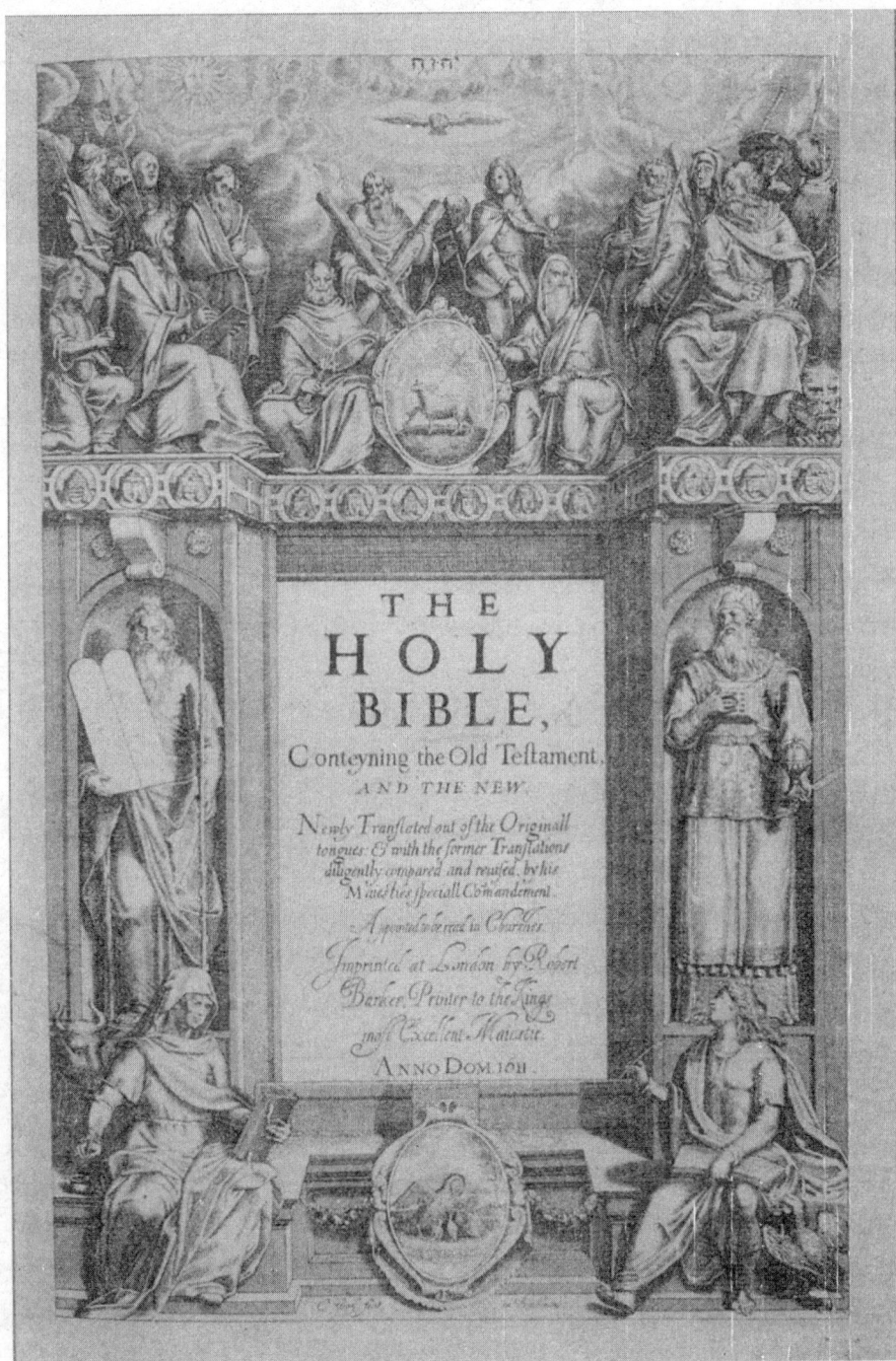

THE
HOLY
BIBLE,
Conteyning the Old Testament,
AND THE NEW.

Newly Transleted out of the Originall
tongues: & with the former Translations
diligently compared and reuised, by his
Maiesties speciall Com̃andement.

Appointed to be read in Churches.

Imprinted at London by Robert
Barker, Printer to the Kings
most Excellent Maiestie.

ANNO DOM. 1611.

詹姆斯国王本《圣经》扉页

2. Charles I and the Civil War

查理一世与内战

Charles I (1600-1649) became king of England, Scotland, and Ireland in 1625. He had a stronger character than his father, but was as unwise as him. Like his father, he also believed in the divine right of kings and in the authority of the Church of England. These beliefs soon brought him into conflict with Parliament.

From 1625 to 1629, Charles called three Parliaments and dismissed each one because the members demanded political and religious reforms that he opposed. In 1628, Parliament passed the famous Petition of Right, designed to limit the power of the king. The document demanded that the king should neither collect taxes without the consent of Parliament, nor imprison any man without a trial. Charles reluctantly accepted the document, but he had no intention of keeping the agreement. In the following year, Charles

查理一世（1600-1649）于1625 年即位，成为英格兰、苏格兰及爱尔兰国王。与他父亲相比，他个性更强，但同样不聪明。跟父亲一样，他相信君权神授和英格兰教会的权威。这些坚定的信念不久就使他与议会发生冲突。

从 1625 年至 1629 年，查理三次召开议会，每次都解散了它，因为议员们要求进行政治和宗教改革，而他却反对改革。1628 年，议会通过著名的《权利请愿书》，以限制王权。这一文件要求未经议会同意，国王不得征税；未经法庭判决，国

穿猎装的查理一世

dismissed Parliament and determined never to call another.

Charles ruled without Parliament for the next 11 years, from 1629 to 1640. He tried to force Scotland to use English forms of worship, and in 1639 the Scots rebelled. Charles had to call Parliament from its long rest and demanded money to fight the rebels. Parliament met in 1640, but it refused his demands unless he again agreed to limit his power. He dismissed the Parliament, called the Short Parliament, after three weeks. When a Scottish army crossed the border and defeated his army, he had to call another Parliament, known as the Long Parliament, because it met until 1653. In 1641, Charles was forced to agree to a series of bills Parliament passed for political and legal reforms to limit the king's power. Later that year, when he tried to have Parliament raise an army to put down an Irish revolt, Parliament refused. It feared that the army, under Charles' control, would be used against itself. Instead, it issued a list of reform demands, including the right of Parliament to approve the king's ministers. Charles reacted angrily, and he went to the House of Commons with several hundred soldiers to arrest its leaders, but they had already escaped. Then all London armed itself to defend Parliament against the king. Charles fled with his family from London. The Civil War broke out between the forces of the king and the forces of Parliament.

The greatest supporters of Parliament were

王不得拘禁任何人。查理勉强接受了这一文件，但无意遵守达成的协议。第二年，查理解散了议会，决心永远不再召开。

从 1629 年至 1640 年，查理在没有议会的情况下统治了 11 年。在此期间，他迫使苏格兰使用英格兰人的礼拜仪式，于是苏格兰人于 1639 年掀起叛乱。查理不得不重新召开议会，以筹集平息叛乱所需要的资金。议会于 1640 年召开，但议员们拒绝满足国王的要求，除非他同意限制王权。查理解散了议会。这届议会只存在了三周，史称短期议会。当苏格兰军队越过边界，打败了国王的军队时，查理不得不再次召开议会。这届议会持续到 1653 年，史称长期议会。1641 年，查理被迫同意议会通过的一系列法案，进行政治和法律的改革，以限制王权。当年晚些时候，当查理试图说服议会招募军队平息爱尔兰人的起义，议会拒绝了。议会担心募集的军队一旦受查理的控制，会被用来对付议会。议会反而提出一系列改革要求，包括国王任命大臣要经议会的批准等等。查理怒不可遏，带着几百名士兵亲临下院去逮捕下院首领，但他们早已逃离。这时全伦敦的市民拿起武器来捍卫议会。查理带着家眷逃离伦敦。国王军队与议会军之间的内战爆发。

religious reformers called Puritans. They were also called Roundheads because they kept their hair cut very short, and disapproved of the long curls worn by noblemen. Charles had the support of many members of the upper classes and of the clergy of the Church of England. These royalists or followers of the king were called Cavaliers, which meant "proud, upper-class horsemen".

The first battles of the war were fought in 1642. Oliver Cromwell, who had won election to Parliament in 1640, became the leading commander of the Parliament army. The army he built up was called the "Ironsides", famous for its strict discipline and desire to fight for freedom. Cromwell had no military experience, but his army defeated the royalists again and again. In 1645, Cromwell won the decisive Battle of Naseby. Charles gave himself up to the Scottish army in May 1646. Then he was turned over in 1647 to the Roundheads.

By this time Parliament's supporters divided into two groups who quarrelled with each other. These two groups were the Presbyterians and the Independents. The Independents, with the support of the chief officers of the army of Parliament, demanded to have complete religious freedom and hold a new general election to reform Parliament. The Presbyterians, who were the majority of Parliament, refused their demands. Both groups wanted to arrange a settlement with the king. They had talks with Charles, but he would not accept their demands,

议会最有力的支持者是称为清教徒的宗教改革者。由于他们将头发剪得短短的，不喜欢贵族们留的长卷发，故称"圆颅党"。查理得到了上层社会人士和英格兰教会教士的支持。这些王党分子称为"骑士派"。

第一场战役于1642年打响。1640年被选入议会的奥立佛·克伦威尔成为议会军的统帅。他建立的军队被称为"铁军"，以严明的纪律、为自由而战的决心闻名。克伦威尔本人并无军事经验，但屡屡打败王党军队。1645年，克伦威尔在纳斯比战役中取得决定性胜利。查理于1646年5月向苏格兰军队投降，次年被移交给圆颅党。

但这一次议会的支持者由于意见不和而分裂成两派，即长老派和独立派。独立派受到议会军上层军官们的支持，要求彻底的宗教信仰自由，举行新的普选以改造议会。在议会中占多数的长老派拒绝了他们的要求。两派都愿意与国王达成妥协。他们与查理谈判，但他不愿接受他们的要求，希望他们之间的分歧使他有可乘之机。但军官们失去了耐心，把长老派议员逐出了议会。余下的议员成立了一个特别法庭审判查理，并以暴君、杀人犯、和国家之敌的罪名将他处以死刑。查理于1649年被推上断头台。

hoping that the quarrel between them would help his cause. But the army officers soon lost patience and drove Presbyterian members out of Parliament. The remaining members set up a special court to try Charles and sentenced him to death as a tyrant, murderer, and enemy of the nation. He was beheaded in 1649.

查理一世的家庭

处决查理一世

克伦威尔驱散议会下院

题外话

- 读英国内战史，一个突出的感觉是英国国王像个叫花子，缺钱花时要向议会伸手，议会乘人之危，提出进一步限制王权的要求。查理忍无可忍，只好来硬的，去逮捕议员。但他必须亲劳大驾，跟在后面的士兵也不过区区数百人。相比之下，同时代的大明皇帝有多么不可一世！缺钱花，有惟命是听的矿监、税监为他们强取豪夺；想把谁除掉，早有宦官们和身边大批阿谀逢迎的小人为他们代劳。

- 佛兰德斯大画家凡·戴克为查理一世画了一幅肖像，《穿猎装的查理一世》。这幅名画给人留下深刻印象。查理面孔清秀，气质高雅，有王者风范。他目光忧郁，略带沉思表情。史家称他为人高尚虔诚，忠于妻子，疼爱孩子，酷爱艺术，并非一个残酷嗜血的人。他走上断头台时也毫无惧色。他的悲剧在于，他顽固地逆历史潮流而动，将自己置于法律之上。他临刑前自称"人民的殉难者"，听起来恬不知耻，但恐怕是他真实的想法。

- 英国革命是不是资产阶级革命，争论很大。内战双方社会阶层的分布大致相当，很难用阶级界线来划分阵营。最明显的界线倒是宗教信仰。总的看来，支持国教的属于王党，反对国教的支持议会。所以英国革命可称为"清教革命"。而清教徒反对国教，实际上是争取信仰上的民主，反对教会专制。所以，英国革命的实质似乎可以说是理性与愚昧、民主与专制的一场较量。

3. Oliver Cromwell

During the English Civil War in the 1640s, Oliver Cromwell (1599-1658), a country gentleman of the east of England became the leader of the armed forces of Parliament. Cromwell was elected to Parliament in 1628. During the 1630s, he became an earnest Puritan. Puritans strongly believed in the right of people to follow more simple forms of worship and church organization than those of the Church of England.

As a commander, Cromwell showed that he was a man of iron will and a military genius. He saw that if the Parliament army was to defeat the king's forces, it must not only be brave and full of faith in its own cause, but must be as well trained as the king's army — and, if possible, better trained. He gathered soldiers among men who had great courage and strength, good horsemanship, and deep religious feelings. He trained them in complete obedience, and filled them with desire to fight for freedom, Parliament and religion. With this army, which became known as the "Ironsides", Cromwell won a series of battles until Charles I

克伦威尔

在 17 世纪 40 年代的英国内战期间，奥立佛·克伦威尔（1599-1658），一位英格兰东部的乡绅，成为议会军的统帅。克伦威尔于 1640 年选入议会。在 30 年代，他成为一个诚心诚意的新教徒。新教徒确信人们有权采用比英格兰教会更简朴的崇拜仪式和教会组织形式。

作为军队统帅，克伦威尔表现出他是个意志刚强的军事天才。他明白，议会军若想打败国王军，光有勇气和对自己事业的信念是不够的，必须像国王的军队一样训练有素，如果可能，训练要更为严格。他招募的军人勇敢强壮、善骑术、

克伦威尔

fell into the hands of Parliament.

When a serious disagreement divided Parliament and its army, Cromwell and his supporters, the Independents, forced Parliament to bring Charles on trial and sentence him to death.

After Charles was beheaded, in 1649, England then became a republic called the Commonwealth of England. A committee of Parliament ruled the country. For the next two years Cromwell remained a soldier in service to the state. The new Commonwealth had powerful enemies, especially in Ireland and Scotland, where Charles II, son of Charles I, was declared king. Cromwell first went to Ireland with his forces and crushed the Irish, mercilessly killing their soldiers and civilians in large numbers. Then he turned to Scotland to prevent the royalists from invading England. There he won a great victory against the Scottish army in 1650. A year later he defeated the combined forces of the Scots and Charles II. Cromwell was now regarded as the savior of the Commonwealth.

Cromwell grew impatient with Parliament, which was unable to make reforms and refused to hold new parliamentary elections. In April 1653 he marched into the House of Commons with his soldiers and drove its members out into the street.

Then the army officers drew up a constitution, called the Instrument of Government, which put the chief power in the hands of Cromwell under the title of Lord Protector. The

有强烈的宗教感情。经过他的训练，这些人有令必从，满怀为自由、议会和宗教而战的强烈愿望。这支军队后来被称为"铁军"，正是依靠它克伦威尔取得了一系列的胜利，直至查理落入议会手中。

当议会与军队产生严重分歧时，克伦威尔与他的支持者独立派迫使议会审判查理，将他判处死刑。

查理于1649年被送上断头台后，英格兰成为共和国。议会的一个委员会治理国家。其后两年，克伦威尔保留军人身份，为国效力。新成立的共和国面对强大的敌人，特别是在爱尔兰和苏格兰。查理一世的儿子查理二世在苏格兰宣布为国王。克伦威尔先率领军队开入爱尔兰，杀死大批爱尔兰军人和平民。然后克伦威尔挥军前往苏格兰，阻止王党军队入侵英格兰。1650年他与苏格兰军队交战，取得重大胜利。一年后，他打败苏格兰人和查理二世的联军。此时，克伦威尔被视为共和国的拯救者。

克伦威尔对议会越来越缺乏耐性，因为议会未能进行改革，而且拒绝举行新的议会选举。1653年，他率领士兵们进入下院，将议员们赶到大街上。

此后，军官们起草一部宪法，称为《政府约法》。这部宪法规定克伦威尔为护国公，负责行政事务。英格兰的共和国实际上到此终

Commonwealth of England was actually ended. During his rule, Cromwell brought Scotland and Ireland under the control of England. His armies swept through both countries and put down all resisting forces.

Cromwell tried to carry out many of the reforms that Puritans had been demanding during the revolution. His government practiced religious toleration and demanded stricter moral standards, and even closed theatres.

He also strengthened England's navy and defeated the Dutch and the Spanish on the sea, and helped to develop English colonies in Asia and North America. Under Admiral Robert Blake, the English navy became a great international power. In 1657, Parliament offered Cromwell the title of king, but he refused it.

When Cromwell died in 1658, his son, Richard, was named lord protector. But Richard could not handle the affairs of government. General George Monk, the commander of the army in Scotland, arranged free elections for a new parliament, which immediately decided to bring back the rule of kings. In 1660 the monarchy was restored in England with Charles II taking the throne.

结。在克伦威尔统治期间，他将苏格兰和爱尔兰置于英格兰的控制之下。他的军队横扫两国，镇压了抵抗部队。

克伦威尔试图实施革命期间清教徒所要求的许多改革。他的政府实行宗教宽容政策，要求人们按照更严格的道德准则行事，甚至关闭了剧院。

克伦威尔还加强了英格兰的海军，在海上打败了荷兰与西班牙，扶植发展了英国在亚洲和北美的殖民地。罗伯特·布雷克海军上将统帅下的英国海军，成为强大的国际威慑力量。1657年，议会要求克伦威尔接受国王的称号。但克伦威尔拒绝了。

克伦威尔于1658年逝世，他的儿子理查继任护国公。但是理查无法控制政府。驻苏格兰的军队指挥官乔治·蒙克将军安排举行了新一届的议会选举，新议会立即决定恢复君主制。1660年君主制在英格兰复辟，查理二世登上王位。

题外话

克伦威尔貌不出众，拙于演说，但品质高尚，性格坚强，是个虔诚的清教徒，天才的军事家。他拒绝王冠，看来并没有权利欲。但革命却把他一步步推向独裁。这究竟是他个人的过错，还是历史的必然？纵观世界历史，革命往往以反抗专制开始，却不得不以新的专制告终，似乎成了规律。

王权复辟后，克伦威尔的尸体从威斯敏斯特大教堂的墓地里掘出，施以绞刑，再枭首示众。

CHAPTER TEN

The Later Stuarts
晚期斯图亚特王朝

1. Charles II and the Restoration

查理二世与复辟时代

Charles II (1630-1685) became king of England, Scotland, and Ireland in 1660, and he died in 1685. The period from 1660 to 1685 is known as the Restoration.

During the civil war of the English Revolution, Charles fled to the Netherlands, from where he made two attempts to save his father, King Charles I. After his father was executed in 1649, he returned to Scotland, and there was declared king. In 1651 he invaded England with 10,000 men, but Oliver Cromwell defeated him, and he fled to France. After Cromwell died in 1658, the English people became increasingly dissatisfied with the government that Cromwell had established. In 1660, Parliament invited Charles to return and declared him king.

Under Charles II, Parliament kept most of

查理二世（1630-1685）于 1660 年登基成为英格兰、苏格兰和爱尔兰国王，1685 年逝世。1660~1685 年这段时期称为复辟时代。

英国革命内战时期，查理逃到荷兰，两次试图营救父亲查理一世。1649 年父亲被处死后，他返回苏格兰，被宣布为国王。1651 年，他率领一万人的军队入侵英格兰，但败于克伦威尔手下，然后逃往法国。克伦威尔于 1658 年去世后，英格兰人对克伦威尔建立的政府日益不满。1660 年，议会邀请查理回国并宣布他为国王。

查理二世统治时期，议会保持了自己争得的大部分权力，与国王

the powers it had won, and ruled the country with the king. The government tried to make peace between the two sides that had fought each other in the civil war, but it was hard to satisfy both of them. England fought two wars against the Dutch, and both of them were unsuccessful and unpopular. Other problems arose during Charles's rule. In 1665, London had a terrible disease, which, like the Black Death of the 14th century, killed 70,000 London citizens. In the next year, a great fire in London destroyed a larger part of the city.

Charles loved having fun and lived an immoral life, but he was one of the most intelligent kings in English history, and his court became a centre of culture. Theatres were reopened. Dramatists wrote comedies to entertain the nobles and upper class, who, like the king, enjoyed carefree and often immoral ways of life. The Restoration was a reaction against Puritanism, not only in behavior, but also in literature; and yet there were notable exceptions. *Paradise Lost*, written by John Milton, was published in 1667 and *Pilgrim's Progress*, by John Bunyan, was published from 1678 to 1684. Charles supported the new Royal Society, which encouraged scientific study in every field. One of its first members was Sir Christopher Wren, who had the chance to prove his skill after the

共同执政。政府试图缓和内战中交战双方的矛盾，但是很难令双方都满意。英格兰与荷兰打了两仗，两仗均未能取胜，因而不得人心。查理统治时期还出现了别的麻烦事。1665年伦敦流行一场可怕的瘟疫，就像14世纪的黑死病，有7万伦敦市民毙命。第二年，一场伦敦大火烧毁了城市的大部分地区。

查理贪图享乐，生活腐化堕落，但他却是英国历史上最聪慧的君王之一，他的宫廷成为一个文化中心。剧院重新开张，剧作家们写喜剧供贵族和上流社会娱乐，而贵族和上流社会也像国王一样过着无忧无虑、腐化堕落的生活。复辟时

查理二世

great fire of London. He helped to build a new London on the burnt ruins. His buildings included St. Paul's Cathedral and over fifty churches.

Under Charles II, the Cavaliers and Roundheads had settled down to become England's first political parties, the Tories and Whigs. Now the king's brother, James, who was a Catholic, was likely to be the next king. Tories were those who supported James; the Whigs were those who tried to prevent him from coming to the throne.

题外话

1679 年，议会两派为废立詹姆斯问题激烈辩论，开始用"托利"和"辉格"对骂。"托利"一词源于爱尔兰，意为"逃犯"或"非法之徒"。"辉格"一词源于苏格兰盖尔语，意为"盗马贼"。托利党和辉格党后来分别演变成保守党和自由党。

代的风尚是对清教主义的反动，不但表现在行为方式上，也表现在文学上。但也有著名的例外。密尔顿的《失乐园》发表在 1667 年；约翰·班扬的《天路历程》也在 1678~1684 年间发表。查理支持皇家学会，这个学会鼓励各个领域里的科学研究。皇家学会的首批会员中有克里斯托弗·雷恩爵士，伦敦大火之后他得到大显身手的机会。在大火废墟之上，他设计建设了一个新的伦敦。他设计的建筑包括圣保罗大教堂和 50 余座别的教堂。

查理二世统治时期，骑士派和圆颅党逐渐演变成英国最初的政党，即托利党和辉格党。此时国王的弟弟詹姆斯会成为继位的国王。他是个天主教徒。托利党是那些支持詹姆斯继位的人；辉格党是那些力图阻止他登上王位的人。

密尔顿口述《失乐园》

2. James II and the Glorious Revolution

Charles died in 1685, and his brother became King James II (1633-1701, king of England, Scotland, and Ireland 1685-1688). The extreme Whigs rose in a rebellion in support of the Protestant Duke of Monmouth, who was Charles's son, but not the Queen's. The rebellion was quickly put down, and James taking a bloody revenge on his enemies. His friend Judge Jeffreys is remembered as the cruellest man in England's history, for he hanged and burned three hundred people and sent a thousand more to work as slaves on American farms. As a result, James quickly lost the sympathy of many people who had supported him.

James was a Roman Catholic, and he wanted to bring back Catholicism as the state religion. He also wanted to become an absolute ruler in England. He tried to put Catholics in control of the army, the Church, the courts and all central and local government. The people disliked his policies but put up with him. They expected James's Protestant daughter, Mary, to become queen after he died. Above all, they did not want another civil war. But when James's wife had a son in June

詹姆斯二世与光荣革命

查理死于 1685 年,他的弟弟继位为詹姆斯二世(1633-1701,英格兰、苏格兰和爱尔兰国王,1685-1688)。极端的辉格党人发动叛乱,支持国王的私生子蒙默斯公爵上台。叛乱很快平息下来,詹姆斯对敌人进行血腥的报复。他的朋友杰弗里斯法官在英国历史上以残酷知名,因为他将三百人处以绞刑或火刑,并将一千余人送往美国庄园做奴隶。结果,詹姆斯很快失去人心,许多先前的支持者不再同情他。

詹姆斯是个天主教徒,他想恢复天主教为国教。他还想成为英格兰的绝对统治者。他设法使天主教徒控制军队、教会、法庭和全部中央和地方政府。人们不喜欢他的政策,但容忍了他。詹姆斯的女儿玛丽信奉新教,人们预期詹姆斯死后玛丽会成为女王。大家毕竟不愿再打一场内战。但当詹姆斯的妻子于 1688 年产下一子,

詹姆斯二世

1688, people realized that they might have another Catholic ruler after James's death, and decided to take action to prevent it.

The Whig and Tory leaders at last united against James. They invited William of Orange, Mary's husband and ruler of the Netherlands, to invade England with Dutch forces. William landed in England in November 1688 and marched on London. He was warmly welcomed, and James, deserted by his troops, fled to France. James's daughter Mary and her husband William became joint rulers. In 1690, with a small French army, James landed in Ireland in an attempt to return to the throne. He was defeated and returned to France, where he lived in exile until his death.

The quick change of rulers in 1688 is called the Glorious Revolution because, unlike that of 1640 to 1660, it was bloodless and successful. It created a constitutional monarchy, which finally put the monarch under the control of Parliament.

人们意识到詹姆斯死后他们会有另一个信奉天主教的统治者，于是决定采取行动来制止。

辉格党和托利党的领袖最终团结起来与詹姆斯对抗。他们邀请玛丽的丈夫、荷兰的统治者奥伦治的威廉率领荷兰军队入侵英格兰。威廉于1688年11月登陆英格兰，向伦敦进军。他受到热烈欢迎，而詹姆斯则被自己的军队所抛弃，仓皇逃往法国。詹姆斯的女儿玛丽和丈夫威廉成为联合执政者。1690年，詹姆斯率领一支人数不多的法国军队在爱尔兰登陆，试图恢复王位。他吃了败仗，返回法国，在流亡中度过余生。

1688年的迅速更换统治者的事件被称为"光荣革命"。与1640~1660年的革命不同，它未经流血就成功了。他开创了君主立宪制，将君主置于议会的控制之下。

🎯 题 外 话

- 查理二世在位时，詹姆斯曾是约克公爵，任英国海军总司令。现在美国的纽约市原属荷兰，名为新阿姆斯特丹。英国海军于1664年夺取该地，以约克公爵的名字将其命名纽约。

- 英国哲学家约翰·洛克在其《政府论》中为光荣革命做了有力的辩护。《政府论》虽然发表于1890年，但据学者考证，其大部分写于1679~1683年间。洛克宣称，如果一个政府不能有效地保护公民的权利，人民有权寻找新的统治者。决定应当由谁来统治人民的，是人民自己。

- 光荣革命的意义不可小觑。它告诉我们，社会制度的变更并非一定要通过暴力冲突来完成。但这种非暴力、低成本变更的前提是：一，有相对文明的社会。文艺复兴开启了民智，理性主义影响增强。1662年成立了皇家学会，极大地促进英国科学的发展。牛顿在1666年前后制定了微积分，从行星运动三定律推出万有引力定律，1687年发表《自然哲学的数学原理》，第一次阐述力学三定律,奠定了经典力学的基础。复辟时代的大哲学家洛克发表了《政府论》,提出了自由主义的政治理论。新闻自由初见端倪。二,有自《大宪章》以来权利制衡的传统。三,有相对成熟的民众。四,有经验丰富的政客,他们懂得妥协,在必要时采取灵活务实、现实主义的策略。

- 光荣革命颇有些不可思议之处。两党领袖果敢打破严格的长子继承制,打乱王位继承顺序,创立了一种奇特的一国二君制。他们胆敢邀请外国军队入侵,在一般人看来,岂非犯了叛国的滔天大罪?这样做需要非同一般的胆识、自信和英国式的务实精神。

- 光荣革命后,和平和渐进的改革成为英国历史发展的特色。英国之所以能率先进入工业化社会,从一个边缘小国走向世界的中心,是与其在不断的和平改革中造就的稳定社会环境分不开的。想到 20 世纪、乃至 21 世纪的很多国家在变更政权时,仍须采用暴力手段,不得不佩服英国人的文明与政治智慧。

3. William III and Mary II

威廉三世与玛丽二世

William III (1650-1702), also known as William of Orange, became King of England, Scotland, and Ireland in 1689. Mary II (1662-1694) became Queen of England, Scotland, and Ireland at the same time. William was the son of a Dutch nobleman, William II, Prince of Orange, and Mary, the oldest daughter of King Charles I of England. In 1672, William was elected governor of the Netherlands to defend his country against the invasions of the French king Louis XIV. In 1677, William married his cousin Mary Stuart. Her father became King James II of England in 1685. William hoped England might side with him against France. However, James II, a Roman Catholic, remained friendly to Louis XIV, who was also a Catholic. William and Mary were Protestants.

In 1689, William and Mary became joint

威廉三世(1650-1702)亦称奥伦治的威廉,于 1689 年登基为英格兰、苏格兰和爱尔兰国王。玛丽二世(1662-1694)同时加冕为英格兰、苏格兰和爱尔兰女王。威廉是荷兰贵族奥伦治亲王威廉二世和英格兰国王查理一世长女玛丽的儿子。1672 年,威廉被选举为荷兰的执政以保卫荷兰,抵御法国国王路易十四的入侵。1677 年,威廉娶表妹斯图亚特的玛丽为妻。玛丽的父亲于 1685 年继位为英格兰的国王詹姆斯二世。威廉希望英格兰会站在他一边反对法国。但詹姆斯是个天主教徒,与同样是天主教徒的路易十四保持友好关系。而威廉和玛丽则是新教徒。

1689 年,威廉和玛丽在接受

rulers of England after accepting what became known as the Bill of Rights. This famous document assured the people certain basic rights and limited the power of the monarchy. It made it illegal for the king to keep an army in time of peace, to put off or stop the enforcement of laws, to collect taxes without Parliament's approval, or to be a Roman Catholic.

After he became king of England, William devoted most of his effort to keep France from becoming a great power in Europe. William brought England into the League of Augsburg, also known as the Grand Alliance. For the next eight years he was busy fighting in wars on the Continent. He skillfully managed to hold the alliance together and forced Louis XIV of France to give up much of the territory he had won and recognized William as England's rightful king.

Near the end of his life, William played a leading role in creating a new alliance of European powers that opposed France in the socalled War of the Spanish Succession (1701-1714). He died in 1702, before he could take an active part in the struggle.

Mary governed England while William was fighting in Ireland (1690-1691) and on the Continent (1692-1694), but for the most part she simply carried out policies decided by her husband. Mary also devoted much of her time to religious and charitable projects. William continued to rule alone after her death.

了后来被称为《权利法案》的文件后，共同登上王位。这个著名文件保障了人民的某些基本权利，而限制了君主的权力。它以法律的形式禁止国王在和平时期保有军队，推迟或中止法律的实施，未经议会批准强征赋税，或信奉天主教。

成为英格兰国王后，威廉将大部分精力用于阻止法国成为欧洲强国。威廉使英国加入奥格斯堡联盟（亦称大同盟），在其后的8年里忙于在欧洲大陆上作战。他巧妙地将同盟国家维系在一起，迫使法国的路易十四放弃他所夺取的大部分领土，并承认威廉为英格兰的合法国王。

在去世前不久，威廉在组建欧洲强国的新同盟中起到领导作用。成立这个同盟是为了在所谓西班牙王位继承战争（1701-1714）中打击法国。但他没有来得及全力参战，便于1702年逝世。

威廉在爱尔兰（1690-1691）和在欧洲大陆作战（1692-1694）期间，玛丽主持政务，但她多半只是执行丈夫的既定政策而已。玛丽也用很多时间从事宗教和慈善事务。在她去世后，威廉继续执政。

🎯 **题 外 话**

1689 年的《权利法案》与 1215 年的《大宪章》和 1628 年的《权利请愿书》，被视为英国人民自由的法律保障。

玛丽二世

威廉三世

4. Isaac Newton

伊萨克·牛顿

Isaac Newton (1642-1727) was one of the greatest scientists and mathematicians in human history. His discoveries and ideas have guided other scientists for nearly three hundred years.

Newton entered Cambridge University in 1661 and graduated in 1665 without any particular distinction. He returned to Cambridge as a fellow of Trinity College in 1667 and became professor of mathematics in 1669. He lectured on arithmetic, astronomy, geometry, optics, or other mathematical subjects. He was elected to the Royal Society in 1672 and became president of the society in 1703 and was reelected every year until his death. Queen Anne knighted Newton in 1705, and after that he became known as Sir Isaac Newton. He died in 1727 and was buried in Westminster Abbey.

One of Newton's greatest contributions to science is his theory of gravitation. The theory says that the gravitational force between two objects is proportional to the size of their masses. That is, the larger their mass is, the larger the force is between the two objects. Newton published his theory of gravitation and laws of motion in 1687 in *Philosophiae Naturalis Principia Mathematica* (Mathematical Principles of Natural Philosophy). This work, usually called *Principia* or *Principia Mathematica*, is considered one of the greatest single contributions in

伊萨克·牛顿（1642-1727）是人类历史上最伟大的科学家和数学家之一。他的发现和思想影响后世科学家达数百年之久。

牛顿于 1661 年就读于剑桥大学，1665 年毕业，当时没有什么名气。1667 年他返回剑桥三一学院任研究员。两年后，他开始担任剑桥大学的数学教授，教算术、天文学、几何学、光学及其他数学课程。1672 年他入选皇家学会，1703 年开始任该学会会长，连任此职直至逝世。1705 年安妮女王授予他爵位，此后被称为伊萨克·牛顿爵士。牛顿死于 1727 年，葬于威斯敏斯特教堂。

牛顿对科学最重大的发现之一是他的万有引力理论。据这一理论，两个物体之间的引力大小与它们的质量大小成正比。也就是说，质量越大，两者之间的引力也越大。1687 年，牛顿将自己的万有引力理论和运动定律发表在《自然哲学的数学原理》一书中。这一著作也简称为《原理》或《数学原理》。这本书被认为是科学史上最大的贡献之一。它是用一个统一的科学原理体系来解释地球和太空物理现象的头一部书。

the history of science. It was the first book to contain a unified system of scientific principles explaining what happens on earth and in the heavens.

Newton invented calculus, a branch of higher mathematics. He also discovered that sunlight contains all the colors of the rainbow. He passed a beam of sunlight through a glass prism and studied the colors that were produced. He believed that green object looks green in sunlight because it largely reflects the green light in the sun and absorbs most of the other colors. Newton also was the first person to show that colored lights can be combined to form white light.

Newton was a bachelor who spent only part of his time studying mathematics, physics, and astronomy. He was also a student of alchemy and made many alchemical experiments. He also spent a great deal of his time on questions of theology and the Bible.

Newton always remained a very modest man. Although other scientists considered him a genius and the greatest thinker of his time, he said of himself shortly before his

牛顿发明了高等数学的一个分支——微积分。他还发现太阳光由七色组成。他让一缕阳光通过三棱镜，研究由此产生的彩色。他认为阳光下的绿色物体之所以是绿色的，是因为它反射了阳光里的绿光，而吸收了其余大部分光。牛顿也是向人们证明彩色光线可以合成为白光的第一人。

牛顿一生未婚，但他只利用部分时间研究数学、物理学和天文学。此外，他还研究炼金术，做了许多相关的实验。他也花费大量时间钻研神学和《圣经》里面的问题。

牛顿毕生保持谦逊的态度。尽管别的科学家将他视为天才和当时

牛顿

death, "I do not know what I may appear to the world, but to myself I seem to have been only like a boy playing on the seashore, and diverting myself in now and then finding a smoother pebble or a prettier shell than ordinary, whilst the great ocean of truth lay all undiscovered before me."

的伟大思想家，他在临终时却说：
"我不知道世人如何看待我，但在我自己看来，我好像是一个在海滩上玩耍的孩子，由于偶尔捡到一颗特别光滑的石子或特别好看的贝壳而自娱自乐，而面前的那个浩瀚的真理的海洋，我却对它一无所知。"

题外话

法国哲学家伏尔泰写道："不久前一些有身份的人在讨论那个陈腐而又浅薄的问题，即谁是最伟大的人物，是恺撒、亚历山大、帖木儿，还是克伦威尔？有人回答说，毫无疑问是牛顿。他答得很对，因为我们尊敬推崇的不是以武力服人者，而是以真理服人者。"

5. War with France

对法战争

During the late 1660s, France became the strongest country on the European mainland. William III had fought against France when he ruled the Netherlands. As king of England, he joined other countries into a union, called the Grand Alliance, to reduce the dangerous power and ambitions of Louis XIV of France. In 1701, the War of the Spanish Succession broke out, with England, the Netherlands, Prussia, Austria, Denmark and Portugal on the one side, against France and Spain on the other. The Grand Alliance tried to prevent Philip of Anjou from becoming king of Spain, and to put the Archduke Charles of Austria on the throne instead, because Philip was the grandson of King Louis

17 世纪 60 年代末，法国成为欧洲大陆上最强大的国家。威廉三世在统治荷兰期间，曾与法国打过仗。作为英国国王，他与其他国家组成联盟，称为"大同盟"，以遏制法王路易十四的危险的势力和野心。1701 年西班牙王位继承战争爆发，英格兰、荷兰、普鲁士、奥地利、丹麦和葡萄牙为一方，法国和西班牙为另一方。大同盟试图阻止安茹的腓力成为西班牙国王，而想将奥地利的查理大公送上王位。腓力是路易十四的孙子，大同盟担心西班牙会成为法国的一部分。

英国的将领马尔伯勒公爵约

XIV, and the Grand Alliance feared that Spain might became part of France.

The English general, John Churchill, the Duke of Marlborough, and the imperial general, Prince Eugene of Savoy, commanded the forces of the Grand Alliance. They were gifted military commanders and defeated the French in several important battles. Under the peace treaty, signed at Utrecht in 1713, Spain agreed that England should keep Gibraltar "absolutely and for ever" as a naval base, to protect her trade. France agreed to give up Newfoundland, Nova Scotia, and the territory around Hudson Bay to England. The Grand Alliance recognized Philip as king of Spain on the condition that Spain and France would never be united.

翰·丘吉尔和奥地利帝国的将领萨瓦的欧根亲王共同指挥大同盟军。两人都是天才的军队统帅，在几次重大战役中打败了法国。1713年在乌得勒支签订的和约里，西班牙同意英格兰将"绝对而永久地"使用直布罗陀作海军基地，以保护它的贸易。法国同意将纽芬兰，新斯科舍以及哈德孙湾周围地区割让给英国。大同盟承认腓力为西班牙国王，条件是西班牙和法国永不合并。

题外话

马尔伯勒公爵约翰·丘吉尔是20世纪英国政治家温斯顿·丘吉尔的祖先。

6. Queen Anne

When William died in 1702, having no children, he was succeeded by his wife's sister, the second daughter of King James II, Queen Anne (1665-1714, queen of Great Britain and Ireland 1702-1714).

In the early years of her rule, Anne favoured John Churchill, making him duke of Marlborough and captain-general of the army. Marlborough won a series of victories over the French in the War of the Spanish Succession. He and his wife, Sarah, had great influence over

安妮女王

威廉于1702年逝世，无嗣。他妻子的妹妹，前国王詹姆斯二世的第二个女儿安妮（1665-1714，大不列颠及爱尔兰女王，1702-1714）继位。

在她统治初期，安妮宠信约翰·丘吉尔，封他为马尔伯勒公爵并任命他为军队总司令。在西班牙王位继承战争中，马尔伯勒打败了法国人，取得一系列的胜利。他与妻子莎拉左右女王多年。

the queen for years.

During Anne's rule, one of the greatest events was the formal union of the kingdoms of England and Scotland in 1707. The parliaments of the two kingdoms each passed the Act of Union, which joined the two kingdoms under one government as the Kingdom of Great Britain. Under the act, Scotland's parliament was joined with that of England. Scotland sent 45 elected members to the British House of Commons and 16 of its noblemen to the House of Lords. Scots received the same trading rights as the English had in England and its colonies. The history of England then became part of the history of Britain.

By 1707, the English Parliament had won a controlling influence over the monarchy, and the Tory and Whig parties had developed. Anne was devoted to the Church of England, and so she favoured the Tory party who supported the Church, rather than the Whig party, especially towards the end

马尔伯勒公爵夫妇

安妮统治时期的一件大事是 1707 年英格兰王国和苏格兰王国的正式合并。两个王国的议会分别通过合并法案，将两个王国统一为大不列颠王国，由一个政府统辖。依照该法案，苏格兰议会与英格兰议会合并，苏格兰派 45 名当选的议员到不列颠议会下院，16 名贵族到上院。苏格兰人享有英格兰人在英格兰及其殖民地同等的贸易权。英格兰的历史从此成为大不列颠历史的一部分。

到了 1707 年，英国议会的势力已大到足以左右君主的地步。托利和辉格两党已发展壮大。

安妮女王

of her rule.

The rule of Queen Anne in early 18th-century England is often called an Augustan age. During this period, the satirist Jonathan Swift, the poet Alexander Pope, and the essayists Joseph Addison and Sir Richard Steele were among the major literary figures. They admired classical art of Rome under the Emperor Augustus and emphasized common sense, clarity, reason and elegance.

Anne was the last monarch of the House of Stuart. She had 5 children, but all of them died before her. She died in 1714, and, having no surviving children, was succeeded by her distant German cousin, George, elector of Hannover, as King George I of Great Britain and Ireland.

安妮信奉英格兰教，因而宠用支持英格兰教会的托利党人，而疏远辉格党，特别是在她统治的后期。

在安妮女王统治下的英国18世纪初常被称为奥古斯都时代。在这一时期，讽刺作家江纳生·斯威夫特、诗人亚历山大·蒲柏、散文家约瑟夫·艾迪生和里查德·斯蒂尔爵士是重要文人。他们崇拜奥古斯都皇帝治下的罗马的古典艺术，强调常识、明晰、理性和雅致。

安妮是斯图亚特王朝的末代君主。她生了5个孩子，但全都在她之前去世。她死于1714年，无嗣，由她的德国远亲汉诺威选帝侯乔治继位，成为大不列颠和爱尔兰国王乔治一世。

诗人亚历山大·蒲柏

讽刺作家江纳生·斯威夫特

CHAPTER ELEVEN

The 18th Century (1714-1815)
十八世纪(1714-1815)

1. The Beginning of Cabinet Government

内阁政府的开端

Queen Anne, the first British monarch, died in 1714. Many people claimed that only her half brother James Francis Edward Stuart, a Roman Catholic and son of King James II, had the right to succeed her. However, Parliament had passed an Act of Settlement that made sure that no Catholic would become monarch. The act stated that Princess Sophia, a Protestant, would succeed Anne as ruler of England if Anne had no children. Sophia was a granddaughter of King James I of England and electress of the German territory of Hanover. Her son George became heir to the throne after her death in 1714 and became king George I (1660-1727, king of Great Britain and Ireland 1714-1427) after Anne's death.

One of the most dramatic events of George's

大不列颠的首任君主安妮女王于1714年逝世。许多人主张，只有她的异母弟弟詹姆斯·弗朗西斯·爱德华·斯图亚特有权继承她。詹姆斯是詹姆斯二世的儿子，天主教徒。然而，议会早已通过了王位继承法，规定天主教徒将不能成为国王。法案规定若安妮无嗣，新教徒索非娅公主将继位成为英国国王。索非娅是詹姆斯一世的孙女，德国汉诺威的女选侯。索非娅于1714年去世,她的儿子成为王位继承人，继而在安妮去世后登基成为国王乔治一世 (1660-1727, 大不列颠及爱尔兰国王,1714-1427)。

乔治在位期间最戏剧性的事件之一是詹姆斯党人叛乱。詹姆斯党

rule was the Jacobite rebellion. Jacobites were supporters of the house of Stuart. They tried to restore the Stuart family as rulers of Great Britain. In 1715 a group of Jacobite nobles led an uprising in Scotland and in the English border area. They supported James's son, James Francis Edward Stuart, who claimed to be the rightful king. In a battle with the government forces, the Jacobites were defeated, and returned to exile in France.

George I did not speak English well, and had little knowledge of British politics. He chose his council of ministers from the Whig Party and kept in close touch with his ministers, of whom the most famous was Sir Robert Walpole (1675-1745). Sir Robert Walpole took control of the council as the chief minister, and this began to develop the British cabinet system of government. The cabinet is a group of leaders of the biggest party in Parliament, and its chief is called the Prime Minister. The members of a cabinet must agree on common aims and they must take joint responsibility for all that they do. Walpole was in fact, though not in name, Britain's first prime minister from 1721 to 1742.

Walpole was a forceful and shrewd statesman. He led the Whig party, but he tried not to stir up trouble between the two parties. During his long term of office he dominated Parliament and gradually weakened all his political rivals. He was not a coward, but he tried to avoid involving Britain in war, because he knew that

乔治一世

人是斯图亚特王朝的支持者。他们试图恢复斯图亚特家族在大不列颠的统治地位。1715 年，一群詹姆斯党贵族在苏格兰和英格兰边境地区发动起义。他们支持詹姆斯的儿子、自称是合法国王的詹姆斯·弗朗西斯·爱德华·斯图亚特。他们与政府军一交火就吃了败仗，返回法国流亡去了。

乔治一世讲不好英语，对英国政治知之甚少。他从辉格党里挑选了一班大臣，与他们保持密切联系。大臣当中最有名的是罗伯特·沃波尔爵士(1675-1745)。沃波尔作为首席大臣主持大臣会议，这就是英国政府内阁制的开端。内阁是议会最大党派的领袖们组成的班

his country needed long years of peace to build up its strength. He insisted on religious and political toleration. Under his leadership the English had freedom of speech and of person, such as no other country had. His government let hard-working men develop trade and agriculture without official interference. He reduced the national debt, land tax and customs duties. He made Britain safer, richer and stronger than it had been.

In the last years of his rule, Walpole became more and more unpopular among Tories and some Whigs. They disliked his way of rule and his foreign policy. Walpole tried to prevent war with Spain, but at the time demand for

子，为首的称为首相。内阁的成员们必须在共同目标上取得一致意见，并对他们所采取的所有行动共同承担责任。沃波尔在 1721~1742 年间是英国首任首相，虽然当时尚没有这一正式称呼。

沃波尔是个精明而有魄力的政治家。他是辉格党的领袖，但小心避免挑起两党的争端。在任职的漫长岁月里，他控制了议会，逐渐削弱了所有政敌的势力。他并非胆小怕事，但他试图避免将英国卷入战争，因为他知道国家需要长期的和平以积蓄力量。他坚持宗教和政治的宽容。在他的领导下，英国人有言论自由和人身自由，这是其他国家所不具有的。他的政府允许勤劳的人发展贸易和农业，而官方不加干预。他削减了国债、土地税和关税。他使英国比以往更安全、更富裕、更强大。

在他任职的末期，沃波尔在托利党人和部分辉格党人中渐失人心。他们不喜欢他的执政方式和他的外交政策。沃波尔试图避免与西班牙交战，而此时国内主张与

沃波尔（左）在下院与议长谈话

such a war was growing in Britain. When war broke out with Spain in 1739 and with France in 1741, he lost a majority in the House. He had to resign in 1742.

西班牙宣战的呼声日益高涨。与西班牙和法国的战争相继于 1739 和 1741 年爆发后，沃波尔在议会里失去了多数的支持。他不得不在 1742 年辞职。

詹姆斯二世的儿子詹姆斯·弗朗西斯·爱德华·斯图亚特（老僭君）

题 外 话

- 光荣革命后的英国可以说已成为世界上政治最文明的国家。当时法国最文明、思想最开放的人伏尔泰到英国住了三年（1726-1729），为英国的文明程度感到惊异。这里的作家，如蒲柏、艾迪生、斯威夫特都有随心所欲的写作自由。这个民族有自己的见解，他们重塑了自己的宗教，处死了国王，又从国外请来一个；他们建立了一个比欧洲任何统治者都更强大的议会。这里没有巴士底狱，也没有王公贵族可以滥用的逮捕证。这里有 30 种宗教，却没有一个教士。这里有一个最勇敢的教派——教友会，他们的真正的基督徒行为使所有的基督教国家惊诧不已。伏尔泰终生羡慕他们。

- 注意，伏尔泰在英国的三年，正是中国的雍正年间，文字狱最烈。1726 年，有位礼部侍郎出试题，其中有"维民所止"一句，皇帝认为他故意砍掉的"雍正"的头。这位礼部侍郎赶紧自杀，但尸体被肢解，儿子们一律处斩，家属们被发配边疆。

2. The Second Jacobite Rebellion

第二次詹姆斯党人叛乱

In July 1745, James II's grandson, Charles Edward Stuart, known as the Young Pretender, landed in Scotland and in September entered Edinburgh with 2000 men. Charles's forces easily defeated the English troops in Scotland and then marched into England. Charles's followers were only the Scottish Highlanders, however; he got little support from the rest of Scotland. In 1746 his forces were completely defeated in the battle on Culloden Moor. Charles fled back to the Highlands and escaped to France. A number of clan chiefs were executed for taking part in the rebellion. Nearly 1000 others were condemned to death. This event marked the end of the armed efforts of the Stuart family to recover the British throne.

1745 年 7 月，詹姆斯二世的孙子查理·爱德华·斯图亚特（史称小僭君)在苏格兰登陆，并于 9 月率领两千人进入爱丁堡。查理的军队轻而易举地打败了驻苏格兰的英军，然后进军英格兰。然而，查理的追随者只是高原苏格兰人，在苏格兰其他地区，他鲜有支持者。

1746 年，在卡洛登漠泽战役中被彻底击败。查理逃回高原，再逃往法国。由于参加叛乱，几个部落酋长被处死，还有近千人被判处死刑。这一事件为斯图亚特家族恢复英国王位的军事行动划上了句号。

詹姆斯二世的孙子查理·爱德华·斯图亚特(小僭君)

题 外 话

历史之所以复杂而有趣，就是因为总有一些顽固不化而又自不量力的人，勇敢地拿鸡蛋往石头上碰。上一代人对之毕恭毕敬的东西，到了这一代可能变得不合时宜，再隆重其事地搬出来，往往显得滑稽可笑。绝对王权早已不合时宜，光荣革命已证明，由谁当君王，不是血统说了算，而是议会或人民说了算。老僭君和小僭君偏偏看不见这一点，自以为正义在身，必一呼百应，可是在旁观者看来，他们上演的都是滑稽剧。

3. The Seven Years' War

七年战争

In the late 17th century, Britain and France came into conflict with each other for the control of the fur trade in North America. Then they began to fight for the land between the Appalachian Mountains and the Mississippi River, and argued over fishing rights off the coast of Newfoundland. Religious hostility made their relationship worse. Almost all the French were Roman Catholics, and most of the English were Protestants. British and French trading companies also competed for control in India. A series of wars had been fought between the two countries, but none of them had settled their conflict. Another war became inevitable.

The Seven Years' War (1756-1763) began in Europe in 1756. It involved nearly every nation in Europe, and extended to America and India. In Europe, Prussia and Austria fought each other for control of Germany. Great Britain aided Prussia, and France helped Austria. Britain

17世纪末，英法两国因北美的毛皮贸易发生冲突。后来，两国开始用武力争夺阿巴拉契亚山脉和密西西比河之间的领土，并就纽芬兰沿岸的捕鱼权发生纠纷。宗教仇恨使两国关系更加恶化。几乎所有的法国人都是天主教徒，而大多数英国人是新教徒。英法两国的贸易公司也在印度争夺控制权。两国之间爆发了一系列的战争，但并没有消除对立。另一场战争已不可避免。

七年战争（1756-1763）于1756年在欧洲爆发。这场战争几乎卷入了所有的欧洲国家，并蔓延到美洲和印度。在欧洲，普鲁士和奥地利为争夺德国的控制权而战。英国支持普鲁士，法国支持奥地利。英国在北美和印度与法国对抗。

1756年，英国历史上的伟人之一威廉·皮特出任英国首相。他决定派遣一支强大的军队到北美制

fought France in North America and India.

In 1756, William Pitt, one of the greatest men in British history, became prime minister of Britain. He decided to send a strong force to North America to conquer the French. He chose young and daring officers, including general James Wolfe, to command the British and colonial troops, and soon the British won a series of victories. The most important French fort in all America was Quebec, which stood on top of a steep cliff overlooking the St. Lawrence River in Canada. Here the French had perfect natural defences. But one dark night in 1759, a little British force under James Wolfe climbed up a steep cliff by a secret path, and at daybreak

服法国人。他挑选了一批年轻而果敢的军官，包括詹姆斯·沃尔夫将军，指挥英军和殖民地军队。不久英国就取得了一系列的胜利。法国在全美洲最重要的要塞是魁北克，它高踞于峭崖之上，俯瞰加拿大的圣劳伦斯河。法国人在这里有理想的天然屏障。但是在1759年的一个漆黑的夜晚，一支英军小分队在詹姆斯·沃尔夫的率领下，沿一条秘密小路攀上峭崖，在拂晓时分偷袭了敌军。战斗中沃尔夫两次受伤，但继续指挥，直至第三颗子弹击中他的胸膛。正当法军溃退时，沃尔夫阵亡。魁北克陷落了，此后一年之

英军攻占魁北克

they took the enemy by surprise. During the battle Wolfe was wounded twice, but he continued in command until a third bullet struck his lungs. He died just as the French troops were breaking. Quebec fell, and within a year all French resistance in Canada was over.

Meanwhile in India the French had attempted to destroy the East India Company. The British and French trading companies had long struggled for control of India, and a series of wars had been fought between them. A daring British military commander Robert Clive won several important victories over the French and their Indian allies, broke French power in southern India and gave the British a stronghold in that region. In 1757 Clive captured Chandernagore, the principal French settlement in India. Soon after that with 3,200 troops he defeated 50,000 troops of the native government of Bengal at the Battle of Plassey. This victo-

内法国人在加拿大的抵抗告终。

与此同时，在印度，法国人试图摧毁东印度公司。英法两国的贸易公司多年争夺印度的控制权，两者之间已发生过多次战争。一位勇猛的英军指挥官罗伯特·克莱武在与法军和他们的印度盟军的战斗中取得多次重大胜利，粉碎了印度南部的法国势力，在该地区建立了英军的据点。1757年，克莱武攻取了法国在印度的重要殖民地金德纳格尔。此后不久，他率领3200人在普拉西战役中打败了孟加拉当地

克莱武在印度

ry enabled the British to gain control of Bengal, the richest province in India. Clive then set up a puppet government in the region controlled by the British.

The Seven Years' War officially ended in 1763. The Treaty of Paris was signed to settle differences between France, Spain, and Great Britain. The treaty gave Britain almost all French lands in Canada and east of the Mississippi River. Britain also received the territory of Florida from Spain, which had become France's ally in 1762. France also gave up its control of India to Britain.

政府的 5 万大军。这次胜利使英国控制了孟加拉，印度最富庶的省份。克莱武在该地区建立起英国控制的傀儡政权。

七年战争于 1763 年正式结束。当年签订的巴黎条约解决了法国、西班牙和英国的争端。根据条约，法国在加拿大和密西西比河东部的几乎全部领土都割让给了英国。西班牙曾在 1762 年成为法国的盟国，英国因此还获得了西班牙的佛罗里达。法国还将印度的控制权让给了英国。

4. The American Revolution

美国革命

During the Seven Year's War the British colonies in America remained loyal to Britain, because they needed her protection. After the war, the French threat was no longer there. The colonists' loyalty to their mother country became weak.

The war against French Canada had cost a lot of money, and it still seemed necessary to keep a small army to defend the colonies. It was reasonable to expect the colonies to help with the cost. But the British Parliament and the governors sent over by the king had never felt the colonists should have as many rights as the people at home in Britain. Since the mid-

七年战争期间，英国在美洲的殖民地一直效忠英国，因为它们需要母国的保护。战后，法国的威胁不复存在。殖民地对母国的忠诚开始弱化。

与法属加拿大的战争耗费了大量资金，而且似乎仍旧需要一支小规模的军队来保卫殖民地。指望殖民地帮助支付这笔费用也合情合理。但是英国政府和国王派驻美洲的总督们从未感到殖民地人民应当像英国国内的人民一样享有许多权利。从 18 世纪 60 年代中开始，英国政府通过一系列法案，特别是

1760s, the British government passed a series of laws, especially tax laws, to increase its control over the colonies. The colonists, who believed that they had certain rights which Britain should respect, strongly resisted the new laws and insisted that Britain had no right to tax them without their approval.

In 1770, in Boston, Massachusetts, the people turned against the British soldiers, who then fired on the un-armed citizens and wounded and killed some of them. This was called the Boston Massacre. In 1773, King George III persuaded Parliament to tax the colonies' imports of tea. Some colonists were angry, and one night, they climbed up British ships carrying tea in Boston Harbour, and dumped the tea into the harbour. This event came to be known as the Boston Tea Party.

In 1775, the British government ordered its troops in Boston to take swift action against the

波士顿惨案

税法，以增加对殖民地的控制。殖民地人民认为他们享有英国应当尊重的某些权利，因而强烈抵制新的法案，坚持认为未经他们的认可，英国无权征税。

1770年，在马萨诸塞的波士顿，人们攻击英军士兵，英军士兵向手无寸铁的市民开枪，打死打伤数人。这一事件被称为波士顿惨案。1773年，国王乔治三世劝说议会向殖民地进口的茶叶征税。一些殖民者感到愤怒。一天夜里，他们

波士顿茶党案

rebels. The Revolutionary War broke out soon afterward. The American Colonies were unprepared for war. They lacked a central government, an army, and a navy. Delegates from the colonies formed the Continental Congress, which served as a national government. The Congress appointed George Washington, a former military officer who had fought against the French, commander in chief of the American forces. On July 4, 1776, the Congress adopted the Declaration of Independence, in which the colonies declared their freedom from the British rule.

Great Britain launched attacks on land and sea to crush the revolution. Britain had a far larger and better-trained army than did the Americans. However, Britain had to transport and supply its army across the Atlantic Ocean. Although the British won many battles, they gained little

爬上波士顿港口的英国运茶商船，将茶叶倾倒在港湾里。这一事件被称为波士顿茶党案。

1775 年，英国政府下令波士顿驻军采取迅速行动镇压叛乱分子。不久后，革命战争爆发。美洲殖民地尚未做好战争准备。他们没有中央政府，没有陆军和海军。各殖民地的代表组建了大陆会议，充当全国政府。会议任命曾经参加对法作战的军官乔治·华盛顿任美国军队的总司令。1776 年 7 月 4 日，大陆会议通过《独立宣言》，殖民地宣告脱离英国统治。

英国在陆地和海上发动进攻以镇压革命。英国军队比美国军队更强大，也更为训练有素。但是英国必须跨越大西洋运送并供给军队。

通过《独立宣言》

from their victories. The American patriots could always form new forces and fight on.

In 1777, the Americans won an important victory at Saratoga. The French, believing that the Americans could win the war and France had the opportunity of winning back Canada, joined the war on the American side. The French provided the Americans with the money and military equipment they badly needed to fight the war. The Spanish and the Dutch were also encouraged to seize the chance of revenge on their old enemy.

Britain lost control of the sea, and in 1781, a large British army was defeated at Yorktown. That defeat led the British government to begin peace talks with the Americans. The Treaty of Paris formally ended the war in 1783.

英国人虽然打了不少胜仗，但从胜利中并没有获取多少利益。美国爱国者总能够组建新的军队，并把战争继续下去。

1777年，美国人在萨拉托加取得重大胜利。法国相信美国人能打赢战争，因而法国能借此机会夺回加拿大，就与美国结盟加入战争。法国人向美国人提供了他们急需的资金和军事装备。西班牙和荷兰也见机行事，出来报复它们的夙敌。

英国失去了海上的控制权，而且在1781年一支英国大军在约克敦战败。这一败仗迫使英国政府开始与美国人和谈。1783年，巴黎条约签订，战争正式结束。

5. Captain James Cook

詹姆斯·库克上校

James Cook (1728-1779) was a British navigator and one of the world's greatest explorers. He changed the map of the world more than any other single man in history.

Cook became an apprentice with a shipping company when he was 18 years old. His earliest voyages gave him best training. He learned how to sail in the most dangerous waters.

Cook joined the British Navy in 1755.

詹姆斯·库克（1728-1779）是英国航海家，世界上最伟大的探险家之一。他对世界地图所做的改动比世界上任何人都要大。

库克18岁时就在一家船运公司当学徒。他早年的航行使他受到最好的训练。他懂得如何在最危险的水域航行。

库克于1755年加入海军。在英法两国的七年战争期间，他于

During the Seven Years' War between Great Britain and France, he carried out a dangerous mission in 1759, when he entered French territory in Canada to survey the St. Lawrence River for the navy. His charts helped General Wolfe's landing there and capture of the French city of Quebec later that year.

Between 1763 and 1768, after the war had ended, Cook command-ed a ship and surveyed the coasts of Newfoundland, sailing most of the year and working on his charts at his base in England during the winters.

In 1768, the navy appointed Cook com-mander of a scientific expedition to Tahiti, a Pacific island. His ship, the *Endeavour*, sailed from England in August and reached Tahiti in April 1769. There, the scientists of the Royal Society on the expedition watched the planet Venus pass across the sun. After this main goal of the voyage had been achieved, Cook was to find an unknown continent in the South Pacific. Geographers had long believed that a southern continent must exist to keep the world in balance.

In October, Cook became the first Euro-pean to visit New Zealand. In April 1770, the Endeavour sailed into Botany Bay on the east coast of Australia. Cook claimed the entire coast for Great Britain and named it New South Wales.

Cook returned to England in July 1771. During the voyage, Cook became the first ship

詹姆斯·库克

1759 年执行了一件危险的使命。他闯入加拿大的法国占领区为海军勘察圣劳伦斯河。他绘制的航图为当年晚些时候沃尔夫将军登陆攻取法国城市魁北克创造了条件。

战争结束后，从 1763~1768 年间，库克指挥一艘军舰勘察了纽芬兰沿岸。他一年间大部分时间用于航行，一到冬天便回到英格兰的基地绘制地图。

1768 年，海军任命库克为探险队指挥官，前往太平洋岛屿塔希提进行科学考察。他的船"努力号"于 8 月从英格兰出发，1769 年 4 月抵达塔希提。探险队里的皇家学会的科学家们在这里观测了金星凌日。完成了这一任务后，库克继续航行，去寻找南太平洋里的未知的大陆。多年来，地理学家们一直认为，南方一定有一个大陆，只有这样地球的南北两半才能保持平衡。

10 月，库克成为踏上新西兰的第一个欧洲人。1770 年 4 月，

commander to prevent an outbreak of scurvy, a disease that had long made sailors sick on long sea voyages. Cook had heard reports that scurvy was caused by a lack of fresh fruits and vegetables, so he was very strict about giving his men fruit and sauerkraut to help prevent the disease.

Back in England, Cook soon began to organize another and even more ambitious voyage.

In July 1772, Cook set out again for the South Pacific with two ships, the *Resolution* and the *Adventure* in another attempt to find the southern continent. Cook sailed farther south than any European had ever gone. Powerful winds, huge icebergs and blinding fog made the voyage full of danger. Cook circled Antarctica, but ice surrounded it and prevented him from seeing land.

In 1773 and 1774, Cook became the first European to visit a number of Pacific islands, including the Cook Islands and New Caledonia. He arrived back in England in July 1775 and was promoted to captain and elected a fellow of the Royal Society, and awarded one of its highest honours, the gold Copley Medal, for a paper that he prepared on his work against scurvy.

Cook set out again in July 1776 with two ships, the *Resolution* and the *Discovery*, to look for the Northwest Passage, a possible northern sea route between Europe and Asia. Cook first sailed to New Zealand and other Pacific islands. In January 1778, he became the first known European to sight the Hawaiian Islands.

"努力号"驶入澳大利亚东海岸的植物学湾。库克宣布整个沿岸地区为英国的领土,将它命名为新南威尔士。

库克于1771年返回英格兰。这次航行中,库克成为成功防止坏血病爆发的头一个船长。坏血病是长期航海的水手们患的一种疾病。库克听说此病是由于缺乏水果和蔬菜引起的,于是严格规定船员们吃水果和泡菜来预防。

库克回到英格兰后不久就开始组织另一次目标更远大的航行。

1772年7月,库克率领两艘船,"坚定号"和"历险号",再次出发前往南太平洋,去寻找南方的大陆。库克航行到欧洲人从未到达过的遥远的南方。狂风、浓雾和巨大的冰山使航行充满了危险。库克环绕南极洲一圈,但冰雪包围着它,使他未能看到陆地。

1773年和1774年,库克成为抵达一系列太平洋岛屿的头一个欧洲人。这些岛屿包括库克群岛和新喀里多尼亚。库克于1775年7月返回英格兰,晋升为上校,被选入皇家学会,他写的预防坏血病的论文获得皇家学会最高奖科普利金奖。

库克于1776年率两艘船"坚定号"和"发现号"再次出发,试图发现连接欧亚的西北航道。他先航行到新西兰和其他太平洋岛屿。1778年1月,他成为望到夏威夷

Later that year, Cook sailed along the west coast of Canada and Alaska, through Bering Strait, and entered the Arctic Ocean. But he failed to discover a Northwest Passage. Yet during this expedition he made detailed charts of the North Pacific. Cook sailed back to the Hawaiian Islands. Soon after that, in a violent conflict with the natives, he was killed.

群岛的头一个欧洲人。

当年晚些时候，库克沿着加拿大和阿拉斯加西海岸向北航行，穿过白令海峡，进入北冰洋。但他未能发现西北航道。但在探险途中，库克绘制了北太平洋的详细海图。库克返回夏威夷后不久，在一次与土著发生了暴力冲突中被杀死。

6. The Industrial Revolution

工业革命

The Industrial Revolution began in Great Britain during the second half of the 18th century and spread through the rest of Europe and to the United States during the following century.

Before the Industrial Revolution, most people of Europe were farmers and lived in small villages. They made most of their own clothing, furniture, and tools from raw materials produced on their farms or in the neighbourhood. They did not buy very much except some iron tools and salt. In the towns, some skilful people worked in their own shops to make such things as jewelry, silverware, hardware, cloth, leather goods, swords and guns. Some products made in the towns were exchanged for food produced in the countryside. The way of life changed little from one generation to the next, and most sons followed their father's trade.

工业革命发生在 18 世纪后半期。它肇始于英国，在一个世纪之内传遍欧洲，远及美国。

工业革命之前，大多数欧洲人是农民，居住在小村庄里。他们用自己的农庄上或邻近地区出产的原材料制作他们自己使用的大部分衣物、家具和工具。除去一些铁制的工具和食盐，他们很少购买其他东西。在城里，有些技术工人在他们自己的作坊里制作首饰、银制餐具、五金工具、布匹、皮革制品、刀剑和枪支。城里制作的一些商品用来交换乡下生产的粮食。人们的生活方式世代相传，很少发生变化。大多数情况下都是子承父业。

大多数人生活艰苦。他们生产的少，赚取的也少。许多人食物粗劣，健康不良，易于患病。只有少

Life was hard for most people. They produced little and earned little. Many of them did not have good food to eat, and they were unhealthy and easy to catch diseases. Only a few people had large incomes, usually because they were landowners, government officials, or successful businessmen.

Before the Industrial Revolution, most European countries were ruled by a powerful monarch. Great landowners, rich merchants, and some members of the clergy also had considerable political influence. But the workers and farmers had no voice in the government. Many countries did not even hold elections. Although Great Britain had a Parliament, only male members of the Church of England who paid a certain amount of taxes could vote. All these social, economic, and political conditions changed in Great Britain as the Industrial Revolution developed.

The Industrial Revolution began in Great Britain because social, political, and legal conditions there encouraged changes. The government adopted a hands-off economic policy and a free-market approach made popular by British philosopher and economist Adam Smith in his book *The Wealth of Nations*. It was easier for ambitious businessmen to make money and become rich through taking risk and investing in business ventures. Scientific and practical knowledge was applied to the process of manufacture and greatly increased technical efficiency. By the mid-18th century, Great Britain had

数人有大宗收入，通常因为他们是地主、政府官员或成功的商人。

工业革命前，大多数欧洲国家由强大的君主统治。大地主、富商和某些教士也有相当大的政治影响。但工人和农民在政府中没有发言权。许多国家甚至不举行选举。虽然英国有议会，但只有男性国教信徒，而且缴纳一定的税额才有选举权。随着工业革命的开展，所有这些社会、经济、政治状况都在英国发生了变化。

工业革命之所以始于英国，是因为社会、政治和法律条件鼓励变革。政府采取了英国哲学家和经济学家亚当·斯密在他的著作《国富论》里宣扬的自由放任的经济政策和自由市场手段。在英国，有雄心的实业家很容易通过冒险和投资企业赚取利润而发家致富。科学理论和实践知识被运用于生产过程，极大地提高了技术效率。到了18世纪中叶，英国已经成为首屈一指的殖民大国。它的殖民地不但提供了原材料，而且为工业产品提供了市场。

工业革命是从棉纺织业开始的。18世纪发明并改进了一些机器，可以廉价而大量地纺线织布。这导致了大工厂的建立，大批工人在工厂里做同样的工作。人们起初用水力转动机器，所以工厂只能建立在有河流的地方。1764年，苏格兰发明家詹姆斯·瓦特（1736-

become the world's leading colonial power. Her colonies not only provided raw materials, but also provided markets for industrial products.

The Industrial Revolution started in the cotton textile industry. In the 18th century a number of machines were invented and improved to spin thread and to make cloth cheaply and in large quantities. This led to the building of big factories in which many people worked at the same job. At first, water power was used to run the machines, and mills could be built only where there were rivers. Then in 1764, Scottish inventor James Watt (1736-1819) made important improvements to the steam engine, so that it could be used widely to provide power for big factories. Factories no longer depended on rivers for power. Steam engines needed coal, and coal mining expanded to meet the demand. Factory towns sprang up around the coalfields. Coal was also needed to make iron. Iron was used to improve machines and tools and to build bridges and ships. Fortunately Britain had large deposits of coal and iron. The growth of industry depended on its ability to transport raw materials and finished goods over long distances. To meet the need for better transportation British engineers widened and deepened many streams and built canals to link cities and to connect coalfields with rivers. They also built many bridges and lighthouses and deepened harbors. In the early 19th century, inventors began experimenting with Watt's steam engine as a means of transportation. In 1829 engineer and

1819) 对蒸汽机做了重大改进，使之可以被广泛利用为大工厂提供动力。工厂不再依靠河流获得动力。蒸汽机需要煤炭，采煤业扩大规模以满足需求。工业城市在煤矿周围兴起。冶铁业也需要煤炭。铁被用来改进机器和工具，建造桥梁和船只。幸运的是，英国有大储量的煤矿和铁矿。工业的发展有赖于长途运输原材料和成品的能力。为满足运输便捷的要求，英国工程师拓宽掘深了很多河流，并开凿运河连接城镇，沟通煤矿与河流。他们还建造了许多桥梁和灯塔，加深了港口。19 世纪初，发明家们开始试验用瓦特的蒸汽机做交通工具。1829 年工程师和发明家乔治·斯蒂芬森建造了首台实用的蒸汽机车。次年，首条重要铁路开通，在曼彻斯特和利物浦之间运送煤炭和大宗货物。不久，乘客的数量便超过货

詹姆斯·瓦特像

inventor George Stephenson created the first successful steam locomotive. The following year the first important railway opened, carrying coal and bulk goods between Manchester and Liverpool. It soon carried more people than products. Passenger travel by rail was faster, cheaper, and more comfortable than travel by coach. By the mid-19th century, steam-powered ships were beginning to carry raw materials and finished products across the Atlantic Ocean.

As the Industrial Revolution grew, private investors and banks were needed to provide money for the further development of industry. Many English merchants who had made fortunes during the 18th century from European wars, from the slave trade with North America, or from commerce with Britain's colonies became financiers, bankers and stockholders. These people were as important as industrialists and factories in the growth of the revolution.

The Industrial Revolution changed people's lives. One of the most obvious changes was that more people moved into the urban areas where there were factories. Many small farms disappeared for various reasons and small farmers were forced to sell their land, and move into cities to find jobs. They provided a work force for the new industries. By 1850 millions of British people lived in crowded, ugly and dirty industrial cities.

As a result of division of labor, each worker did one piece of a task, rather than the entire task. Such division of labor greatly increased

物。人们乘火车旅行比乘马车更快、更便宜、也更舒适。到了 19 世纪中叶，蒸汽动力的轮船开始跨越大西洋运送原材料和工业产品。

随着工业革命的开展，需要私人投资者和银行为工业的进一步发展提供资金。许多在 18 世纪从欧洲战争、北美奴隶贸易或与英国殖民地的贸易中大赚了一笔钱的英国商人成了金融家、银行家和股东。这些人在工业革命的进程中所起的作用与工业家和工厂同样重要。

工业革命改变了人们的生活方式。最明显的变化之一是越来越多的人移居有工厂的城市。许多小农庄由于各种各样的原因消失了，小农户们被迫出售土地，迁居城镇寻找工作。他们为新建的工厂提供了劳力。到了 1850 年，已有数百万英国人居住在拥挤、丑陋和肮脏的工业城镇里。

由于工厂里实行分工，每个工人只做一道工序，而不接触全部工序。这样的分工极大地提高了效率，但工人们每天必须成百上千遍地重复同一简单的动作，工作变得极端乏味。工人们必须在恶劣的条件下长时间地工作，但报酬却很低。贪婪的工厂主常常雇佣妇女和儿童，付给他们极低的工资。大多数工厂工人极端贫困，不会读书写字。他们居住在日益扩大的工业城市里拥挤的贫民窟里，生活条件十

efficiency, but workers had to repeat the same simple movements again and again for hundreds of times each day, so their job became extremely boring. Workers had to work long hours under bad conditions, but they were very poorly paid. Greedy factory owners often hired women and children and paid them very low wages. Most factory workers were extremely poor and could not read or write. They lived in crowded slums in the growing industrial cities in extremely unhealthy conditions.

Although the workers did not at first benefit from the development of industry, members of the middle and upper classes did from the beginning. Many people made fortunes during the period. The revolution provided new comforts and conveniences to those who could afford them. The middle class, which consisted of business and professional people, became better educated and more important politically. By the mid-19th century, business leaders called capitalists largely controlled British government policies.

One of the results of the revolution was the improvement of education. Before the revolution, England had only two universities, Oxford and Cambridge. The revolution created a need for engineers, professional workers and better-educated people. Private persons or groups set up schools, universities, and libraries to meet the need.

By about the 1820s, income levels for most workers began to improve. Although vast

分有害健康。

　　虽然工人们起初并没有从工业发展中得到好处，但社会的中上阶层从一开始就获得了利益。在这一时期，很多人发了财。工业革命为有钱人提供了新的舒适与方便。由工商和专业人士构成的中产阶级受到更好的教育，政治地位得到提高。到了 19 世纪中叶，被称为资本家的工商业的领袖很大程度上控制了英国政府的政策。

　　工业革命的成果之一是教育的发展。工业革命前，英国只有两所大学，即牛津与剑桥大学。工业革命创造了对于工程师、技术工人和受过良好教育的人的大量需求。个人或集团出资建立学校、大学和图书馆以满足需求。

　　大约在 19 世纪 20 年代，大多数工人的收入水准开始提高。虽然贫富差别依然巨大，大多数人还是享受到了经济发展的部分成果。中上阶层有更好的食物可吃，生活环境更加清洁舒适，患病更少，寿命更长。工人阶级的物质条件也得到了改善。部分由于生活条件的改善，人口迅速增加了。

题外话

• 工业革命之所以称为“革命”，因为它在较短的时间内给社会带来了翻天覆地的变化。在人类历史上，只有一次变革与工业革命有同等的重大意义。

differences existed between the rich and the poor, most of the people enjoyed some of the fruits of economic growth. As people of the middle and upper classes had better food to eat and lived in cleaner and more comfortable conditions, they suffered less from disease and lived longer. The material condition of the working class also improved. Partly as a result of these improved conditions, the population grew rapidly.

这就是人类学家所谓的"新石器革命"。在这场革命中，以渔猎和采集为基础的社会转变成以农业和畜牧业为基础的更为复杂的社会。由此产生了定居的生活方式和城市文明。而工业革命则将农业社会进一步转变成现代工业社会。

- 有些历史学家对"工业革命"这一提法不以为然。首先，它不仅仅是一场工业上的变革，它也是社会和文化上的变革。其次，它的发生也不够突然，实际上是一个渐变的过程，其肇端远在 18 世纪之前，对英国社会的影响在 1830 年后继续存在。但大多数人仍沿用这一传统提法。

7. The Age of Enlightenment

The Age of Enlightenment began in the 17th century and lasted until the late 18th century. This period is also called the Age of Reason or the Age of Rationalism. During this period, philosophers emphasized the use of reason as the best method of learning truth. They believed that nature is vast and complex but well ordered, and everything in the universe behaves according to a few simple laws. As the English poet Alexander Pope described, nature is "a mighty maze, but not without plan". So they had the confidence that powerful human reason can understand universe. Isaac Newton, for example, had solved the greatest problem in the history of science up to that time, the problem of how and why the universe worked as it did. In praise of Newton's work Pope wrote:

启蒙时代

启蒙时代开始于 17 世纪，持续到 18 世纪末。这一时代又称理性时代。在这一时期，哲学家们强调理性是获得真理的最佳手段。他们认为自然界虽然庞大而复杂，但有其秩序，宇宙万物都要遵循几条简单的定律来运行。正如英国诗人亚历山大·蒲柏所说，自然界是"巨大的谜团，但并非没有规则"。他们因而确信人类强大的理性可以了解宇宙。例如伊萨克·牛顿就解决了当时科学史上的最大问题，即宇宙如何运行以及为何那样运行。为赞扬牛顿的成就，蒲柏写道：

　　自然，和自然的规律都曾在黑夜中隐藏；

Nature and nature's Laws lay hid in Night;
God said, Let Newton be: and all was Light.

If human beings could understand the laws of the universe, God's own laws, why could they not also discover the laws underlying all nature and society? Philosophers of the Age of Enlightenment believed that the scientific method could be used in the study of human society. They studied problems in education, law, philosophy, politics and economy and attacked tyranny, social injustice, superstition, and ignorance.

Perhaps the earliest thinker in the English Enlightenment was Thomas Hobbes (1588-1679). Hobbes had a strong interest in physical science, and believed that human knowledge begins with the senses. His important contribution to thought was in political and social organization. He believed that people are selfish. They are moved chiefly by desire for power and by fear of others. Thus, without an all-powerful sovereign to rule them, their lives would be "poor, nasty, brutish, and short". Hobbes' most famous work is *Leviathan*. In the book, he argues that in a state of nature, human beings are not cooperative, but competitive, and live in an unending state of war. To escape this intolerable condition, human beings

上帝说,"让牛顿出生!"于是一切都被照亮。

倘若人类能够理解宇宙的规则,即上帝本人制定的规则,那他们为什么不能同样发现隐藏在所有自然和社会现象背后的规律?启蒙时代的哲学家们认为在人类社会的研究中可以采用科学的方法。他们研究教育、法律、哲学、政治和经济问题,攻击暴政、社会不公、迷信和愚昧。

英国启蒙运动中最早的思想家应当是托马斯·霍布斯(1588-1679)。霍布斯对自然科学有强烈的兴趣,相信人类的知识源于感觉。他的最大贡献是他关于政治和社会组织的思想。他认为人们都是自私的。他们的行为动机主要是权利欲以及对他人的戒惧心。因而,若没有强大的君主统治他们,他们的人生将是"可悲、险恶、野蛮而短暂的"。霍布斯的最著名的著作是《利维坦》。在这本书里,他试图说明在自然状态下,人类不是合作而是竞争,生活在一种永无止境的战争状态之中。为逃避这种难以忍受的处境,

托马斯·霍布斯

contracted to form a society in order to keep peace among themselves. So they have to choose a government, either a single person such as a king, or of a body of people such as the English parliament.

One of the most influential leaders of this age was British philosopher John Locke (1632-1704). Locke wrote that reason is "the candle of the Lord set up by himself in men's minds" and "must be our last judge and guide in everything." Locke stressed the importance of the senses. He believed that all human thought and knowledge is based on the direct experience of the world through the senses. This idea is known as empiricism. Therefore the environment is very important in shaping the individual. He described the human mind as a blank slate that gathered all its information through education and experience.

Locke's theory encouraged the optimistic idea of the 18th century that new experiences, produced by improved education and a better environment, could create a new and superior human race. His theory greatly influenced education in Great Britain and the United States.

《利维坦》扉页

人类订立契约而组建社会，以在他们之间维持和平。因而他们必须选择一个政府。这个政府可以是一个人，如国王，也可以是一个团体，如英国的议会。

这一时代最有影响的领袖人物之一是英国哲学家约翰·洛克(1632-1704)。洛克写道，理性是"上帝亲手在人心中点燃的蜡烛"，"必定是我们在一切事务中的最终法官与指导。"洛克强调感觉的重要性。他认为人类的一切思想与知识都建立在通过感官所获取的直接经验之上。这种观点称为经验主义。因而环境对人的塑造非常重要。他将人心说成是一块白板，通过教育与经验来积聚信息。

洛克的理论助长了18世纪的一种乐观的想法，即改良的教育和改善的环境所产生的新经验可以创造出崭新的和更高级的人类。他的理论对英美两国的教育有重大影响。

In his *Two Treatises of Government,* Locke attacked the theory of divine right of kings. Locke believed reason teaches that people are "all equal and independent, no one ought to harm another in his life, health, liberty, or possessions". He insisted that the government is responsible to the people, rather than the other way round. He emphasized the importance of private property. He advocated a system of checks and balances in government. Perhaps most importantly, he supposed that the people have the right to rebel against and overthrow the government when the government rules cruelly and unfairly.

Locke also insisted on the right of free speech, toleration for conflicting ideas, freedom of religion and separation of church and state.

David Hume (1711-1776), another most important British philosophers in the age, developed Locke's empiricism to the logical conclusion of extreme skepticism. Hume maintained that people's impressions and ideas are different things. Impressions come directly from experience. Ideas do not come directly from experience, but are formed from previous impressions.

洛克在他的《政府论》里抨击了君权神授论。洛克认为，理性告诉人们，人们"都是平等而独立的，任何人都不应损害他人的生命、健康、自由或财产。"他坚持认为政府应对人民负责，而不是相反。他强调私有财产的重要性。他鼓吹建立政府中的制约与平衡系统。或许最重要的是，他认为当政府施行残酷和不公的统治时，人民有权反叛并推翻政府。

洛克还极力主张言论自由权，对不同思想的容忍，宗教自由和政教分离。

大卫·休谟（1711-1776），这一时代的另一个最重要的哲学家。他发展了洛克的经验主义，从中导出极端怀疑主义的逻辑结论。休谟主张人们的印象和观念是两码事。印象直接来自经验，而观念并非直接来自经验，而是由先前的印象构成的。既然观念必须建立在经验的基础之上才是真实的，因而凡是无此基础的观念就无法确定其真实性。休谟力图证明传统哲学里的几

约翰·洛克

Since ideas must be based on experience to be true, ideas without such basis are uncertain. Hume argued that a number of ideas central to traditional philosophy are doubtful in this way. For example, people generally believe that a relationship exists between a cause and the effect that it has. But we never observe anything that actually connects the two events. So this idea is a belief without basis in experience.

Hume also studied the nature of happiness. He believed that virtue is the cause of happiness, both in ourselves and others, and that the two kinds of happiness are in agreement with each other. The highest human virtue is the kind and generous effort to increase the happiness of others. This idea had great influence over the reformers in the 19th century.

Another influential leader in the Age of Enlightenment was Adam Smith (1723-1790), a British philosopher and economist. Smith was strongly opposed to government's restriction on business. In his book *The Wealth of Nations* (1776), Smith showed that there would be social order and human progress when all individuals in a society freely followed their own self-interests. He argued that freedom in trade would bring about social harmony, because in order to make money, people

个中心观念因此而值得怀疑。例如，人们普遍认为，原因和其结果之间存在着联系。但是我们从未观察到任何事物真的将两个事件联系在一起。所以这一观念只是一种信念，而无经验的根据。

休谟还研究了幸福的本质。他认为美德是幸福的原因，既是自己的幸福的原因，也是他人的幸福的原因。这两种幸福是一致的。人类最高的美德是为增进他人的幸福而做出仁慈和慷慨的努力。这一思想对19世纪的改革家们有很大影响。

另外一个启蒙时代有影响的人物是英国哲学家和经济学家亚当·斯密（1723-1790）。斯密强烈反对政府约束工商业。在他的著作《国富论》（1776）里，斯密证明，当一个社会里的所有个人都自由地追逐个人利益时，就会产生社会秩序和人类进步。他力图说明，买卖的自由会带来社会和谐，因为为了赚钱，人们总要生产他人愿意购买的东西。而买方则花钱购买他们所最需要的东西。斯密认为，追求自己利益的私人企业最有效地组织了经济，"好像有一只看不见的手"

大卫·休谟

produce things that other people are willing to buy. Buyers spend money for those things that they need or want most. Smith believed that private businesses seeking their own interests organize the economy most efficiently, "as if by an invisible hand". Government interference would certainly be harmful to free competition. Smith insisted that the only job government is supposed to do is to keep law and order, enforce justice, defend the nation, and provide for a few social needs that could not be met through the market. Smith's opinions became increasingly influential and finally the government policy toward business in the first half of the 19th century.

亚当·斯密

在操控。政府的干涉必然会对自由竞争造成伤害。斯密坚持认为,政府的唯一任务应是维持法律与秩序,主持公道,保卫国家,确保少数通过市场无法满足的社会需求得到满足。斯密的观点后来影响日益增大,最终在 19 世纪前半期成为政府对待工商业的政策。

题外话

- 注意亚当·斯密不但写了《国富论》,强调自由竞争会给整个社会带来好处,而且此前写过《道德情操论》(*The Theory of Moral Sentiments*),专门讨论人们在受私利驱动时,如何又能具有道德判断的能力。斯密的回答是,人的内心深处都有另一个人(inner man),扮演不偏不倚的检察官的角色,赞同或谴责自己或他人的行为。这内心深处的另一个人的声音是无法漠视的。(比起弗洛伊德的 superego,即"超我",斯密的 inner man 略显幼稚。)所以,人的理性或他们的同情心,与他们追逐私利的本能同等重要。只有看到这一点,自由竞争才不致变成恶性的。《道德情操论》实际上为《国富论》奠定了心理学基础。有人误把亚当·斯密看做一个鼓吹冷酷无情的竞争的人,他们应当读一读他的《道德情操论》。

- 理性时代于 18 世纪末结束。此时人们的思想感情发生了重大转变。他们开始看重情感而不是理性,偏好激情、个性、本能,摒弃约束、规则与克制。这一变化,标志着理性时代的结束和浪漫主义运动的开端。

8. The War Against Napoleon

拿破仑战争

The French Revolution began in 1789. At first, most British people welcomed the ideas of the French revolutionaries, for many of the changes happening in France had already occurred in England and brought freedom to the British people. As for the British politicians, they were divided between the Whigs on the left who were more or less sympathetic to the revolution, and the Tories on the right who were frightened by the radical social and political changes in France. But the British generally changed their mind when the revolution grew more violent, and many members of the French upper classes were executed. Yet they did not try to interfere until the new French government seized Belgium in 1792 and threatened the Netherlands. Britain began to fear that France might destroy the balance of power in Europe, and so it joined Austria, Prussia, Spain, the Netherlands and the Kingdom of Sardinia in a war against France.

The British government, under William Pitt, was unwilling to make a direct attack. For the next 15 years, British navy fought the French at sea while the powers of central Europe fought them on land.

The war on land at first went badly. In 1796 the French government put an army under Napoleon's command to attack Austrian forces

法国革命于 1789 年爆发。起初，大多数英国人欢迎法国革命理想，因为法国正在发生的事件，正是曾经在英国发生过，并给英国人民带来自由的事件。英国的政治家们的态度则有分歧。辉格党人偏左，或多或少对革命抱有同情心；托利党人偏右，他们对法国剧烈的社会和政治变动感到惊恐。但当革命的暴力倾向日增，许多法国上层人士被处决后，英国人普遍改变了他们的态度。但他们没有试图干涉。直至法国新政府于 1792 年夺取了比利时，并进逼荷兰，英国开始担心法国会打破欧洲的权力平衡，于是加入了奥地利、普鲁士、西班牙、荷兰和撒丁王国的联盟，与法国对抗。

威廉·皮特领导的英国政府不愿发动直接进攻。在其后的 15 年里，英国海军在海上打击法国，而欧洲中部的大国则在陆地上与法国作战。

陆地上的战事起初很不顺利。1796 年，法国政府拨给拿破仑一支军队，命令他进攻意大利北部的奥地利军。在不到一年的时间里，拿破仑击败了四支军队，每一支都比他自己的兵力更强。1797 年初，

in northern Italy. In less than a year, Napoleon defeated four armies, each larger than his own. He won a final victory by marching over the Alps and threatening Vienna in early 1797. In 1798, Napoleon persuaded the French government to let him take an army to conquer Egypt as a base for future attack against India, the richest British possession. Napoleon was very successful with his army in Egypt, but his plan was wrecked when the greatest naval hero, Horatio Nelson, defeated the French fleet in the Battle of Nile. Without naval control the French could not send supplies across the Mediterranean Sea to Napoleon's army in Egypt, so Napoleon gave up that plan and returned to France.

When Napoleon was in Egypt, however, a new alliance against France was formed in 1798. The alliance included Russia, Great Britain, Austria, the kingdom of Naples, Portugal, and the Ottoman Empire. Wars broke out at the end of 1798, and were fought during the following year in northern Italy and in Switzerland.

Back in France, Napoleon seized control of the French government in 1799. In 1800, he led a famous march across the Alps into northern Italy with a newly raised army of 40,000 men. His army surprised and defeated the Austrians in the Battle of Marengo.

With Austria defeated, the British, now tired of war, agreed to peace in 1802 in the Treaty of Amiens. Russia had dropped out of the coalition against France in 1799. For the

他越过阿尔卑斯山，进逼维也纳，取得最后一次胜利。1798年，拿破仑说服法国政府让他率军征服埃及，再利用埃及为基地攻打印度，因为那是英国最大的财源。拿破仑的军队在埃及打得很顺利，但当伟大的海军英雄霍拉修·威尔逊在尼罗河战役中打败了法国舰队时，拿破仑的计划被打破了。没有海上优势，法国就无法跨过地中海向拿破仑在埃及的军队运送作战物资。拿破仑放弃了原计划，返回法国。

1798年，拿破仑还在埃及期间，一个新的反法联盟又形成了。联盟包括俄国、英国、奥地利、那不勒斯王国、葡萄牙和奥斯曼帝国。战争于1798年末爆发，次年在意大利北部和瑞士进行。

回到法国后，拿破仑于1799年夺取了法国政府的权力。1800年，他率领一支新近征集的4万大军，经过一次著名的行军，翻越阿尔卑斯山，偷袭了奥地利军，在马伦戈战役中打败了奥军。

奥地利被打败后，英国厌倦了战争，1802年同意议和，签署了亚眠条约。俄国于1799年退出反法联盟。经过10年的战乱，欧洲首次恢复和平。

但和平并未持久。1805年，奥地利、俄国和瑞典再次联合英国组成反法联盟。拿破仑率军进入德国，在乌尔姆战役中俘获奥军。当

first time in 10 years, Europe was at peace.

But peace did not last long. By 1805, Austria, Russia, and Sweden had joined Britain in a new coalition against France. Napoleon led his troops into Germany and captured an Austrian army at Ulm. By the end of the year, the French army, under the command of Napoleon, defeated a larger, combined army of Austria and Russia at Austerlitz. This battle was one of the greatest victories won by Napoleon.

Napoleon's greatest ambition was to invade and conquer England. To achieve this purpose, he had first to take control of the seas. In 1805, the French and Spanish fleets fought the British fleet in a battle at Trafalgar, off the southern coast of Spain. The French and Spanish fleets had 33 ships, while the British fleet, under the command of Admiral Horatio Nelson, had only 27. But Nelson surprised the enemy by having his ships cut through the French battle line. The British fleet did not lose a ship in the battle, but it destroyed or captured over half the French and Spanish ships. The Battle of Trafalgar crushed Napoleon's naval power, gave Britain control of the seas and ended all his hopes of invading Britain. But Nelson was wounded and died during the battle.

When Napoleon became master of all Europe except Russia and Britain, his power began to decline, mainly because of the rise of a nationalistic spirit in the defeated nations of Europe. In 1808 Spanish and Portuguese forces rebelled against French rule. Soon after the war

年年末，法国军队在拿破仑的指挥下在奥斯特利茨战役中打败了兵力更强的俄奥联军。这次战役是拿破仑取得的最辉煌胜利之一。

拿破仑的最大野心是入侵并占领英国。为达到这一目标，他必须首先取得海上霸权。1805年法国和西班牙舰队在西班牙南部海岸附近的特拉法尔加与英国舰队会战。法西舰队共有33艘战舰，而舰队司令纳尔逊指挥的英国战舰只有27艘。但是纳尔逊下令突袭敌军，将法军阵线切割开。英国舰队在战斗中没有损失一只战舰，但摧毁或俘获了超过一半的法西战舰。特拉法尔加战役粉碎了拿破仑的海军力量，使英国得到了制海权，使拿破仑入侵英国的希望彻底破灭。但是，纳尔逊在战斗中负伤后死去。

当拿破仑成为除俄国和英国之外的全部欧洲的统治者时，他的权势开始衰落，主要因为欧洲战败国民族主义情绪的高涨。1808年西班牙和葡萄牙军队发动反对法国统治的叛乱。此后不久战事又起，英国军队加入反法战争。这场战争，由于在葡萄牙和西班牙所在的半岛上进行，史称"半岛战争"(1808-1814)。在战争中，亚瑟·韦尔斯利，即后来的威灵顿公爵，被公认为最伟大的英军统帅。到了1814年4月，所有的法国军队已被逐出半岛。为继续在西班牙的战争，法

began, British troops joined the fight against France. This war, which was fought on the peninsula that consisted of Portugal and Spain, became known as the Peninsular War (1808-1814). During the war, Arthur Wellesley, later the Duke of Wellington, became recognized as the greatest British general. By April 1814, all French forces had been driven from the peninsula. The constant demand for men and money to continue the war in Spain greatly weakened France and finally contributed to Napoleon's final defeat in Europe.

Meanwhile Napoleon was fighting a trade battle with Britain. His ports were forbidden to export anything to the island, and the British navy in return would not allow any ship to enter them. But this caused troubles with the Americans and led to the War of 1812 between Britain and the United States. The war began when the United States insisted that Britain had no right to stop, search, or seize ships belonging to neutral countries.

Napoleon's downfall came after he decided to attack Russia in 1812. His army failed stand up to the extreme cold of the Russian winter and had to retreat, but in the march across Russia most of the soldiers died.

After he returned to Paris, Napoleon faced a new alliance of Austria, Great Britain, Russia, Prussia, and Sweden. He raised a new army and attacked the allies. But his forces were greatly outnumbered. Napoleon was defeated, and the allies captured Paris in March 1814. Napoleon

威灵顿公爵

国不断投入兵力和财力，大大削弱了法国，最终促成拿破仑在欧洲的彻底失败。

与此同时，拿破仑与英国在进行一场贸易战。法国港口禁止任何货物出口不列颠，而英国海军则阻止任何船只进入法国港口。但这一举措与美国发生摩擦，导致1812年的英美战争。战争的起因是美国坚持英国无权阻止、搜查或扣押属于中立国的船只。

拿破仑在1812年决定进攻俄国后，他的末日来临了。他的军队未能经受住俄国冬季的严寒，只得撤退，但在跨越俄国的行军中士兵们死去大半。

拿破仑

gave up his imperial throne, and was exiled from France and made ruler of the tiny island of Elba off the northwest coast of Italy.

Early in 1815, Napoleon made a last attempt to return to power. He escaped from Elba and landed in southern France with a thousand supporters. He gathered an army as he marched north to Paris. Louis XVIII, who had been placed on the French throne, fled.

Napoleon advanced into Belgium with a powerful army, hoping to defeat the separate armies of Britain's Duke of Wellington and the Prussian Marshal Gebhard von Blücher. Napoleon first defeated Blücher, and then met Wellington at Waterloo, a small town near Brussels, Belgium. The French started a fierce attack, and Wellington's troops held out stubbornly. When Blücher arrived with what was left of his Prussian troops to reinforce Wellington, the joint forces defeated the French army decisively. The Battle of Waterloo marked the end of the Napoleonic Wars.

返回巴黎后，拿破仑面对着一个由奥地利、英国、俄国、普鲁士和瑞典组成的新联盟。他募集了一支新的军队进攻联盟国家。但是敌国军队的数量大大超过了法军。拿破仑被打败，盟国军队于1814年3月占领巴黎。拿破仑放弃帝位，离开法国，流亡到意大利西北方小岛厄尔巴，任该岛的统治者。

1815年初，拿破仑为了夺回政权，做了最后一次尝试。他逃离厄尔巴，率领一千名支持者在法国南部登陆。在向北方进军巴黎时，他聚集了一支军队。重登王位的路易十八逃离巴黎。

拿破仑率领一支大军开入比利时，试图分别击败英国威灵顿公爵和普鲁士布吕歇尔元帅的军队。拿破仑先打败了布吕歇尔，然后与威灵顿在比利时布鲁塞尔附近的小镇滑铁卢相遇。法军发动猛攻，威灵顿的军队顽强抵抗。后来，布吕歇尔率普鲁士军残部赶来增援威灵顿，两军合力彻底击溃法军。滑铁卢战役标志着拿破仑战争的结束。

题外话

拿破仑是历史上最伟大的军事统帅之一。但他也常被人描绘成一个权力欲极大的征服者。拿破仑本人则否认他是这样的征服者。他声称他的目标在于建立一个自由欧洲人民的同盟，由一个自由主义的政府管辖。就算他说的是真心话，但他为达到此目标而采取的手段却是将权力集中在自己手中。但无论如何，在他重建的那些国家里，拿破仑允许它们制订自己的宪法，引入法典，废除封建制，建立有效的政府，并扶植教育、科学、文学和艺术。

9. Horatio Nelson

Horatio Nelson (1758-1805) was Britain's greatest admiral and national hero, famous for his victories in the battles of the Nile and Trafalgar. These victories broke France's naval power and established Britain's rule of the seas for the rest of the 19th century.

Nelson fell in love with the sea early in life and made up his mind to be a sailor. He entered the British navy when he was 12 serving under his uncle, Captain Maurice Suckling. He owed much of his early training to Captain Suckling. By 1779 he had attained the rank of captain.

In 1793, Nelson was placed in command of the *Agamemnon* in the Mediterranean Sea. In the following years he fought in a series of battles at sea. Nelson was one of the British commanders who blockaded Toulon, France, and captured Corsica. He was wounded at Calvi, on the Corsican coast, and lost his right eye. After that, he wore a black patch over the eye.

霍雷肖·纳尔逊

霍雷肖·纳尔逊（1758-1805）是英国最伟大的海军统帅和民族英雄，以其在尼罗河战役和特拉法尔加战役取得的胜利闻名于世。这两场胜利粉碎了法国的海军力量，奠定了19世纪英国在海上的霸权地位。

纳尔逊从小就热爱大海，决心长大成为一名水手。他12岁就加入海军，在舅舅毛利斯·萨克林舰长的指挥下服役。他早年受到的良好训练，与萨克林舰长的培养分不开。到1779年，他就获得了舰长的职务。

1793年，纳尔逊受命指挥地中海上的军舰"阿加门农号"。在此后数年里，他参加了一系列的海战。他参加了对法国土伦港的封锁和夺取科西嘉岛的战斗。他在攻占科西嘉海岸的卡尔维时

纳尔逊

Nelson next distinguished himself at the Battle of Cape St. Vincent, Portugal, in 1797. He played a very important part in the defeat of the combined French and Spanish fleets. A few months later, Nelson led a rash attack by small boats on the strongly fortified port of Santa Cruz de Tenerife in the Canary Islands. But this attack failed. The British were driven off with heavy losses and Nelson's right arm was badly wounded and had to be cut off.

After Napoleon had won victories in Europe, he began to gather a French fleet for an expedition to conquer Egypt. Nelson was sent to watch the French ships at Toulon. A storm came up, and under its cover the French fleet escaped. Nelson followed it in a long pursuit. He finally cornered the French ships in Abu Qir Bay, at the mouth of the Nile. The French fleet lay in the harbour and was protected by shore guns. Any ships that wished to attack had to pass by dangerous rocks in the harbour. Nelson skilfully led his fleet into the harbour during the night, and although outnumbered, his fleet attacked and almost destroyed the French fleet on August 1, 1798. This battle is known to history as the Battle of the Nile. It cut off Napoleon's army in Egypt and ruined his Egyptian campaign. The victory over Napoleon made Nelson famous. He was made Baron of the Nile and given a large sum of money.

Nelson was wounded again in this battle, and he went to Naples to recover. Emma Lady Hamilton, wife of Sir William Hamilton, the

负伤，失去右眼。此后，右眼总是戴着黑色眼罩。

1797 年，纳尔逊在葡萄牙的圣文森蒂角战役中再次崭露头角。他为打败法国和西班牙联合舰队做出重要贡献。数月后，他率领几艘小船贸然进攻加那利群岛防守严密的圣克鲁斯-德内里费，但未能得手。英国人被赶下海，损失惨重。纳尔逊的右臂受重伤，不得不截肢。

拿破仑在欧洲打了胜仗后，开始聚集一支法国舰队远征埃及。纳尔逊受命监视土伦港法国舰队的动向。一场风暴袭来，法国舰队乘机逃出港口。纳尔逊穷追不舍，最终将法国舰队堵在尼罗河口的阿布吉尔湾。法国舰队在港口内停泊，受岸上的炮火保护，企图进攻港口的任何船只都必须通过港口内布满危险暗礁的水域。纳尔逊在夜间率领舰队巧妙地突入港口，在敌强我弱的情况下发起攻击，于 1798 年 8 月 1 日将法国舰队摧毁殆尽。这次战役史称尼罗河战役。它切断了拿破仑军队在埃及的供给线，挫败了拿破仑在埃及的战略计划。纳尔逊由于此次大捷而成名。他受封为尼罗河男爵，并得到一大笔奖金。

纳尔逊在此次战斗中再次负伤，到那不勒斯疗伤。英国驻那不勒斯大使威廉·汉密尔顿爵士的妻子，汉密尔顿夫人爱玛爱上了这位

British ambassador to Naples, fell in love with the one-eyed, one-armed naval hero and became his mistress. Later, Nelson separated from his wife and Lady Hamilton from her husband.

Nelson became a vice admiral in 1801, and sailed for Copenhagen, Denmark, to make the attack on the Danish fleet. In the following Battle of Copenhagen, the British destroyed the Danish fleet in the harbor of the capital. Nelson, although second in command, took entire charge of the British operations. Admiral Parker, who was the commander of the British fleet, later became doubtful of the attack's outcome and signaled Nelson to withdraw. It is said that Nelson put his telescope to his blind eye and declared he could not see the signal, and went on fighting. His decision turned out right, and the British won a great victory. After the Battle of Copenhagen, Nelson was given the title of viscount.

Nelson was made commander in chief of the fleet in May 1803. Sailing on the flagship *Victory*, he once more went in search of the French. He found the French fleet at Toulon, but it slipped away from him. Nelson chased the French to the West Indies and back, and finally caught up with the French fleet off Cape Trafalgar on the coast of Spain, in October 1805. Nelson hoisted his famous signal, "England expects that every man will do his duty." With only 27 ships, Nelson attacked the combined French and Spanish fleets. One of the great naval battles of all time followed.

独眼独臂的海军英雄，成了他的情妇。后来纳尔逊与妻子分手，汉密尔顿夫人也与丈夫脱离了关系。

1801年，纳尔逊升任舰队副司令，受命前往丹麦的哥本哈根，攻击丹麦舰队。在接下来的哥本哈根战役中，英国舰队在这座首府的港口摧毁了丹麦舰队。虽然纳尔逊只是副司令，却指挥了整个战役。英国舰队司令帕克上将担心进攻会失利，向纳尔逊发出撤退信号。据说纳尔逊把单筒望远镜放在失明的眼睛上，宣布说他无法看到信号，于是继续作战。他的决定结果证明是正确的，英军大获全胜。哥本哈根战役后，纳尔逊受封为子爵。

1803年5月，纳尔逊被任命为舰队总司令。他乘旗舰"胜利号"再次出发搜寻法国舰队。他在土伦发现敌舰，但法国舰队乘他不备，溜出港口。纳尔逊一路追逐到西印度群岛，再返回欧洲，于1805年10月在西班牙的特拉法尔加角附近追上法国舰队。纳尔逊升起信号旗，发布他那著名的动员令："英国要每位将士恪尽职守"。尽管只有27艘战舰，纳尔逊下令向法国和西班牙联合舰队发起进攻。接着，历史上最大的海战之一打响，拥有33艘战舰的拿破仑舰队被摧毁了。

纳尔逊在战斗中身负重伤，不久死去，但在死前得知英国舰队打

Napoleon's fleet, which had 33 warships, was destroyed.

Nelson was mortally wounded and died during the battle, but he lived long enough to know that the British fleet had defeated the French and Spanish fleets. Nelson's last words were, "Thank God I have done my duty."

Today Nelson is remembered as the most famous of all British naval heroes. His statue stands high above Trafalgar square in the heart of London, and navy leaders gather there each year to do him honour on Trafalgar Day.

败了法西联合舰队。纳尔逊的最后一句话是，"感谢上帝，我已尽职了。"

纳尔逊至今被视为最著名的英国海军英雄受到人们的怀念。他的雕像高高矗立在伦敦中心的特拉法尔加广场上。每年的特拉法尔加节海军将领们都要聚集在雕像周围，向纳尔逊致敬。

题 外 话

- 在英国历史上，有三位军事统帅最受推崇，他们是马尔博罗、威灵顿和纳尔逊。马尔博罗即约翰·丘吉尔，英国首相温斯顿·丘吉尔的祖先。他背弃詹姆斯二世，转而支持威廉三世，为光荣革命作出贡献，因而受赏识，被封为马尔博罗伯爵。安妮女王即位后，他成为宠臣，被封为公爵。他是个作战勇猛的军事天才，在西班牙王位继承战争中打了一系列的胜仗，因而名声显赫。他的妻子与女王关系密切，但由于试图操纵女王而失宠。马尔博罗为人圆滑，惟利是图的人品颇受后人诟病，所以人缘不好。威灵顿在拿破仑战争中屡建战功，最后在滑铁卢彻底击败拿破仑，有"铁公爵"之称。但他缺乏政治头脑，担任首相期间反对议会改革，也没有多少人缘。人缘最好的是纳尔逊。英国诗人罗伯特·骚塞谈到纳尔逊时写道："英国有许多英雄人物。但没有一个受到同胞们如此全心全意的爱戴。所有的人都知道他的心既无所畏惧又充满人情……所有的人都知道他为了祖国鞠躬尽瘁。因而，人们就像热爱英国一样真挚地热爱他。
- 纳尔逊临终时究竟说了些什么，其说不一。通常认为他说的是："感谢上帝，我已尽职了。"这是不是杜撰，不得而知。反正凡夫俗子们乐于相信伟人临终必有豪言壮语在胸，不吐不死。再说，他不是提出"英国要每位将士恪尽职守"吗？总要有个呼应才对。据另一说法，他说的是："可怜的爱玛，现在她可怎么办。"然后转向自己的副手，"吻一吻我，哈代。"哪一种说法更符合纳尔逊的性格，只好由人们自己判断了。

CHAPTER TWELVE
The 19th Century (1815-1914)
十九世纪(1815-1914)

1. The Act of Union of 1800

Troubles with Ireland became serious during the Napoleonic Wars. The English had governed Ireland for centuries, but the Irish hated English rule.

After the Normans conquered England in the 11th century, they also tried to conquer Ireland. But they did not control most of Ireland until 14th century. However, as the Normans married Irish girls and adopted Irish language and customs, they lost touch with their own people and were no longer loyal to England. By the early 15th century, England actually controlled only a small area around Dublin called the Pale.

The relations between England and Ireland became hostile in the 16th century, when the English attempted to establish Protestantism in Ireland and aroused strong resistance. Elizabeth I declared Roman Catholic services illegal and

1800 年的合并条例

在拿破仑战争期间，英国与爱尔兰的纠纷加剧了。英国人统治爱尔兰长达几世纪，但爱尔兰人憎恨英国人的统治。

诺曼人于 11 世纪征服了英格兰之后，他们也曾试图征服爱尔兰。但他们直到 14 世纪才控制了爱尔兰的大部分。然而，随着诺曼人与爱尔兰女子通婚，接受了爱尔兰人的语言和习俗，他们与自己的人民失去接触的机会，不再忠于英格兰。到了 15 世纪，英格兰实际上只控制都柏林周围的一小片称为佩尔的英国统治区。

16 世纪，英格兰人试图在爱尔兰建立新教，激起强烈反抗。此时，英爱关系恶化。伊丽莎白一世宣布罗马天主教礼仪非法，处决了

executed a number of bishops and priests. But as a result, the Irish Catholics became more united and more hostile to the English than ever. They rose in a series of revolts against the English in Ulster, a large province in northern Ireland, but their revolts were put down.

James I tried to prevent further revolts by settling Protestants in Ireland. He seized land in Ulster and gave it to English and Scottish Protestants, so that the Protestants became the majority that still exists in Northern Ireland.

During the English Civil War the Irish Catholics feared that the Puritans, who grew powerful, would persecute them. In 1641, they rose up against the Protestants. They took revenge on the settlers who had seized their lands, killing thousands. In 1649 Cromwell brought an army to Ireland and cruelly crushed the revolt. Cromwell gave even more land to English Protestants and deprived the Catholics of many political rights.

After James II, who was a Catholic, became king of England in 1685, he abolished many of the laws against Catholics. In the Glorious Revolution of 1688, all the Irish Catholics supported James II. In 1689, when James landed in Ireland to raise an army to fight the English, many Irish Catholics were ready to help him. William III quickly defeated James II and his Irish supporters, and severely punished Irish Catholics. Irish Catholics lost more land and more political rights, and their religious rights were restricted.

In the 18th century, the British continued

几个主教和教士。但结果却适得其反，爱尔兰天主教徒们比以往更加团结，更加仇视英格兰人。他们在爱尔兰北部的大省阿尔斯特发起一系列反抗英格兰人的起义，但起义都被镇压下去。

詹姆斯一世采用派送新教徒移居爱尔兰的方法防止爱尔兰人起义。他夺取阿尔斯特地区的土地，将土地赐予英格兰和苏格兰的新教徒，使新教徒成为爱尔兰北部居民的大多数。这种局面一直持续到现在。

在英国内战期间，爱尔兰天主教徒担心政治势力越来越大的清教徒会迫害他们。1641年，他们掀起反对新教徒的起义。他们报复夺取他们土地的移居者，杀死数千人。1649年，克伦威尔率领一支军队进入爱尔兰，残酷地镇压了起义。克伦威尔将更多的土地分给英格兰的新教徒，剥夺了天主教徒的许多政治权利。

詹姆斯二世于1685年登基，由于他是天主教徒，废除了许多压迫天主教徒的法律。1688年的光荣革命中，所有的爱尔兰天主教徒都支持詹姆斯二世。1689年，当詹姆斯在爱尔兰登陆以募集军队与英格兰人作战时，许多爱尔兰天主教徒都乐于协助他。威廉三世迅速击败了詹姆斯二世及其爱尔兰支持者，严厉地惩罚了爱尔兰天主教

their control over Ireland with a strong hand. They limited the powers of the Irish Parliament. In 1770s, under the influence of the American Revolution, the Irish demanded more freedom and rights. Protestants formed volunteer military groups, supposedly to defend the island from a French invasion. Backed by these groups, the Irish Protestants put pressure on the British government until it gave greater independence to the Irish Parliament in 1782. Catholics regained their rights to hold land, and the restrictions on their religious rights were removed. But still they did not have any political rights.

Some Protestants in Parliament tried to gain more rights for Catholics. After their attempts failed, they formed a group called the Society of United Irishmen in 1791. This society wanted to bring the democratic ideals of the French Revolution to Ireland and create an independent, religiously tolerant state. In 1798, with the help of the French, the United Irishmen raised a rebellion, but it was harshly put down by British forces. After the rebellion, the British prime minister, William Pitt, the Younger, proposed that the British and Irish parliaments should be united and give Irish Catholics political rights. He thought that was the only way to end Roman Catholic rebellion and Protestant cruel and unfair rule in Ireland. The two parliaments approved his proposal, and passed the Act of Union. Under the act, which went into effect in 1801, Ireland officially became part of the United Kingdom of Great Britain and Ireland. The Irish Parliament

徒。爱尔兰天主教徒失去了更多的土地、更多的政治权利，他们的宗教权利也受到限制。

在 18 世纪，英国人继续对爱尔兰采取高压政策。他们限制爱尔兰议会的权力。18 世纪 70 年代，在美国革命的影响下，爱尔兰人要求更多的自由和权利。新教徒组建了志愿军，声称要保卫爱尔兰，使之免遭法国的入侵。在这些军事组织的支持下，爱尔兰新教徒向英国政府施压，直至它于 1782 年给爱尔兰议会以更大的自主权。天主教徒重获了拥有土地的权利，他们宗教权利的限制也被取消。但他们仍然没有任何政治权利。

议会里的某些新教徒试图为天主教徒争取更多的权利。他们的努力失败后，于 1791 年成立了一个称为爱尔兰人联合会的组织。该组织想在爱尔兰宣传法国革命的民主理想，创建一个独立的、宗教宽容的国家。1798 年，在法国人的帮助下，爱尔兰人联合会发动叛乱，但遭到英国军队的残酷镇压。叛乱发生之后，英国首相小威廉·皮特建议英国和爱尔兰议会合并，并给爱尔兰天主教徒以政治权利。他认为这是结束天主教徒叛乱和新教徒在爱尔兰残酷而不公正统治的唯一办法。两个议会赞同他的建议，通过了合并条例。条例于 1801 年开始实施。根据这一条例，爱尔兰正

was ended, and the Irish were allowed 32 members in the British House of Lords and 100 members in the House of Commons. Owing to the opposition of George III, however, Pitt was unable to make good his promise of giving Catholics political rights. The Catholic Irish could not serve in the British Parliament or hold public offices. They felt betrayed.

The Act of Union of 1800 brought England, Scotland, Ireland, and Wales under the rule of a central government headed by a common monarch and controlled by a single parliament. When Ireland (except its northern part) became independent in 1922, the kingdom was renamed the United Kingdom of Great Britain and Northern Ireland.

式成为大不列颠及爱尔兰联合王国的一部分。爱尔兰议会解散，爱尔兰人在英国议会上院拥有 32 席，在下院拥有 100 席。但是，由于乔治三世的反对，皮特未能实现给天主教徒政治权利的承诺。爱尔兰的天主教徒不能担任英国议会的议员，也不能担任公职。爱尔兰的天主教徒感到受了欺骗。

1800 年的合并条例将英格兰、苏格兰、爱尔兰和威尔士置于一个中央政府的管辖之下。这个政府，由一位共同的君主做首脑，并受单一的议会控制。爱尔兰（除去它的北部以外）于 1922 年独立后，王国重新命名为大不列颠及北爱尔兰联合王国。

威廉·皮特

英国国旗

题外话

• 18 世纪初，爱尔兰人的生活依然十分悲惨。大多数人没有政治权利，经济上受英国商人和爱尔兰地主的双重剥削。若想形象地了解他们的悲惨生活，可以读斯威夫特的著名讽刺文章《一个温和的建议》。

- 合并条例（The Act of Union）亦可指 1536 年威尔士与英格兰的合并条例，当时亨利八世在位。他的父亲亨利七世是威尔士贵族埃德蒙•都铎的儿子，所以英格兰兼并威尔士也顺理成章。合并条例亦可指 1707 年英格兰和苏格兰的合并条例。在使用这一名词时应标明年代。
- 英格兰的国旗本是白底正红十字旗，即圣乔治旗。1707 年英格兰和苏格兰合并时，詹姆斯一世在圣乔治旗上加上代表苏格兰的圣安得烈蓝底白斜十字。1800 年的合并条例通过后，代表爱尔兰的圣帕特里克白底斜红十字也叠加在旗子上。从此，由 3 个十字叠加而成的大不列颠及北爱尔兰联合王国的国旗称为 Union Jack。

2. The Era of Reform

Social, economic, and political reform had been needed in Britain for many years. A few years before the French Revolution, the younger Pitt had proposed a reform bill. But reform could not succeed when the English, who feared the French Revolution, became more conservative. After the Napoleonic Wars, however, the people's demands for reform became strong again, and forced Parliament to act. Many people had the ideas of the Enlightenment, and thought that a political reform would cure all social and economic evils.

Britain's criminal laws badly needed reform. In the 18th-century, more than 200 crimes, including those that today would not earn a month in prison, were punished by death. Prisons were so crowded that the government sent tens of thousands of convicts to the Americas to do hard work and established the colony of Australia as a prison colony at the end of the

改革时代

社会、经济和政治改革已是英国多年来需要解决的问题。法国革命之前几年，小皮特就已经提出的改革法案。但由于英国人害怕法国革命，变得更加保守，改革不可能成功。然而，在拿破仑战争之后，人们改革的要求再次变得强烈，迫使议会采取行动。许多人已接受了启蒙运动的思想，认为政治改革会医好所有社会和经济的弊病。

英国的刑法急需改革。在 18 世纪，有 200 多种罪行，包括今天只会得到监禁一个月的处罚的轻罪，都要被判处极刑。监狱人满为患，政府将数以万计的罪犯遣送美洲做苦工。到了世纪末，政府在澳大利亚建立殖民地关押囚犯。19 世纪 20 年代，许多苛刻的法律得到纠正。1824 年，议会废除了禁止工人成立工会的法律。1828 年，

century. During the 1820s, many of the harsh laws were corrected. In 1824, Parliament abolished the laws forbidding workers to form trade unions. In 1828, under increasing pressure from Protestants who were not members of the Church of England, Parliament ended the Test Acts. These acts had prevented the group of Protestants from working in government jobs and the professions, and from studying in universities. In the following year, after a long struggle in Ireland, Parliament removed the legal restrictions that had prevented Catholics from holding public office in the United Kingdom. In 1833, Parliament abolished slavery in the colonies and in the Factory Act of that year, restricted child labour in the textile industry.

But the most burning issue was reform of the system of the election of members of Parliament. Great landowners had most seats in Parliament, and the large and growing middle class had few. Some members of Parliament represented empty country places that had no or very small populations, and they were easily bribed. On the other hand, many towns with large populations had few or no representatives.

In 1830, the Tory Party's 60 years in office ended. The Whigs had promised parliamentary reform and they came to power. The Tories had led the country to victory over Napoleon and changed it into a great industrial power, but on matters of reform they were divided. The majority, under Wellington, opposed parliamentary reform. In 1831, the Whigs introduced a reform

在非国教新教徒日益增长的压力下,议会废止了宗教考查法。宗教考查法曾禁止这些新教徒担任公职,从事知识性专业,或进入大学学习。第二年, 在爱尔兰人的长期斗争之后, 议会废除了天主教徒在联合王国担任公职的法律限制。1833 年,议会废除了殖民地奴隶制。同年的工厂法禁止纺织工业使用童工。

但是最急迫的问题是议会议员选举体制的改革。大土地所有者在议会里占据了大多数席位,而人数众多且日益扩大的中产阶级的席位却很少。有些议员代表的是没有人口或人口稀少的农村地区,他们很容易受贿。而许多人口众多的大城市在议会里只有很少或干脆没有代表。

1830 年, 托利党长达 60 年的执政结束了。辉格党由于许诺进行议会改革而上台执政。托利党曾领导英国战胜了拿破仑, 使之发展成强大的工业国, 但在改革问题上, 党内产生了分歧。威灵顿领导下大多数托利党人反对议会改革。1831 年, 辉格党在议会提出一项改革法案。经过激烈的辩论,议会最终通过法案, 这就是 1832 年的改革法案。

1832 年的改革法案取消了人口稀少的农村选区在下院的 143 个议席, 将它们按人口比例分配给城镇。这意味着该法案剥夺了大土

bill in Parliament. After a heated argument, Parliament finally passed the bill, which became the Reform Act of 1832.

The Reform Act of 1832 took away 143 seats in the House of Commons from empty country places and gave them to towns, corresponding to their large population. That means it took away the political power from the large landowners and gave it to the middle class, and Parliament became more democratic. Yet only about 15 percent of Britain's adult males could vote because right to vote was limited to people who had a level of income not lower than that of the middle class. The working class and women had no right to vote.

After 1830 the two chief political parties in Britain, the Tory Party and the Whig Party, followed each other in and out of power. The Tories supported the king and the official Church of England and were concerned about keeping the established order. The Whigs supported reforms that would make the government more democratic. They were sympathetic to freedom of speech and of the press and favoured greater religious liberty for those people who did not belong to the Church of England. Before long the parties changed their names into Conservative and Liberal Parties respectively. The first leader of the Conservative Party was Sir Robert Peel. Peel served as British prime minister in 1834 and 1835 and from 1841 to 1846. As home secretary in 1829, he reorganized the London police, who have

地所有者的政治权力，将它交给了中产阶级，因而议会将更加民主。但是，仍只有百分之十五的英国成年男性有权选举，因为选举权仅限于收入不低于中产阶级水准的人。工人阶级和妇女没有选举权。

1830年以后，英国的两个主要政党，托利党和辉格党开始轮流上台执政。托利党人支持国王和官方的英国国教，关心如何维持现成秩序。辉格党人支持使政府民主化的改革。他们赞成言论和出版自由，愿意给非国教教徒以更大的宗教自由。不久后，两党的名称分别改为保守党和自由党。保守党的头一个首领是罗伯特·皮尔爵士。皮尔于1834~1835年，再于1841~1846年任英国首相。皮尔于1829年任内务大臣时期，改组了伦敦警察，此后伦敦警察被称为"博比"。"博比"是皮尔的教名"罗伯特"的昵称。这个名字很合

罗伯特·皮尔

been called "bobbies". "Bobby" is the friendly form of Peel's first name Robert. It was a suitable name, for the British police have always been friendly and helpful when controlling traffic or directions to a passer-by.

Leading intellectuals in the 19th century played an important role in reforms. One of them was British philosopher and economist Jeremy Bentham (1748-1832). He accepted David Hume's idea that the highest human virtue is the kind and generous effort to increase the happiness of others and build up his own theory of utilitarianism. One of the principles of the theory is that the function of government should be to secure the greatest happiness for the greatest number of people. This theory was influential and in part responsible for the reforms. Romantic poets early in the 19th century, such as William Wordsworth, Samuel Taylor Coleridge, Lord Byron and Percy Bysshe Shelley, also advocated freedom for the individual and criticized restricting social conventions and unjust political rule.

The Reform Act of 1832 brought few benefits to workers, the biggest class. They still lived in poverty

适,因为英国警察在维持交通秩序和为行人指路时,一贯态度友好,乐于助人。

19世纪的著名知识分子在改革中扮演了重要角色。其中一个是哲学家和经济学家杰里米·边沁(1748-1832)。边沁接受了休谟的思想,认为人类最高的美德是为增进他人的幸福而做出仁慈和慷慨的努力,因而创立了他自己的功利主义的学说。功利主义的一条原则是政府的功能在于保障最大多数人民的最大幸福。这一理论影响很大,是促成改革的部分原因。19世纪初的浪漫主义诗人如威廉·华兹华斯、塞缪尔·泰勒·柯尔律治、拜伦勋爵和珀西·比西·雪莱,也鼓吹个人自由,抨击束缚人的社会传统和不公正的

杰里米·边沁

拜伦

珀西·比西·雪莱

and had few rights. They demanded more re-forms in working conditions, political rights, and economic justice that might improve their lives.

In the mid-19th century two groups of peo-ple struggled hard for more reforms. One was the Anti-Corn Law League and the other the Chartists.

The Anti-Corn Law League was made up of Whigs, or middle-class radicals who believed in free trade rather than protection. They argued that the Corn Laws only benefited rich landowners by causing higher food price. Then a terrible famine broke out in Ireland in 1845 when potato crop failed due to a plant disease. The famine lasted for several years and about 1 million people died of hunger or disease, and

政治制度。

1832 年的改革没有给人数最多的工人阶级带来多少利益。他们依然生活在贫困之中，没有多少权利。他们要求在工作条件、政治权利、经济公正方面进行更多的改革，以改善他们的生活。

19 世纪中叶，有两个组织为进一步改革进行艰苦的斗争。一个是反谷物法同盟，另一个是宪章派。

反谷物法同盟由辉格党人，即激进的中产阶级组成，他们主张自由贸易，反对贸易保护。他们争辩说，谷物法引起食品价格上涨，只对富裕的土地所有者有利。1845 年爱尔兰的马铃薯遭受病害，当地发生严重饥荒。饥荒持续了几年，

another million left the country. Prime Minister Robert Peel finally made up his mind to abolish the Corn Laws in 1846.

The Chartists fought for the cause of workers by demanding that they receive full political rights. In imitation of the Magna Carta, which had secured the rights of the nobles from the king in 1215, the Chartists produced a People's Charter. The charter set forth six points: (1) votes for all adult males; (2) secret voting; (3) no property qualifications for members of Parliament; (4) salaries for members of Parliament so that poor men could have political careers; (5) annual elections, and (6) seats in Parliament distributed on the basis of population. The Chartists presented their program to Parliament in 1839, 1842, and 1848. Each time Parliament rejected it. Finally, however, all of the Chartist demands except the fifth were met. The Reform Bill of 1867 extended the vote to all male members of the working class in the towns, and the Reform Bill of 1884 extended the vote to the rural working class. Both bills further took seats from places with small populations and gave them to cities with big populations. Secret voting was introduced in 1872.

大约一百万人死于饥饿或疾病，另有一百万人逃离爱尔兰。1846年，首相罗伯特·皮尔终于下决心废除谷物法。

宪章派为工人的利益而斗争，要求得到充分的政治权利。他们模仿1215年贵族们从国王手中获得权利的《大宪章》，起草了《人民宪章》。宪章提出六点要求：一，所有成年男子获得选举权；二，秘密投票；三，取消要求议员具备的财产条件；四，为议员提供薪金，使穷人可以从政；五，选举每年举行一次；六，议会席位数目按人口分配。宪章派将他们的纲领于1839年、1842年和1848年三次提交议会。每次都被议会否决。但是，宪章派提出的所有要求，除去第五项，最终都得到了满足。1867年的改革法案将选举权扩大到城市里所有男性工人，1884年的改革法案再将选举权扩大到农村的工人阶级。两项法案进一步将人口稀少地区的席位转交给人口众多的城市。秘密投票于1872年开始实行。

题外话

- 成熟的社会，有表达民意渠道的社会，总可以通过和平手段改变国家体制，而无须诉诸暴力。英国人比起其他民族似乎更成熟，更理性。暴力的成本过高，往往两败俱伤。该妥协时便妥协，这是英国人的聪明之处。

- 在英国，30岁以上妇女于1918年获得选举权；21岁以上妇女于1928年获得选举权；1969年，男女两性选举人的年龄限制降低至18岁。

3. The Victorian Age

Queen Victoria came to the throne in 1837, when she was 18 years old. She ruled for 63 years until 1901, longer than any other British king or queen had ever ruled. This period came to be known as the Victorian Age. During this period, great economic, social, and political changes took place and Great Britain became the strongest and richest country in the world. The British Empire, which included Canada, Australia, India, New Zealand, and large parts of Africa, had about a quarter of the world's land and about a quarter of the world's people. Wealth poured into Britain from its colonies. Industry and trade expanded rapidly, and the country became known as the workshop of the world, though by the end of the age, Britain was becoming more the banker of the world. Railways and canals covered Britain, and telephone and telegraph lines linked the big cities. Science and technology made great advances. People were better educated. The middle class grew enormously. Literature flourished. In addition, the government introduced democratic reforms.

In spite of the prosperity of the Victorian Age, workers in both factories and farms still lived in terrible poverty. Benjamin Disraeli, one of the period's outstanding prime ministers, described England as two nations, one rich and

维多利亚时代

维多利亚女王于 1837 年登基，当年 18 岁。她在位 63 年，直至 1901 年逝世，比任何其他男女君主统治时间都长。这一时期史称维多利亚时代。在这一时期，经济、社会、政治发生了一系列的重大变化，英国变为世界上最强大富有的国家。大英帝国囊括加拿大、澳大利亚、印度、新西兰、非洲大部分地区，拥有世界四分之一的土地和大约世界四分之一的人口。财富源源不断地从殖民地流入英国。工业和贸易迅速扩大，英国被称为世界的工厂，虽然到了维多利亚时代末期，英国正在成为世界的银行家。铁路和运河遍布不列颠，电话和电报线连接大城市。科学技术取得了重大进步，人们受到更好的教育，中产阶级人口猛增。文学也进入繁荣时期。此外，政府进行了民主改革。

维多利亚时代尽管十分繁荣，但工厂和农庄的工人们仍然生活在可怕的贫困中。这一时期杰出的首相之一本杰明·迪斯累里将英国描写成两个国度，一贫一富，界线分明。维多利亚时代最伟大的小说家查尔斯·狄更斯也在他的小说里描写了穷人们的悲惨生活和受到的虐

one poor. Charles Dickens, the greatest novelist of the age, also described in his novels the miserable life and the cruel treatment of the poor.

The prosperity of the age encouraged the spread of materialism. The British middle class were proud of their wealth and the comforts and conveniences industrialization had brought to them. Their materialistic attitude was shown in the Great Exhibition held in Hyde Park, London, in 1851. The Exhibition was the first great international exhibition of the products of industry. Great Britain, the host of the Exhibition and at that time the world's most advanced industrial country, contributes almost half of the exhibits. The Great Exhibition was housed in the Crystal Palace, a huge building made of glass set in a light, iron framework. The building itself represented the greatest advance in architecture.

The peace, prosperity and scientific advances of the day also encouraged optimism and belief in progress, especially during the early and middle Victorian Age. People tended to believe that wars could be

待。

时代的繁荣使物质主义盛行。英国的中产阶级为工业化给他们带来的财富、舒适和方便感到自豪。他们的物质主义态度体现在 1851 年伦敦海德公园举行的大博览会上。这个博览会是首届工业产品的大型世界博览会。英国是博览会的主办国,也是当时最发达的工业国,提供了近一半的展品。大博览会的举办场所是水晶宫,这是一座用重量轻的钢材做骨架的巨大玻璃建筑。建筑本身代表了建筑业最伟大的成就。

当时的和平、繁荣和科学的发

维多利亚女王在水晶宫里举办的大博览会上

avoided as better communications created understanding among the peoples of the world, and as political power passed from warlike nobles to the peace-loving middle class.

Today people tend to laugh at the middle class of the Victorian Age, because they always tried to behave in a way that was considered socially acceptable, they were too easily shocked by things relating to sex, and they were too self-satisfied and unwilling to listen to others' opinions. Many Victorians regarded pleasure as sin, and poverty as God's punishment for laziness. Daily family prayer and Sunday Bible-reading reminded their children that obedience was the greatest virtue. The early Victorian father was like a king in the home, and he expected to be obeyed by all the other members of the family. His wife was supposed to be his faithful companion, her place was in the home, and she had no right to look for jobs outside the home. Even in the home, her interests and conversation were strictly controlled. The highest virtue of the Victorian women was sexual purity; adultery was the worst of all possible sins. Her dress concealed her whole body except her hands and face, and to show an ankle or a shoulder was considered "improper".

展也促使人们产生乐观主义和对进步的信心，特别是在维多利亚早期和中期。人们倾向于相信，通讯技术的改善会加强世界各国人民之间的了解，而且政权已从好战的贵族转入爱好和平的中产阶级手中，因而战争是可以避免的。

今天，人们往往嘲笑维多利亚时代的中产阶级，因为他们总是循规蹈矩，对与两性关系有关的事物太容易感到震惊，他们过于自满，过于刚愎自用。许多维多利亚时代的人将娱乐视为罪恶，将贫穷视为上帝对懒惰的惩罚。人们每天在家里祈祷，礼拜天要朗读《圣经》，这些做法提醒孩子们服从是最大的美德。维多利亚早期的父亲像家中的国王，他希望所有的家庭成员都服从他。他的妻子应当是他忠实的伴侣，她的活动场所是家庭，家庭之外的事务她无权过问。即使在家里，她们的兴趣和谈话也受到严格的限制。维多利亚妇女的最大美德是性的纯洁，通奸是一切罪恶中之最大者。她的衣服要遮盖手和面

维多利亚女王，她的家庭和其他欧洲皇族

查尔斯·达尔文

部之外的所有部分，露出脚踝或肩部被视为"不正经"。

维多利亚时代的人非常虔诚。他们相信《圣经》上每个字都是真理，所以当查尔斯·达尔文发表了他关于人类起源的科学理论时，激起愤怒的抗议。主教们愤怒地表示，他们决不能同意自己是猴子的后代的暗示；而科学家们则回答说，他们宁可当猴子的后代，也不愿当主教的后代。达尔文是个虔诚的基督徒，他相信对上帝创造的世界做科学的研究可以使人更好地了解上帝的意图和人类的责任。然而，达尔文和其他科学家的理论还

The Victorians were extremely religious. They believed every word of the Bible, so that when Charles Darwin published his scientific idea about the origin of man, it caused an angry protest. Bishops angrily resisted the suggestion that they were descended from monkeys; the scientists replied that they would rather be descended from monkeys than from bishops. Darwin was a good Christian, and he believed that a scientific study of God's world could lead to better understanding of God's purpose and man's duty. Yet the theories of Darwin and other scientists led many people to feel that traditional values could no longer guide their lives.

Queen Victoria herself became a model of Victorian morality. She was opposed to women

反进化论者讽刺达尔文的漫画

marrying again after the death of their first husbands. She never married after her husband, Prince Albert, died in 1861. She believed in womanly modesty, and often criticized Queen Elizabeth I for lack of it.

Victorian literature includes some of the greatest and most popular novels ever written. The novels of Charles Dickens are well-known for their colorful characters. In *Oliver Twist and*

查尔斯·狄更斯

是使许多人感到传统价值不再能够指导他们的生活了。

维多利亚女王本人成为维多利亚时代道德的样板。她反对妇女在头一个丈夫去世后再婚。她的丈夫艾尔伯特亲王于 1861 年去世，此后她再没有结婚。她主张谦逊的妇德，常常批评伊丽莎白一世不够谦逊。

维多利亚时代的文学包括一些历史上最伟大、最受欢迎的小说。查尔斯·狄更斯的小说因其中丰富多彩的人物而著名。在《奥列佛·特维斯特》和《大卫·科波菲尔》里，狄更斯描写儿童们由于成年人的残酷和冷漠过着悲惨的生活。《远大前程》是狄更斯小说里情节最复杂的一部。其主题是只有建立在同情，而不是虚荣、财产和社会地位基础上的生活，才具有真正的价值。《双城记》是狄更斯小说里结构最完美的一部。它讲述法国革命

矿井里的童工

David Copperfield, Dickens described the lives of children made miserable by cruel or thoughtless adults. *Great Expectations* is Dickens' most complicated novel with the theme that only a life on a foundation of sympathy, rather than on vanity, possessions, and social position, has real value. *A Tale of Two Cities* is the best constructed novel that Dickens wrote. It tells of the heroism of fictional Sidney Carton during the French Revolution. William Makepeace Thackeray created a masterpiece of Victorian fiction in *Vanity Fair*. The story pictures the lives of many characters at different levels of English society during the early 19th century. The novels of the Bronte sisters — Emily's *Wuthering Heights* and Charlotte's *Jane Eyre* are also ranked among the greatest works of Victorian fiction.

Several writers wrote nonfiction that dealt with social problem. Thomas Carlyle attacked the evils of materialism and gave romantic praise to the heroes of world history. John Stuart Mill discussed the relationship between society and the individual in his long essay *On Liberty*. Matthew Arnold criticized the Victorian values in his critical essays on culture, literature, religion, and society. Many of the essays were collected in *Culture and Anarchy*.

The most important Victorian poets were Lord Tennyson and Robert Browning. Tennyson discussed intellectual and religious problems of the time in his long poem *In Memoriam*. Browning is most famous for the development of the

威廉·梅克匹斯·萨克雷

期间一个名叫西德尼·卡顿的英雄事迹。威廉·梅克匹斯·萨克雷的《名利场》是维多利亚时代小说的代表作之一。小说描绘了19世纪初英国社会各阶层人物的生活。勃朗蒂姊妹的小说——艾米莉的《呼啸山庄》和夏洛特的《简·爱》也在维多利亚时代的伟大作品之列。

有几个作家写散文讨论社会问题。托马斯·卡莱尔批判物质主义的丑恶,对世界历史上的英雄人物给予浪漫的赞扬。约翰·斯图亚特·密尔在他的长文《自由论》里讨论了社会和个人之间的关系。马修·阿诺德在他关于文化、文学、宗教和社会的批评文章里抨击了维多利亚时代的价值观。他的许多文章搜集在《文化与无政府主义》一书里。

维多利亚时代最著名的诗人是丁尼生和勃朗宁。丁尼生在他的长

勃朗蒂三姊妹

丁尼生

勃朗宁

萧伯纳

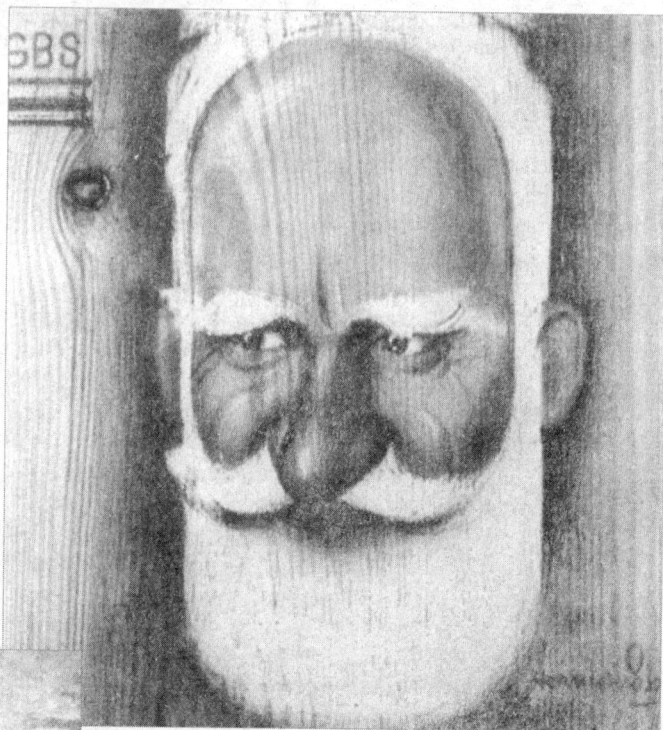

王尔德

dramatic monologue, for his psychological insight, and for his forceful, colloquial poetic style.

The leading late Victorian novelists were George Eliot, George Meredith, Anthony Trollope, and Thomas Hardy. Eliot's novels, such as *Adam Bede* and *Middlemarch* deal with social and moral problems. Meredith wrote satirical novels of the upper classes, with complex psychological treatment of character. *The Egoist* is one of his best novels. Trollope's novels, including *Barchester Towers*, are gentle satires of life in rural England. They often tell of conflicts within the Church of England, always in a humorous way. Hardy described in his realistic novels how the characters are defeated by a hostile fate. *The Return of the Native*, *The Mayor of Casterbridge* and *Tess of the D'Urbervilles* are among his best novels.

British playwrights revived the English theater by the end of the 19th century. Oscar Wilde wrote witty comedies, such as *Lady Windermere's Fan* and *The Importance of Being Earnest*. George Bernard Shaw also wrote witty plays, but most of his works, including *Arms and the Man, Candida,* and *Pygmalion*, show that Shaw was concerned about serious social problems of the time.

诗《悼念集》里讨论了当时的思想和宗教问题。勃朗宁的诗歌最著名之处是戏剧独白的发展，人物的心理刻画以及有力的口语风格。

维多利亚时代晚期的重要小说家有乔治·艾略特、乔治·梅瑞狄斯、安东尼·特罗洛普和托马斯·哈代。艾略特的小说，如《亚当·比德》和《米德尔马契》探讨了社会和道德问题。梅瑞狄斯的讽刺小说描写上流社会，探索人物的复杂心理。《利己主义者》是他最好的小说。特罗洛普的小说，包括《巴塞特寺院》，是对英国乡村生活的温和的讽刺。这些小说常常讲述教会内部的冲突，叙述的方式总是幽默的。哈代在他的现实主义小说里描述人物如何在残酷命运的打击下失败。《还乡》、《卡斯特桥市长》、《德伯家的苔丝》是他最好的小说。

英国的剧作家在 19 世纪末复兴了英国的戏剧。奥斯卡·王尔德写机智俏皮的喜剧，如《温德梅尔夫人的扇子》和《认真的重要性》。乔治·萧伯纳也写机智俏皮的喜剧，但他的大部分作品，包括《武器与人》、《康蒂姐》和《皮格马利翁》，表明萧伯纳关注当时严肃的社会问题。

题 外 话

　　维多利亚女王有"欧洲的祖母"之称。她的子孙，包括 40 个孙子、孙女，几乎与欧洲所有皇族联姻。

4. Palmerston and His "Gunboat" Diplomacy

帕默斯顿与"炮舰"外交

During the Victorian Age, the three most outstanding Prime Ministers after Peel were Palmerston (1784-1865), Gladstone and Disraeli.

Viscount Palmerston's full name was Henry John Temple. He entered Parliament in 1807 as a member of the Tory Party. From 1809 to 1828 he served as secretary of war in several Tory governments. Then he had a quarrel with the party and joined the Whigs. Palmerston served as foreign minister almost continuously from 1830 to 1851 and as home secretary from 1852 to 1855. He was prime minister from 1855 to 1858 and from 1859 to 1865.

Palmerston was a skillful diplomat and tactician, well-known for his aggressive foreign policy or so-called "gunboat" diplomacy. This policy was criticized abroad and in Parliament, but popular among the British people. He once sent a fleet to Greece after the Greek government refused to compensate a British subject whose house in Athens had been looted and burned. In a speech he made before Parliament to defend his policy, he said that a citizen of ancient Rome felt

在维多利亚时代，皮尔之后的三位最著名的首相是帕默斯顿(1784-1865)、格莱斯顿和迪斯累利。

帕默斯顿子爵的全名是亨利·约翰·坦普尔。他于1807年以托利党党员的身份进入议会。自1809~1828年他在几届托利党政府中任陆军大臣。此后他与托利党发生争吵，加入辉格党。帕默斯顿自1830~1851年担任外交大臣，几乎从未间断；继而自1852~1855年担任内务大臣。他从1855~1858年，再从1859~1865年担任首相。

帕默斯顿是个老练的外交家和策略家，以其侵略性的外交政策，或所谓的"炮舰外交"著称于世。这一政策在国外和英国议会中受到批评，但在英国人民中颇受欢迎。曾有一个英国公民的房子在雅典遭抢劫后被焚毁，希腊政府拒绝赔偿，帕默斯顿竟然派

帕默斯顿

safe anywhere in the Roman Empire, because his country was able to protect him. So his government should have aggressive means to win respect for his country from other nations so that British subjects could not be wronged anywhere in the world. He regarded Britain as the world's greatest country and felt contempt for all foreigners. He dealt with foreign affairs like mischievous schoolboy.

Palmerston helped Belgium gain independence in 1830, which was the first of his successful diplomatic achievements. Then he established friendly relations with France. In the 1840s, he forced China to open its ports to British trade and acquired Hong Kong in the Opium Wars with China (1839-1842, 1856-1860). From 1854 to 1856, he led Britain in the Crimean War against Russia and brought the war to a successful end. He resigned as prime minister in 1858 because he was criticized for his policy in China, but came back to office the next year as Britain's first Liberal prime minister. He supported the Italians' effort to unite their land into a single country. But he remained neutral during the American Civil War.

Although Palmerston supported political reform in other countries, he promoted only minor reforms in Britain. After Palmerston's death in 1865, a struggle began between two great party leaders — William Gladstone of the Liberal Party and Benjamin Disraeli of the Conservative Party.

遣一支舰队到希腊。在对议会做的一次演说里,他为自己的外交政策辩护,说古罗马的公民在罗马帝国的任何地点都感到安全,因为他的国家能够保护他。因而他的政府应当拥有强硬的手段为英国赢得外国的尊重,这样英国公民才不致在世界任何地方受到欺侮。他把英国看做世界上最伟大的国家,蔑视所有其他国家。他处理外交就像一个调皮的学童,喜欢用拳头说话。

帕默斯顿于 1830 年帮助比利时赢得独立,这是他最初的外交成就之一。接着,他与法国建立了友好关系。在 19 世纪 40 年代,他迫使中国对英国贸易开放口岸,并在鸦片战争 (1839-1842, 1856-1860) 中夺取香港。从 1854~1856 年,在与俄国进行的克里米亚战争中,他领导英国战胜了敌人。1858 年,由于他在中国的外交政策而受到批评,辞去首相职务,但在次年又以英国首任自由党首相官复原职。他支持意大利人统一国家的努力。但在美国南北战争中他保持了中立。

帕默斯顿虽然支持其他国家的政治改革,但在英国却仅仅提倡微小的改革。帕默斯顿于 1865 年逝世,此后,两大政党首领——自由党的威廉·格莱斯顿与保守党的本杰明·迪斯累里之间的一场较量开始了。

题外话

　　腐败愚昧的中国政府与英国一交手，正好碰上强硬好战的帕默斯顿，所以只剩下割地赔款一着儿。如果碰上的恰巧是格莱斯顿（他反对帕默斯顿针对中国的帝国主义的外交政策），也许下场会略好些。但细想来，中国与英国的交手，实际上是君主专制与议会民主制两种政治制度的交手。即使英国的政客们全是格莱斯顿，中国有无数的林则徐，后果也大同小异。鸦片战争后的一百年中，中国与列强交手，每战必败，就是明证。

5. Two Political Giants: Gladstone and Disraeli

两大政界巨人：格莱斯顿与迪斯累里

Gladstone (1809-1898) and Disraeli (1804-1881) were two of the most influential men in Victorian Britain. They took turns to be prime minister from 1868 to 1885. They were lifelong political rivals.

Gladstone served as prime minister of Britain four times: from 1868 to 1874, from 1880 to 1885, in 1886, and from 1892 to 1894. He was a well-educated man, a classical scholar and an excellent speaker. He entered the House of Commons as a member of the Tory Party (later called the Conservative Party), but later broke with the main body of the party when he supported Prime Minister Robert Peel's effort to end the Corn Laws. In 1859 Gladstone joined the Liberal Party (earlier called the Whig Party), and finally became its leader. Under his leadership the Liberal Party advocated reforms to improve the lives of the working class and fought for Irish home rule (self-government). During

　　格莱斯顿（1809-1898）与迪斯累里（1804-1881）是英国维多利亚时代影响力最大的两个人。他们两人从 1868 至 1885 年间轮流上台任首相，是毕生的政敌。

　　格莱斯顿四次出任英国首相：从 1868~1874 年，1880~1885 年，于 1886 年，再从 1892~1894。格莱斯顿受过良好教育，是个研究古典文化的学者，杰出的演说家。他作为托利党（日后改称保守党）党员进入议会下院，但后来与托利党的主流分裂，因为他支持罗伯特·皮尔首相废除谷物法。1859 年格莱斯顿加入自由党（前身为辉格党），最终成为该党领袖。在他的领导下，自由党鼓吹改革以改善工人阶级的生活，并争取爱尔兰的自治。在他的头一任期（1868-1874）内，他的政府进行

his first term, which lasted from 1868 until 1874, his government made some of the most liberal reforms of the 19th century to make the British government more democratic.

Disraeli served as prime minister of Britain in 1868 for 10 months and again from 1874 to 1880. He was also a novelist, and wrote with sympathy about the condition of the working class. A character in one of his novels declares that Britain is made up of two vastly different nations: the rich and the poor. As a Conservative, he supported the Corn Laws and remained in the main body of the party. Disraeli and the Conservatives represented the interests of the queen, the church, landowners, and tried to strengthen the British Empire. Nevertheless, he also supported important parts of social reforms.

In 1866, Gladstone introduced a reform bill to give more people the right to vote. But Parliament, considering the bill too radical, did not pass it. Disraeli knew that a bill had to be passed because it was the will of the people. In 1867, he introduced his own bill, which Parliament passed. The Reform Act of 1867 gave all city workers the

了 19 世纪最具自由主义色彩的几项改革,使英国政府更加民主。

迪斯累里于 1868 年任首相 10 个月,然后在 1874~1880 年间再次出任。他是个小说家,带着同情心描写工人阶级的状况。他的小说里有个人物宣称英国是有两个截然不同的国度组成的,一贫一富,界线分明。作为保守党党员,他支持谷物法与党的主流保持一致。迪斯累里代表女王、教会和土地所有者的利益,努力巩固大英帝国。然而,他也支持大部分社会改革。

1866 年,格莱斯顿提交一份给更多人以选举权的改革法案。但

格莱斯顿

right to vote in national elections.

In 1868, Disraeli became prime minister when the Conservative Party leader Derby resigned. Disraeli hoped the new voters would be grateful to Conservatives and elect them in the next election. But, contrary to his expectation, Liberals won a big victory in 1868 national election. Gladstone became prime minister.

The first thing Gladstone decided to do was to solve the problem of Ireland. Under the control of the English, the Irish people had been extremely poor for centuries. They thought the British government was unfair to them, and demanded independence. Their demand became even stronger after the famine between 1845 and 1847, which reduced the Irish population by 25 percent. In 1867 Irish nationalists formed a secret society, the Fenians, to overthrow British rule and win Ireland's independence. Violence against British officials also increased. In 1869 Gladstone caused the Irish Church Act to pass Parliament. Under this act, the Irish, most of whom were Roman Catholic, no longer had to pay taxes to the Church of England, which had few Irish members. In the following year, a Land Act was passed to protect Irish peasants who rented their land from others.

Under Gladstone many other reforms were made. The Education Act of 1870 established a system of primary schools, supported by the state and open to all children. In the same year, competitive examinations were introduced in the civil service system. Government officials

议会认为该法案过于激进，未能通过。迪斯累里明白通过一项法案是大势所趋，因为这是人民的意愿。1867年，他提出自己的法案，结果获得通过。1867年的改革法案使所有的城市工人获得了大选的选举权。

1868年，保守党领袖德比辞职，迪斯累里出任首相。迪斯累里希望新增的选举人会出于对保守党的感激在下届选举中投保守党的票。但出乎他的预料，自由党在1868年的大选中大获全胜。格莱斯顿出任首相。

格莱斯顿决定要做的头一件事是解决爱尔兰问题。在英国人的统治下，爱尔兰人民几世纪以来极端贫困。他们认为英国政府歧视他们，因而要求独立。1845~1847年爱尔兰发生饥荒，人口减少四分之一。此后，他们独立的要求更为强烈。1867年，爱尔兰民族主义者成立了一个秘密组织"芬尼党"，旨在推翻英国统治，赢得爱尔兰的独立。与此同时，反抗英国官员的暴力活动也增加了。1869年，格莱斯顿敦促议会通过了《爱尔兰教会法》。根据这项法案，天主教徒占大多数的爱尔兰人无须再向爱尔兰人人口极少的英国国教纳税。次年，议会又通过了《土地法》，以保护租用土地的爱尔兰农民的利益。

could no longer simply give civil service jobs to friends or relatives. Gladstone's government ended the remaining laws that were unfair to Protestants who did not belong to Church of England. In 1872, the secret voting was introduced. Gladstone made various groups of people unhappy with each of these reforms and lost the election of 1874.

Disraeli then served as prime minister until 1880. While Gladstone opposed in principle the policy of imperialism, Disraeli followed a strong foreign policy and tried to extend Britain's control over its colonies and over other countries. Under Disraeli Britain developed into a powerful imperialist country. In 1875, he raised money and bought for Great Britain the control of the Suez Canal to make it safe to connect Britain and its vast empire in India and the Far East. In 1876, he declared Queen Victoria empress of India. At the Congress of Berlin in 1878, Disraeli helped prevent Russian expansion in the Balkans, and he won Cyprus for Britain. Britain also expanded its influence in China, the

迪斯累里

格莱斯顿执政时期进行了多项改革。1870 年的教育法建立了初等教育体系，由国家提供资金，向所有儿童开放。同年，竞争性考试引入公务员制度。政府官员不再允许将公务员职务赠送亲友。格莱斯顿的政府废止了歧视非国教新教徒的残余法规。1872 年开始实行秘密投票制。每项改革都使各种各样的人群感到不快，格莱斯顿于 1874 年落选。

迪斯累里接任首相直至 1880年。格莱斯顿在原则上反对帝国主义政策，而迪斯累里却奉行强硬的外交政策，努力扩大英国对殖民地和其他国家的控制。在迪斯累里执政时期，英国发展成一个强大的帝国主义国家。1875年，迪斯累里筹款为英国买下苏伊士运河的控制权，使之成为连接英国和它在印度和远东的庞大帝国的安全通道。1876 年，迪斯累里宣布

Middle East, and Africa.

Disraeli also wanted to make social reforms to help the lower classes. But his party, which included many wealthy people, supported only minor reforms. In spite of that government took actions to improve living conditions and working conditions of the poor.

In the election of 1880, Gladstone attacked Disraeli's imperialistic policies. He led the Liberals to victory and again became prime minister. Disraeli died the next year.

In 1882, Gladstone ordered a British invasion of Egypt to protect British interests there. In 1884, Gladstone succeeded in persuading Parliament to pass a reform bill that extended the vote to the rural working class. After that almost all adult males got their right to vote.

The Liberals won the 1885 election, and Gladstone became prime minister for a third time in February 1886. Gladstone was sympathetic to the Irish and attempted to make further reforms to protect them. He introduced a Home Rule Bill, which would have given the Irish Parliament the right to appoint the head of Ireland's government, although the power to tax was still supposed to be in the hands of the British Parliament. But Gladstone had little support even within his own party. The bill failed to pass the House of Commons and he resigned in July of that year.

In his final term, at the age of 83, Gladstone made a final attempt to win home rule for Ireland. The bill was passed in the House of

维多利亚女王为印度女皇。在1878年的柏林会议上，迪斯累里与其他国家一起阻止了俄国在巴尔干的扩张，为英国赢得塞浦路斯。英国也在中国、中东地区和非洲扩大了影响。

迪斯累里也愿意进行社会改革以帮助下层社会。但在党内有许多有钱人只支持微小的改革。但迪斯累里的政府还是采取了行动，改善了穷人的生活和工作条件。

在1880年的选举中，格莱斯顿攻击迪斯累里的帝国主义政策。他领导自由党取得胜利，再次出任首相。迪斯累里次年逝世。

1882年，格莱斯顿命令英国军队入侵埃及，以保护英国在埃及的利益。1884年，他说服了议会通过一项法案，将选举权扩大到农村的劳工阶级。此后，几乎全部成年男子都获得了选举权。

自由党在1885年的选举中获胜，格莱斯顿于1886年2月第三次出任首相。格莱斯顿同情爱尔兰人，试图进行进一步的改革来保护他们的利益。他提出了爱尔兰自治法案，该法案将给爱尔兰议会以任命爱尔兰政府首脑的权力，虽然课税权仍在英国议会手中。但即使在自己的党内，格莱斯顿只得到很少的支持。法案未能在下院通过，格莱斯顿于当年7月辞职。

格莱斯顿最后一次出任首相，

Commons, but defeated in the House of Lords. Gladstone retired from office in 1894.

已是 83 岁高龄。他为争取爱尔兰自治做了最后一次努力。他的提案在下院通过,却在上院受挫。格莱斯顿于 1894 年退休。

题 外 话

- 爱尔兰自治法案直到 1914 年才成为正式法律,但为时已晚。英国政府忙于战争,无暇顾及该法律的执行。战后爱尔兰民族独立运动风起云涌,法案被弃置一旁。在爱尔兰问题上,格莱斯顿是个有远见的政治家。
- 政客们给人的印象常常是枯燥乏味,缺少文化修养。但英国有几位首相非同一般。格莱斯顿毕生坚持研究古典著作,写出巨著《荷马与荷马时代研究》。迪斯累里也不差,他写过多部小说,其中以创作于 40 年代的三部曲最受欢迎。它们是《科宁斯比:或新的一代》、《西比尔:或两个民族》和《坦克雷德:或新改革运动》。当然还不能忘记 20 世纪的丘吉尔,他由于文学和历史学著作而获得诺贝尔文学奖。此外,20 世纪三次出任首相的斯坦利·鲍德温也是个著述甚丰的学者;爱德华·希思是个具有专业水准的乐队指挥家。

6. Florence Nightingale

弗洛伦斯·南丁格尔

Florence Nightingale (1820-1910) was the founder of the profession of modern nursing for women. She was named after Florence, Italy, where she was born. Her parents were rich and expected her to become a graceful, well-educated woman who was able to run a large household. But from the time she was a little girl Florence Nightingale had always enjoyed taking care of babies and sick people. At the age of 16, Florence thought she heard the voice of God telling her to devote her life to helping other people. She then turned down suitors, declined many parties, and spent much of her time studying nursing.

When Florence grew up she visited hospitals in many parts of Europe. Then she went to

弗洛伦斯·南丁格尔 (1820-1910) 是现代妇女从事的护理专业的创始人。她出生于意大利的佛罗伦萨,所以取名弗洛伦斯。她的父母很富裕,希望她能够成为一个优雅而有教养的女人,有能力操持家政。但从童年起,弗洛伦斯就一直喜欢照看婴儿或病人。16 岁那年,弗罗伦斯认为自己听到了上帝的呼唤,上帝叮嘱她将自己的一生用于救助他人。她谢绝了求婚者,不再接受舞会的邀请,将大部分时间用于学习护理。

弗洛伦斯长大后,参观了欧洲的许多医院。然后她去了德国,在

Germany and studied nursing in a school for training nurses. At 33, she became superintendent of a women's hospital in London.

Britain and France went to war with Russia in the Crimea in 1854 to keep Russian influence out of the Balkans. The English newspapers told how the English troops had been sent to battle without enough supplies, and how they died of wounds because they did not receive proper care. Florence had friends in the government, and she persuaded them to let her go to Crimea and care for the wounded soldiers. Then the secretary of war put her in charge of all nursing operations at the front. Florence organized a group of 38 women and sailed for the Crimea in 1854.

The hospital at the front was in a terrible condition. The wounded and the sick lay in long lines on the floor, without anybody to take care of them. There were not enough beds, mattresses, or bandages, and no washbasins, soap, or towels. Nightingale found a few men well enough to clean the place, and she put them to work at once. She set up a nursing schedule and laid down strict rules and regulations.

Things soon changed and fewer and fewer soldiers died of wounds or disease. Living conditions were bad at the front. Nightingale was sick herself, but she never deserted her patients. Soldiers who were wounded in the Crimean War called

一所护士学校学习护理。33 岁时，她成为伦敦的一所妇女医院的总监。

1854 年，英法两国与俄国在克里米亚交战，以阻止俄国在巴尔干扩张势力。英国报纸上报道英国军队在装备不足的情况下投入战斗，受伤的士兵们由于得不到适当护理而死去。南丁格尔有朋友在政府里，她劝说他们允许她到克里米亚护理伤员。于是，陆军大臣委派她全面负责前线的伤员护理。南丁格尔组建了一个有 38 位妇女的护士团，于 1854 年乘船前往克里米亚。

前线医院的条件十分恶劣。伤病员躺在地板上排成长长的一排，没有任何人照看他们。没有足够的床位、床垫和绷带，没有用来洗浴的盆、肥皂和毛巾。南丁格尔找到几个身体还算健康的人来打扫医院，立即给他们分配了工作。她还建立了护理日程表，制定了严格的规章制度。

局面不久便发生了变化。死于伤病的士兵越来越少。前线的生活条件很艰苦，南丁格尔自己也病倒了，但从未抛下她的病人不管。克里米亚战争中的伤兵们称

南丁格尔

her "Lady with the Lamp" because she walked the long corridors of their hospital every night, with a lamp in her hand, giving them comforts and advice. By the end of the war, Nightingale had saved many lives and had brought about reforms in running hospitals and in nursing.

Nightingale worked in Crimea for two years. When she returned home the English people raised a large amount of money to give her so that she could open a school to train nurses. This school was called the Nightingale School for Nurses at Saint Thomas's Hospital, and it was opened in London in 1860. The opening of this school marked the beginning of professional education in nursing. Nightingale became a world authority on scientific care of the sick. The United States asked her advice for setting up military hospitals during the American Civil War. Nightingale received many honors and was the first woman to receive the British Order of Merit.

7. The British Empire

During the rule of Queen Victoria, the British Empire reached its height. It included about a quarter of the world's land and about a quarter of the world's people.

The British Empire began when the English merchant explorers of Elizabethan days went in search of new land for trade, and established colonies in North America and the West Indies.

她为"提灯女士",因为她每天晚上都要手提一盏油灯,沿着医院长长的走廊巡视伤员,给他们以安慰和叮嘱。到战争结束时,南丁格尔拯救了许多生命,同时也给医院管理和护理职业带来了变革。

南丁格尔在克里米亚工作了两年。她回到英国后,英国人为她捐献了一大笔钱,使她能够开办学校,培训护士。这所学校称为圣托马斯医院南丁格尔护士学校,1860年在伦敦开办。这所学校的开办标志着护理职业教育的开始。南丁格尔则成为科学护理学的世界权威。美国人在南北战争中为建立战地医院曾向她征求意见。南丁格尔获得过许多荣誉,她是荣获英国功绩勋章的头一位妇女。

英帝国

在维多利亚时代,英帝国臻于鼎盛,拥有世界大约四分之一的土地和四分之一的人口。

当伊丽莎白时代的英国商人探险家到海外寻找新的陆地进行贸易,并在北美和西印度群岛建立殖民地时,大英帝国便开始形成。到了1670年,英国在美洲的殖民地

By 1670 there were British American colonies in New England, Virginia, and Maryland and settlements in the Bermudas, Honduras, Antigua, Barbados, and Nova Scotia. The British took Jamaica from Spain in 1655, and began their formal control of the island in 1670. During the 1670s, British pirates in the Caribbean used Jamaica as a base to attack Spanish ports and ships. The British took control of almost all French lands in Canada in 1763, and the Hudson's Bay Company gained almost complete control of the fur trade in the region. The East India Company, which was formed in 1600, opened India and the Far East to English trade and finally brought India into the British Empire. The first permanent British settlement on the African continent was made at James Island in the Gambia River in 1661. Then Sierra Leone was brought under British control in 1787. Britain acquired the Cape of Good Hope in 1806, and the South African interior was opened up by Boer and British pioneers under British control. Nearly all these early settlements were made by particular companies and ambitious businessmen rather than from any effort on the part of the British government. So at first the empire was formed slowly without any plan or organization. In the 17th and 18th centuries, the British government controlled British colonies mainly in the areas of trade and shipping. The colonies were regarded as a source of necessary raw materials for England and markets for British manufactured goods.

During the Seven Years' War (1756-1763)

已有新英格兰、弗吉尼亚和马里兰，并在百慕大、洪都拉斯、安提瓜、巴巴多斯和新斯科舍拥有居民点。英国于1655年从西班牙手中夺取了牙买加，1670年正式控制了这个岛屿。70年代，英国的加勒比海盗利用牙买加为基地，袭击西班牙的港口和船只。1763年，英国夺取了加拿大的几乎全部法国领土，哈德孙湾公司几乎控制了该地区的全部毛皮生意。1600年成立的东印度公司为英国贸易开辟了印度和远东的市场，最终将印度纳入英帝国。英国在非洲大陆的头一个永久定居点于1661年建立在冈比亚河的詹姆斯岛。1787年，塞拉里昂开始受英国控制。1806年英国占领好望角，在英国控制下的布尔人和英国移居者开始进入南非腹地。几乎所有这些早期的居民点都是由某些公司和野心勃勃的商人们建立的，英国政府并未参与。因而，帝国起初是缓慢形成的，没有任何规划或组织。在17和18世纪，英国政府对英国殖民地的控制主要在贸易和航运方面。殖民地被视为英国所必需的原材料的供应地和英国工业产品的市场。

七年战争（1756-1763）期间，英国的陆军和海军在詹姆斯·沃尔夫和罗伯特·克莱武等人的率领下为英国夺取了帝国内两个最重要的地区——加拿大和印度。但此

British military and naval power, under the leadership of such men as James Wolfe and Robert Clive, gained for Britain two of the most important parts of its empire — Canada and India. But soon after that, Britain lost its 13 American colonies in the War of American Independence (1775-1783). The loss, however, was balanced by the rapid growth of Upper Canada (now Ontario) after many people who remained loyal to Britain moved into that area from what had become the United States.

The new settlements in Australia from 1788 also made up for the loss of American colonies. For a long time, British courts had punished criminals by sending them to the American colonies. After Americans became independent, criminals were sent to Australia instead, and Sydney became the first of their settlements. Ordinary settlers soon followed and began to raise sheep and cattle. Freed prisoners chose to remain as farmers, so did their guards when they were retired. Colonies began to grow all round the coast.

The Napoleonic Wars added more colonies to the empire. The Treaty of Amiens (1802) made Trinidad and Ceylon (now Sri Lanka) officially British, and in the Treaty of Paris (1814) France gave up Tobago, Mauritius, Saint Lucia, and Malta to Britain. Malacca joined the empire in 1795, and all of Singapore came under British control in 1824. Canadian settlements in Alberta, Manitoba, and British Columbia extended British influence to the Pacific, while further British

后不久，英国又在美国的独立战争（1775-1783）中失去了 13 个美洲殖民地。但这一损失又得到了补偿，因为许多仍旧忠于英国的人从成为美国的地区移居到上加拿大（现在的安大略省），使该地区得到迅速发展。

1788 年后在澳大利亚新建的殖民地也补偿了美洲殖民地的损失。长期以来，英国法庭惩处罪犯的方法是将他们遣送美洲殖民地。美国人独立后，罪犯们则被遣送到澳大利亚，悉尼成为他们的头一个定居点。普通人不久也随之定居下来，开始饲养牛羊。刑满释放的囚徒愿意留下来务农，退休后的监狱看守们也是如此。殖民地开始沿海岸发展起来。

拿破仑战争使帝国增加了更多的殖民地。亚眠条约（1802）正式将特立尼达和锡兰（现在的斯里兰卡）划归英国。在巴黎和约（1814）里，法国又将多巴哥、毛里求斯、圣卢西亚和马耳他割让英国。马六甲于 1795 年加入帝国，1824 年整个新加坡开始受英国控制。艾伯塔、马尼托巴和不列颠哥伦比亚的加拿大定居点，将英国的影响扩大到太平洋。同时，英国在印度的进一步征服将更多的省份纳入帝国。

库克上校于 1769 年考察了新西兰沿岸，但 60 年之后才开始有

conquests in India brought more provinces into the empire.

Captain Cook explored the coasts of New Zealand in 1769, but organized settlement was not begun until 60 years later. The islands became officially British in 1840. British control was further extended to Fiji, Tonga, Papua, and other islands in the Pacific Ocean. The British took over the Burmese government and Burma became a British colony in 1886, and at the same time they conquered new territory in the India. When the Suez Canal was opened in 1869, Britain had a much shorter sea route to India. It took this opportunity, and expanded its port at Aden (in what is now Yemen), took over much of northern Somalia, and extended its influence in the sheikhdoms of southern Arabia and the Persian Gulf. Cyprus, which was, like Gibraltar and Malta, a link in the chain of communication with India through the Mediterranean, was occupied in 1878.

Elsewhere, British influence in the Far East expanded with the develop ment of the British colonies in what is now Malaysia and Singapore. During the Opium War between China and Britain, China was defeated and Britain took control of the island of Hong Kong as part of the Treaty of Nanjing in 1842. In 1860, Britain gained control of the Kowloon Peninsula as part of a settlement of further trade disputes with China. In 1898, China leased the New Territories to Britain for 99 years.

The greatest extension of British power took

组织地定居。这一群岛于 1840 年正式成为英国领土。英国的控制进一步延伸到斐济、汤加、巴布亚及其他太平洋岛屿。英国控制了缅甸政府，缅甸于 1886 年成为英国殖民地。同时，英国人又征服了更多的印度领土。苏伊士运河于 1869 年开通，此后英国有了一条到达印度的较短的海路。英国利用这一机会，扩大了其在亚丁（现在的也门）的港口，占领了索马里北部大部分地区，并在阿拉伯半岛南部和波斯湾地区的酋长国扩大影响。塞浦路斯与直布罗陀和马耳他一样，是通过地中海前往印度交通链条上的一环。塞浦路斯于 1878 年被英国占领。

随着英国殖民地在现在的马来西亚和新加坡的发展，英国在远东地区的影响扩大了。在中英鸦片战争中，中国战败，英国根据 1842 年的南京条约占据了香港岛。1860 年，作为与中国贸易争端解决方案的一部分，英国占领了九龙半岛。1898 年，中国又将新界租给英国 99 年。

然而，19 世纪英国势力的最大扩张发生在非洲。英国于 1882 年打败埃及军队后，实际上操纵了埃及的事务。1899 年，英国进一步控制了苏丹。19 世纪后半期，皇家尼日尔公司开始在尼日利亚和黄金海岸（现在的加纳）扩大英国

place in the 19th century in Africa, however. Britain actually directed the affair of Egypt after it defeated the Egyptian army in 1882 and it further took control of Sudan in 1899. In the second half of the century, the Royal Niger Company began to extend British influence in Nigeria, and the Gold Coast (now Ghana) and the Gambia also came under British rule. The Imperial British East Africa Company operated in what are now Kenya and Uganda, and the British South Africa Company operated in what are now Zimbabwe (formerly Southern Rhodesia), Zambia (formerly Northern Rhodesia), and Malawi. Britain's victory in the Boer War (1899-1902) enabled it to control the Transvaal and the Orange Free State in 1902 and to create the Union of South Africa in 1910. As a result a chain of British territories was formed, stretching from South Africa northward to Egypt, and it realized an enthusiastic British public's idea of an African empire extending "from the Cape to Cairo".

的影响，接着冈比亚也被英国人所控制。帝国不列颠东非公司在现在的肯尼亚和乌干达经营；不列颠南非公司在现在的津巴布韦（前南罗得西亚）、赞比亚（前北罗得西亚）和马拉维经营。英国在布尔战争（1899-1902）中的胜利使它于1902年控制了德兰士瓦和奥兰治自由邦，并于1910年创立南非联邦。由于英国的领土结成了一根从南非向北直达埃及的链条，热心的英国公众心中的一个"从好望角到开罗"的非洲帝国的梦想实现了。

吉普林

题 外 话

- 英帝国与其他一些帝国相比，带有较多的自由主义色彩。它更注重殖民地的生产性开发及其商业价值，而不是一味地掠夺。在政治上，它扶植殖民地政府，很大程度上缓和了母国与殖民地的矛盾。这就是为什么英帝国瓦解后仍能留下一个英联邦。
- 英帝国主义在文学上的代表是诗人和小说家吉普林。他在作品中表现出一种对英国统治之下人民的傲慢态度。他夸耀英帝国的军威和"白种人的责任"。若想了解他的态度，或当时英国人普遍的想法，可以读一读他的诗《白种人的责任》（*The White Man's Burden*）。

8. David Livingstone

大卫·利文斯敦

David Livingstone (1813-1873) was one of the greatest explorers who went into the unknown wilds of the African continent.

Livingstone was born in Scotland. He was a poor boy and began working in the local cotton mill at the age of 10, but studied hard when not at work. He received a medical degree from the University of Glasgow and became a doctor. He was sent as a medical missionary to southern Africa.

Livingstone arrived at Cape Town on Africa's southern tip in 1841. To convert more Africans to Christianity he went northward to explore Bechuanaland (what is now Botswana) and the Limpopo River. In 1844, when he was on a journey to establish a mission station, a lion attacked him and injured his left arm, but he went right on with his work. In 1845 Livingstone married Mary Moffat, the daughter of a notable Scottish missionary in southern Africa.

大卫·利文斯敦（1813-1873）是进入非洲大陆蛮荒地带的最伟大的探险家之一。

利文斯敦出生于苏格兰。他家里很穷，10岁时就开始在家乡的棉纺厂干活，但他在业余时间努力学习。他在格拉斯哥大学获得医学学位，成为一名医生。他被派往非洲南方做一名医生兼传教士。

利文斯敦于1841年抵达非洲大陆最南端的开普敦。为使非洲人改信基督教，他向北方旅行去考察贝专纳兰(即现在的博茨瓦纳)和林波波河。1844年，他在去建立传教站的途中受到狮子的攻击，左臂受伤，但他继续工作。1845年利文斯敦娶玛丽·莫法特为妻。玛丽是非洲南部一位著名苏格兰传教士的女儿。利文斯敦探险考察的最初几年,玛丽和孩子们跟他一起旅行,

Through the early years of his explorations, Mary and their children travelled with Livingstone, facing considerable hardship as they did so. Livingstone made several difficult journeys further north, making maps of the land and searching for rivers that ships could travel on so that British missionaries and traders could use them. In 1849, he arrived at Lake Ngami, in what is now Botswana. In 1851, Livingstone travelled with his family to the Zambezi River, on the border between present-day Zambia and Zimbabwe.

Livingstone returned to Cape Town in 1852, sent his wife and four children back to Britain, and then made preparations for another journey into the interior of Africa. He made his purpose clear in his famous statement: "I shall open up a path into the interior, or perish." During his amazing journey in the next few years Livingstone first travelled back to the Zambezi, then west across Angola to Luanda on the Atlantic Ocean. But he failed to find a waterway to connect the Zambezi and the coast. He then returned to the Zambezi and headed down the river. In spite of disease and hunger, he kept careful geographical records, which would fill huge gaps in European knowledge of central and southern Africa. In 1855, Livingstone became the first European to see Victoria Falls on the Zambezi River. He named the falls

吃了不少苦头。利文斯敦不畏艰难，数次北上，绘制地图、寻找可以通航的河流，使英国的传教士和商人可以利用它们。1849 年，他抵达了现在的博茨瓦纳的恩加米湖。1851 年，利文斯敦携家属到达赞比西河。这条河就在现在的赞比亚和津巴布韦的边界上。

利文斯敦于 1852 年返回开普敦，把妻子和四个孩子送回英国，然后准备做另一次深入非洲腹地的旅行。他的一句名言清楚地表达了他的目标："我要么开辟一条进入腹地的通道，要么死去。"此后几年，利文斯敦的旅行取得令人惊异的成果。他先返回赞比西河，然后向西，穿过安哥拉，抵达濒临大西洋的罗安达。但他未能找到连接赞比西河与大西洋的水路，然后返回赞比西河，沿河而下。他忍受疾病和饥饿的折磨，做了详尽的地理记录，填补了欧洲人在非洲中部和南部地理知识上的巨大空白。1855 年，利文斯敦成为观看到赞比西河上的维多利亚瀑布的头一个欧洲人。

他以维多利亚女王的名字为瀑布命名。1856 年，利文斯敦抵达濒临印度洋的赞比西河河口，也就是现在的莫桑比克。他成为横穿非洲南方的头一个欧洲人。

大卫·利文斯敦

after Queen Victoria. Livingstone reached the mouth of the Zambezi on the Indian Ocean in what is now Mozambique in 1856, becoming the first European ever to cross the full width of southern Africa.

Livingstone returned to England in 1856, as a national hero. He made speeches across the country and his book *Missionary Travels and Researches in South Africa* sold widely. Honours were heaped upon him. His income was increased and he was now able to provide adequately for his family, which had lived almost in poverty since returning to Britain.

Between 1859 and 1863, with half a dozen British assistants and a number of steamboats Livingstone once again explored the interior of Africa. He became the first European to see Lakes Nyasa and Chilwa, in what is now Malawi. In the late 1860s, Livingstone began to explore the Lake Tanganyika region, trying to find the source of the Nile River. But illness made him so weak that he had to be carried on a stretcher, and finally he could not travel at all. He died in a village in present-day Zambia in 1873. His body was carried back to England and buried in Westminster Abbey in London.

Livingstone learned more about African geography, customs, and the slave trade than any other European of his day. For more than 30 years he traveled across one-third of the continent, making careful observations of people and places. His discoveries led to a great competition among European nations for control

利文斯敦于 1856 年返回英国时受到欢迎，被当做民族英雄。他到英国各地演讲，他的著作《南非的传教旅行与研究》成为畅销书。他获得许多荣誉称号。他的收入增加了。他的家属返回英国后一直处于贫困的边缘，现在他有了足够的钱来供养他们了。

从 1859~1863 年，利文斯敦再次进入非洲腹地考察。这一次，他带了五六名英国人做助手，还带了几条汽船。他成为头一个看到尼亚萨湖和奇尔瓦湖的欧洲人。这两个湖位于现在的马拉维。60 年代末，利文斯敦开始考察坦噶尼喀湖地区，试图找到尼罗河的源头。但他病倒了，身体虚弱，必须用担架抬着旅行。最后，他无法再走了。他于 1873 年病死在现在的赞比亚的一个村庄里。他的遗体运回了英国，葬在威斯敏斯特教堂里。

利文斯敦是他那个时代对非洲地理、风土人情和奴隶贸易了解最多的欧洲人。他花费 30 多年，穿越了三分之一的非洲大陆，仔细观察了当地的人文和地理。他的发现引发了欧洲国家对非洲的争夺。19 世纪末和 20 世纪初欧洲列强瓜分了几乎全部非洲。利文斯敦本人像大多数西方帝国主义分子一样，认为非洲应当向基督教和西方文明开放。但他又痛恨奴隶贸易，相信非洲人自己有能力实现祖国的现代

of Africa. European powers seized almost all Africa in the late 19th century and early 20th century. Livingstone himself, like most European imperialists, believed that Africa should be open to Christianity and Western civilization. But he also hated slave trade and believed that the Africans had the ability to modernize their homeland. He was, in this sense, a forerunner not only of European imperialism in Africa but also of African nationalism.

化。在这种意义上，他不但是欧洲帝国主义在非洲的先驱，也是非洲民族主义的先驱。

题 外 话

由于利文斯敦在非洲的巨大影响，以他的名字命名的地方很多。如赞比亚南方省省会称为利文斯敦；刚果河上的大瀑布称为利文斯敦瀑布；坦桑尼亚尼亚萨湖北岸的山脉称为利文斯敦山脉。

9. Cecil Rhodes

Cecil Jo hn Rhodes (1853-1902) was a British businessman and statesman. In 1870 he was sent to live with his brother in Africa, in what is now South Africa. In 1873, when he was only 19, he had become the owner of a diamond mine and made a big fortune. He returned to England the same year to study at the University of Oxford. He spent half of each year at the university and half in his diamond mine in Africa until he received his degree in 1881.

In 1881, Rhodes

塞西尔·约翰·罗得斯

塞西尔·罗得斯

塞西尔·约翰·罗得斯 (1853-1902) 是英国商人和政治家。1870 年他被送往非洲，即现在的南非，与哥哥一同生活。1873 年，当时他只有 19 岁，就已成为一个钻石矿的矿主，因而发了大财。同年，他返回英国，就读于牛津大学。他每年用一半时间上学，另一半时间经营非洲的钻石矿，直到 1881 年才获得学位。

1881 年，罗得斯当选开普殖民地议会议员，终身保持这一席位。在他认为自己可以在非洲南部扩大英帝国的版图和巩固英帝国的统治的场合，他毫不吝惜自己的钱财。在英国控制贝专纳兰（即现在的博茨瓦纳）并于 1885 年将它纳

was elected to the Cape Colony Parliament and held the seat for the rest of his life. He used his wealth in politics to gain control of most of southern Africa. He spent his fortune freely when he thought he could enlarge and strengthen the British Empire in southern Africa. He was largely responsible for taking control of Bechuanaland (now Botswana) and adding it to the territory of the British Empire in 1885. In 1888, Rhodes combined all his mines into the De Beers Consolidated Mines, which controlled almost all diamond production of southern Africa. By now Rhodes had become extremely rich and powerful. In 1889, he forced the native peoples to give up most of their land to Britain. This huge territory was named Rhodesia (what is now Zimbabwe and Zambia) in honour of Rhodes. The British South Africa Company, which Rhodes had created, ruled this territory until 1923.

In 1890, Rhodes became prime minister of the Cape Colony. He never regarded money-making as an end in itself. His ambition was to bring all of southern Africa into the British Empire. He dreamed of building a railroad from Cape Town in the south to Cairo in the north, passing only through British controlled territory in Africa. He tried to unite the British and the Boers, who were white settlers, mainly of Dutch descent and had lived in African for generations. But he was cruel and greedy in taking land from Africans and he was a racist when treating black people. He refused to give the colony's blacks the right to vote and restricted

入大英帝国的版图一事中，罗得斯发挥了重要作用。1888 年，罗得斯将自己所有的钻石矿合并为德比尔斯采矿公司，控制了非洲南部几乎全部的钻石生产。此时罗得斯已富甲天下，权势显赫。1889 年，他迫使土著将大部分土地割让给英国。这一大片土地以罗得斯的名字命名为罗得西亚（即现在的津巴布韦和赞比亚）。罗得斯组建的不列颠南非公司统治这片领土直至 1923 年。

1890 年，罗得斯担任开普殖民地的首相。他从未将赚取利润当做目的。他的雄心是将非洲南部全部纳入大英帝国的版图。他梦想修筑一条铁路，从南方的开普敦一直通向北方的开罗，只通过英国的非洲领土。他试图使英国人和布尔人联合起来。布尔人多是荷兰人的后裔，在非洲定居已历经几代。但罗得斯在攫取非洲人的土地时，残酷而贪婪。在对待黑人时，他是个种族主义者。他拒绝给殖民地的黑人以选举权，限制黑人拥有土地的数量。

罗得斯明白倘若英帝国想扩张在非洲南部的统治，它必须夺取布尔人定居的大片土地。1895 年，他支持德兰士瓦（即现在的南非北部）的英国定居者推翻共和国政府的阴谋，因为该政府是由布尔人控制的。阴谋未能得逞，而且遭到广泛的批评。罗得斯因此被迫辞去开普殖民地的首相的职务，将精力用

the amount of land blacks could own.

Rhodes saw that if the British Empire wanted to expand its rule in southern Africa, it would have to take the large areas of land settled by the Boers. In 1895 he supported a plot made by British settlers in the Transvaal, in what is now northeastern South Africa, to overthrow the government of the republic, which was dominated by the Boers. This plot was unsuccessful and widely criticized. For this Rhodes was forced to resign as prime minister of the Cape Colony and then devoted himself to the development of Rhodesia. But his efforts to enlarge the territory of the British Empire finally caused the Boer War (1899-1902), in which British troops fought Dutch colonists for controlling some of the richest gold and diamond mining areas of southern Africa. During the war he took part in the defense of Kimberley. He died at Cape Town in March 1902, before the war was over.

In his will Rhodes left most of his fortune to Oxford University for the establishment of the Rhodes scholarships.

10. Boer War

Boer War is also called the South African War, which was fought from 1899 to 1902 between the British and the Boers (now called

于开发罗得西亚。但他扩张英帝国领土的努力终于引发布尔战争（1899-1902）。这是英国军队与荷兰殖民者之间的战争，目的是控制非洲南部黄金和钻石储量最大的矿区。战争期间，他参加了金伯利的保卫战。战争结束前，罗得斯于1902年3月在开普敦逝世。

在遗嘱中，罗得斯将自己的大部分财产留给牛津大学，建立了罗得斯奖学金。

题外话

罗得斯的遗嘱于1902年4月公开后，他的名望创了新高。他用大部分遗产在牛津大学设立奖学金，资助来自英国殖民地、美国和德国的青年男子受教育。由于遗嘱禁止在资格审批上有种族歧视，许多有色人种的学生也从中受益。但人们怀疑这是否罗得斯的本意。他曾声称自己的原则是"赞比西河以南所有白人男子权利平等"。后来，在自由主义的压力之下，他又将"白人"改为"文明人"。但他可能认为，非洲土著的文明化太遥远，这两个词的意义差别并不大。

布尔战争

布尔战争又称南非战争，是英国人与南非北部的布尔人（现称阿非利堪人）之间于1899~1902年

Afrikaners) of the northern South African regions.

The Boers' ancestors were the Dutch, who were the first Europeans that settle in what is now South Africa. In 1657, the Dutch East India Company began to allow some employees to leave the firm and start their own farms. These people became known as *Boers*, which means "farmers" in the Dutch language. Later, more Dutch farmers, as well as French and German settlers, joined what became known as the Cape Colony. By 18th century, whites occupied most of the good farmland around Cape Town. During the Napoleonic Wars British troops occupied the Cape Colony to keep it out of French hands. In 1814, the Netherlands formally gave the Cape to Britain. The first British settlers arrived in 1820. They extended the territory of the colony by taking more land from the black African peoples. The government made English the colony's only official language in 1828. In 1833, Britain abolished slavery throughout its empire, ruining some Boer farmers who depended on slave labor to work their fields. The Boers hated the newcomers and many decided to leave the Cape Colony to get away from British rule. Beginning in 1836, several thousand of the Boers made a historic journey called the Great Trek. They moved their entire households 500 or more miles to the northeast into lands of black African peoples. The Boers defeated the African peoples and settled in what became Natal, the Orange Free

间进行的一场战争。

布尔人的祖先是荷兰人,是在现在的南非定居的头一批欧洲人。1657 年,荷兰的东印度公司开始允许某些雇员离开公司开办自己的农场。这些人被称为"布尔",在荷兰语里是"农夫"之意。后来,更多的荷兰农民,还有法国和德国的移居者聚居在一起,形成开普殖民地。到了 18 世纪,白人占据了开普敦周围大部分肥沃的土地。拿破仑战争时期,英国军队占领了开普敦,使之不落入法国人之手。1814 年,荷兰正式将开普割让英国。头一批英国人于 1820 年到达。他们从非洲黑人手中夺取更多土地,扩张了殖民地的领土。1828 年,政府规定英语为殖民地的唯一官方语言。1833 年英国在整个帝国废除奴隶制,使一些依靠奴隶在田间干活的布尔农夫破产。布尔人痛恨这些后来者,许多人决定离开开普敦,躲避英国人的统治。从 1836 年开始,数千布尔人开始了一次历史上著名的迁徙,史称"大迁徙"。他们带着全部家当向北跋涉 500 多英里,进入非洲黑人的土地。布尔人打败了非洲人,在后来称为纳塔尔、奥兰治自由邦和德兰士瓦的地方定居下来。英国于 1843 年控制了纳塔尔。但它于 1852 年承认了德兰士瓦的独立,又于 1854 年承认了奥兰治自由邦的独立。

State, and the Transvaal. Britain took control of Natal in 1843. But it recognized the independence of the Transvaal in 1852 and the Orange Free State in 1854.

In 1886, a gold field was discovered in the Transvaal. British miners, traders and other people rushed to the country and by 1895, these newcomers made up about half the Transvaal's white male population. To keep control of the Transvaal, the Boers taxed the British newcomers heavily and denied them voting rights. As a result, tension grew between Britain and the Transvaal.

In 1895, Cecil Rhodes, the prime minister of the Cape Colony, plotted to overthrow the Transvaal government. He sent a force to invade the country. But the Boers defeated the invaders. Relations between Britain and the Transvaal became worse.

In 1899, the Transvaal and the Orange Free State declared war on Britain. Though Great Britain was then the strongest power on earth, South Africa was far away and the Boers knew the country better, so for several months the Boers seems to be winning. Their forces invaded Natal and Cape Colony. Within days they succeeded in surrounding British forces at Ladysmith, Natal, and at Mafeking and Kimberley, Cape Colony. But soon many more British troops arrived. The British captured the capitals of the two republics early in 1900. General Louis Botha's Boer army surrendered to Lord Roberts in September. The remaining Boer

1886 年，德兰士瓦发现金矿。英国采矿者、商人和其他人蜂拥进入这个国家，到了 1895 年，这些新来者大约占了白人人口的一半。为控制德兰士瓦，布尔人向新来的英国人征收重税，并拒绝给他们选举权。结果，英国和德兰士瓦的关系紧张起来。

1895 年，开普殖民地的首相塞西尔·罗得斯阴谋推翻德兰士瓦政府。他派了一支军队入侵德兰士瓦，但是布尔人打败了入侵者。英国和德兰士瓦的紧张关系加剧了。

1899 年，德兰士瓦和奥兰治自由邦向英国宣战。虽然英国当时是世界上最强大的国家，但南非是个遥远的地方，而布尔人更熟悉这个国家，因而在几个月内，布尔人似乎将取得胜利。他们的军队侵入纳塔尔和开普殖民地。数日内，他们将英军围困在纳塔尔的莱迪史密斯和开普殖民地的马弗京和金伯利。但不久后大批英国军队抵达。1900 年初，英国占领两国首都。路易斯·博塔将军的布尔军队于 9 月向罗伯茨勋爵投降。布尔人的残余部队退入农村，坚持游击战直至 1902 年 5 月。为对付游击队，英国人破坏布尔人的农场，将成千的妇女和儿童投入集中营。按照 1902 年 5 月签署的一个条约，这两个布尔共和国沦为英国的殖民地。

在布尔战争期间，英国损失

forces went to the countryside, where they fought on as guerrillas until May 1902. To deal with the guerrillas the British destroyed the farms of the Boers and put thousands of women and children in concentration camps. Under the terms of a treaty signed in May 1902, the two Boer republics became British colonies.

In the course of Boer War, British lost about 28,000 men. Boers lost about 4000 men, plus more than 20,000 civilians who died from disease in concentration camps. Thousands of black Africans also died in the camps.

28000 名士兵。布尔军队损失了大约 4000 人，另有两万多平民病死在集中营里。成千上万的非洲黑人也死于集中营。

题外话

有人将布尔战争视为英帝国发展史上的分水岭。此后如日中天的帝国开始走下坡路。这场局部战争竟持续三年，英军付出惨重的代价，英国在国际上也失尽人心。英国人的手毕竟伸得太长了。

11. The Early 20th Century

20 世纪初年

In the late 19th century Britain had followed a foreign policy of isolation. But at the turn of the century, it began to feel the threat of Germany. Germany had grown too strong. It had the best army in Europe and had begun to build a very large navy. Britain now needed friends for its safety. It first made an alliance with Japan in 1902. Two years later it signed a treaty of friendship with France. In 1907, Russia joined Britain and France and the three became allies.

In 1906, the Liberal Party won a great election victory. The government introduced free school meals in 1906, and pensions for the elderly two years later. In 1909 politician David Lloyd

19 世纪末，英国一直奉行一种孤立的外交政策。但在世纪之交，它开始感到德国的威胁。德国已发展得十分强大。它拥有欧洲最精锐的部队，而且已开始建立一支庞大的海军。英国现在需要朋友以保障自身的安全。它先是于 1902 年与日本结盟，两年后又与法国签署友好条约。1907 年，俄国加入英法同盟。

1906 年，自由党在选举中大获全胜。政府于 1906 年开始实行免费校餐，两年后实行老年人养老金制。1909 年，威尔士社会主义

George, a Welsh socialist, introduced what became known as "the people's budget". The budget raised taxes on the rich to help the poor, especially the old, the sick and the unemployed. The House of Lords did not like the budget and refused to pass it. A political struggle followed over the veto power of the Lords. The struggle ended in 1911, when George V (1910-1936) threatened to create more than 250 new peers who would vote for the budget. The Lords were forced to agree to a bill that allowed them to delay—but not to veto—bills passed by the House of Commons. Liberal reforms between 1906 and 1914 laid the foundation for the establishment of Britain's welfare state.

At the beginning of the 20th century some changes took place in British society. The classes mixed more freely in towns, and women discarded old-styled clothing and began to wear dresses that made them easier to move about. Many of them took to traveling by bicycle. As railroads and buses became common, the suburbs began to develop. The middle classes built large houses in the suburbs, where their children could be kept away from crime and social problems, and yet they could still go to work in urban areas.

Many British people began to believe socialism. Among the socialists there were not only industrial workers, but also middle-class intellectuals. One of the most important groups of socialist intellectuals was the London Fabian Society, led by Sidney and Beatrice Webb. The society was founded in 1884. It was named for

者大卫·劳合·乔治提出一个预算案，日后被称为"人民预算案"。预算案提高针对富人的税收，以救助穷人，特别是老人、病人和失业者。议会上院不喜欢这一预算案，拒绝通过它。接着，预算案的支持者和反对者就上院的否决权问题展开了一场政治较量。1911年，乔治五世（1910-1936）威胁说要加封250名新贵族，使预算案获得通过，这场较量终于结束。上院被迫同意一项法案，该法案只允许上院延迟通过而不能否决下院通过的法案。自由党在1906~1914年的改革为英国福利国家的建立奠定了基础。

20世纪初，英国社会发生了一些变化。城里各阶层更为自由地融合在一起，妇女们抛弃了老式的服装，穿上使她们更易于活动的衣服。许多妇女开始骑自行车。随着火车和公共汽车的普及，城郊开始得到发展。中产阶级在城郊建起宽敞的住宅，他们的孩子在那里可以远离犯罪和社会问题，而他们仍可以在城里上班。

许多英国人开始相信社会主义。社会主义者当中不但有工业工人，也有中产阶级知识分子。社会主义知识分子最重要的团体之一是伦敦的费边社，由西德尼·韦伯和妻子比阿特丽斯·韦伯领导。费边社成立于1884年，以罗马将军昆

费边社集会

Quintus Fabius Maximus, a Roman general who avoided defeat by refusing to fight any decisive battles against Hannibal. The Fabians disagreed with the Communists, who believed that the people could gain ownership of the means of production only through revolution. They taught that socialism could be achieved gradually, through a series of reforms. Members of the Fabian Society included novelist H. G. Wells and Irish playwright George Bernard Shaw. Fabian ideas became the basis of the British Labour Party.

During the early 20th century workers in coal mines, on railways, and on the London docks often went on strike. These strikes paralyzed the economy and showed the power of a unified labor movement. Under the leadership of

塔斯·费边·马克西姆斯的名字命名。这位将军拒绝与汉尼拔展开决战，以避免失败的结局。费边社不赞成共产主义，因为共产主义者认为只有通过革命人民才能拥有生产资料。费边社主张，社会主义可以通过一系列的改革逐步实现。费边社成员包括小说家 H. G. 威尔斯和爱尔兰剧作家乔治·萧伯纳。费边社的思想为英国工党的成立打下基础。

20 世纪初，煤矿、铁路和伦敦码头工人经常举行罢工。这些罢工使经济瘫痪，显示出统一劳工运动的力量。在费边社和独立工党的

the Fabian Society and the Independent Labour Party, the Labour Party was created in 1900 to gain representation in Parliament for workers. It was at first called the Labour Representation Committee. The committee included representatives of trade unions and socialist groups. In the election of 1906, 29 Labour members were elected, and they formed a union with the Liberals. The Labour Party claimed to represent the interest of the working class, and the majority of its supporters were working classes, but it also had middle-class supporters among intellectuals. The party was to become one of two major parties that took power by turns in Britain.

While industrial workers were fighting for higher wages and better working conditions, women began to fight for their voting rights. The first women's movements arose as a result of great economic and political changes that had taken place in the industrial age. As women's roles became different, they began to question their status and situation. The first thing they demanded to have was their political rights. A woman called Emmeline Pankhurst led the fight for women's voting rights. In 1903, she helped organize the National Women's Social and Political Union, with the slogan "Votes for Women". The members of this organization often used violence to call attention to their struggle. They broke glass windows, blocked traffic, and went on hunger strikes when put into prison. London police were unwilling to use force against these middle-class women. This movement was the

领导下，工党于 1900 年成立，为工人们争取议会里的代表权。它起初称为劳工代表委员会。委员会包括工会和社会主义团体的代表。在 1906 年的选举中，有 29 个工党党员获选，他们与自由党结成联盟。工党自称代表工人阶级利益，其大多数支持者也是工人阶级，但它在知识分子中也有中产阶级的支持者。工党日后成为英国轮流执政的两大政党之一。

当工业工人们为提高工资和改善工作条件而斗争时，妇女们也开始为争取选举权而斗争。工业时代巨大经济和政治的变革导致妇女运动的兴起。妇女担任的角色发生了变化，她们开始对自己的社会地位和处境提出了疑问。她们的头一个要求就是政治权利。一位叫做埃米琳·潘克赫斯特的妇女领导了为妇女争取选举权的斗争。1903 年，她参与组织了全国妇女社会和政治联盟，提出"为妇女争取选举权"的口号。这个组织的成员常用暴力来唤起公众对她们斗争的关注。她们打碎玻璃窗，阻挡交通，被囚禁后便绝食。伦敦警方不愿对这些中产阶级妇女使用武力。这场运动是议会最棘手的问题。1918 年，30 岁以上英国妇女获得选举权。但 21 岁以上妇女获得选举权要等到 1928年。

most difficult issue for Parliament to handle. British women over 30 were given the vote in 1918, but women over 21 were to wait until 1928.

题外话

从 1688 年光荣革命后，英国的几乎所有争取社会变革的斗争都是"费边"式的。很少发生暴力

冲突。最大的暴力冲突莫过于 1819 年曼彻斯特的彼得卢大屠杀，死 11 人，伤数百人。但比起其他国家争取改革所付出的代价，仍不算大。英国的社会压力，总能通过某种渠道得以释放，不致形成爆炸性局面。改革势力，一般不愿走极端；保守势力，则懂得妥协常常是明智之举。

埃米琳·潘克赫斯特在示威时被捕

CHAPTER THIRTEEN

From 1914 to the Present
从 1914 年 至 今

1. World War I

第一次世界大战

World War I was one of the most violent and destructive wars in European history. It lasted four years, and involved many of the countries of Europe as well the United States and other nations throughout the world. It took the lives of nearly 10 million troops.

World War I began in 1914. The two sides that fought each other were called the Allies and the Central Powers. The Allies included Britain, France, Russia and Serbia. Later Italy, Rumania, Greece, Japan, the United States and other countries joined the Allies. The Central Powers were Germany, Austria-Hungary, the Ottoman Empire, and Bulgaria.

During the years before 1914 the important countries of Europe got into political and economic rivalry and more and more suspicious of one another. Part of this rivalry was between

第一次世界大战是欧洲历史上最残酷、破坏性最大的战争之一。战争持续了四年，欧洲许多国家参与其中，美国和全世界其他国家也卷入其中。阵亡将士将近一千万。

第一次世界大战始于 1914 年。交战双方称为协约国和同盟国。协约国包括英国、法国、俄国和塞尔维亚。后来意大利、罗马尼亚、希腊、日本、美国等国家也加入了协约国。同盟国包括德国、奥匈帝国、奥斯曼帝国和保加利亚。

1914 年以前，欧洲的大国就开始了政治和经济的角逐，相互之间越来越缺乏信任。英国和德国也是竞争对手。德国已成为世界最强大的国家之一，对英帝国的安全构成威胁。欧洲国家分成两个集团，

Britain and Germany. Germany had become one of the strongest countries in the world and a threat to the safety of the British Empire. European countries had divided into two groups, which were called the Triple Entente (England, France and Russia) and the Triple Alliance (Germany, Austria and Italy). Because each group was afraid that the other would start a war, every nation made preparations by building up armed forces. Great Britain was afraid of Germany because Germany was building a great fleet of warships that might threaten British control of the sea.

On June 28, 1914, Archduke Francis Ferdinand, heir to the throne of Austria-Hungary, went to Sarajevo, the capital of Austria-Hungary's province of Bosnia-Herzegovina. As he and his wife rode through the streets in their automobile, a young Serbian nationalist fired two shots at them and they died almost instantly. Austria-Hungary believed that Serbia's government was behind the assassination. It seized the opportunity to declare war on Serbia.

When the fighting began, the Allies, including France, Britain and Russia were on the side of Serbia. They opposed the Central Powers, made up of Austria-Hungary and Germany. Britain entered the war in August 1914, when German troops marched through the small country of Belgium to attack France. Great Britain had promised to protect Belgium and so declared war on Germany and Austria. Italy broke its alliance with Germany and a year later joined

称为三国协约(英、法、俄)和三国同盟（德、奥、意）。由于每个集团都害怕另一集团发动战争，所以所有的国家都扩军备战。英国害怕德国，因为德国正在建立一支强大的舰队，可能威胁到英国的制海权。

1914 年 6 月 28 日，奥匈帝国王储弗朗西斯·斐迪南大公前往奥匈帝国的波斯尼亚-黑塞哥维那省的首都萨拉热窝访问。当他和妻子乘车穿过大街时，一个年轻的塞尔维亚民族主义分子朝他们开了两枪，二人很快死去。奥匈帝国认为塞尔维亚政府策划了刺杀，借机向塞尔维亚宣战。

战争开始时，协约国，即法国、英国和俄国都站在塞尔维亚一边。他们反对同盟国奥匈帝国和德国。英国于 1914 年 8 月参战，当时德国军队穿越小国比利时向法国发动进攻。英国曾许诺要保护比利时时，所以向德奥宣战。意大利脱离与德国的联盟，一年后加入英法一方作战。

第一次世界大战初期，德国在欧洲主要战场上取得了胜利。在不到一月的时间里德国军队横扫比利时。一支英国军队开赴法国，但得到援助的法国军队起初仍未能阻挡住德军。1914 年 9 月初，德军已抵达马恩河，距离巴黎只有大约 30 英里。在这里，法国聚集一支军队，在 9 月 6 日的第一次马恩河战役

Britain and France in the war.

Germany won early victories in World War I on the main European battlefronts. German armies swept through Belgium in less a month. A British army quickly went to France, but even with this help the French could not stop the Germans at first. By the beginning of September 1914, the Germans had reached the River Marne, only about thirty miles from Paris. There the French got together an army and stopped the Germans on September 6 in the first Battle of Marne, one of the fiercest battles in history. This battle destroyed Germany's plan for a quick and decisive victory over France. On September 9, German forces started to withdraw.

The German army stopped its withdraw near the Aisne River. From there, the Germans and the Allies fought a series of battles. Germany wanted to seize ports on the English Channel and cut off supply lines between France and Britain.

中阻挡住了德国的攻势。这是历史上最激烈的战役之一，它使德国取得迅速而决定性胜利的计划受挫。9月9日，德国军队开始后撤。

后撤的德军在埃纳河附近停下来，与协约国军展开一系列战斗。德军企图占领英吉利海峡上的港口，切断法国和英国之间的供应线。但在比利时进行的第一次伊普尔战役中，英军阻挡住德军向海边的推进。

在以后的三年半里，战争处于胶着状态。交战双方挖掘壕堑以防御敌人炮火的袭击，阵地上形成了一条东起北海海岸，穿越比利时和法国北方直至瑞士边界的连续不断的壕堑线。在壕堑的泥水里，士兵

壕堑战在西线造成的破坏

But the British stopped the German advance to the sea in the First Battle of Ypres in Belgium.

For the next three and half years, the war was fought basically along the same line. The opposing armies dug trenches to protect themselves from enemy bullets and shells, until there were two continuous lines of trenches running from the coast of the North Sea across Belgium and northeastern France to the border of Switzerland. Soldiers lived a terrible life in the mud of the trenches, never knowing when the enemy would bombard them with shells or when they would be ordered to make an attack. Machine guns began to be used in defence, and they could kill hundreds of charging soldiers in a minute. Attacks all failed and millions of lives were lost for the purpose.

Both the Allies and the Central Powers developed new weapons, which they hoped would break the stalemate. In April 1915, the Germans started using poison gas over Allied lines in the Second Battle of Ypres. Soon the Allies began to use it too. Then gas masks became necessary equipment in the trenches. The next year the British used tanks for the first time against the Germans in the Battle of the Somme. The early tanks were slow and clumsy, but they were used successfully in the Battle of Cambrai in 1917. For the first time in a great war, airplanes were used, but they were very small and could do little damage.

In early 1916 the Germans decided to attack the French city of Verdun. They believed that

们的生活极其艰苦。他们不知道敌人会何时轰炸他们，也不知道何时会接到命令发起进攻。此时，在防御中已开始使用机枪，很短时间里可以杀死大量进攻的士兵。但进攻都未能成功，数百万士兵阵亡。

协约国和同盟国都研制了新武器，企图打破胶着状态。1915 年 4 月，德国开始在第二次伊普尔战役中使用毒气。不久，协约国方面也开始使用毒气。在壕堑里，防毒面具成为必需的装备。第二年，英军在索姆河战役中首次使用坦克。早期的坦克缓慢而笨重，但在 1917 年的康布雷战役中发挥了作用。飞机也首次用于大战，但它们很小，造成的破坏有限。

1916 年初，德国决定进攻法国城市凡尔登。他们认为法国军队会不惜一切代价保卫这座城市，以此消耗法国的兵力，直至它无力再

戴防毒面具的士兵

France would defend Verdun at whatever cost, until it would not have enough troops to continue the war. The Battle of Verdun continued to the end of the year. The German army made one attack after another on the city, but the French defended it desperately and the Germans never took it. The Battle of Verdun became a symbol of the terrible destructiveness of modern war. The losses on both sides were high. The city itself was practically destroyed.

To relieve the German pressure on Verdun, the Allies began in the same year a major offensive near the Somme River in France. The Allies attacked on July 1, 1916. Within hours, 60,000 British soldiers were killed or wounded. Fierce fighting went on into the autumn. In September, Britain used tanks for the first time in an attack. But the tanks were too unreliable and too few in number to make a difference in the battle. The Allies' offensive ended in November. Although the line of the Allies moved forward only about 11 kilometers, the Battle of the Somme is often considered the real turning point in the war for the Allies.

On the Eastern Front, a Russian army attacked Austria in 1914, and won a victory. But the Germans soon pushed them back. As the war

第一次世界大战中的坦克

战。凡尔登战役一直打到年底。德军向这座城市发动一次又一次的进攻，但法国军队拼死守城，德军一直未能占领它。凡尔登战役成为现代战争可怕的破坏力的象征。双方兵力损失惨重。这座城市几乎被夷为平地。

为解除德军对凡尔登的压力，协约国于同年在法国的索姆河发起一次大反攻。反攻于 1916 年 7 月 1 日打响。几小时内，英军士兵死伤 6 万人。激烈的战斗持续到秋天。9 月，英军首次在进攻中使用坦克。但坦克太不可靠，而且数量太少，不足以改变战局。协约国的进攻于 11 月结束。虽然协约国的战线仅向前推进大约 11 公里，但索姆河战役常被视为战争的转捩点。

在东线，一支俄国军队于 1914 年进攻了奥地利，取得胜利。但德

continued, the Russians lost many battles and the Russian people suffered greatly. In 1917, the Communists led a revolution and gained control of Russia's government. The new government immediately called for peace talks with Germany. Now the Germans were able to use their troops fighting on the Eastern Front on the Western Front. The Allied situation seemed even more difficult.

During the war Britain had the most powerful navy in the world. With it Britain tried to stop any food and supplies from reaching Germany. Germany's navy was strong, but not as strong as Britain's. So most of the time Germany's big ships had to stay in its home waters, and the Germans sent out their submarines, called U-boats, to sink Allied and neutral ships that were carrying supplies to England. On May 7, 1915, a U-boat sank without warning the British passenger liner Lusitania off the coast of Ireland. Among the 1,198 passengers who died were 128 Americans. The U.S. government protested, and for a while the Germans stopped attacking neutral or passenger ships.

国军队不久就将他们击退了。随着战争的继续，俄国打了多次败仗。俄国人民由于战争而苦难深重。1917 年，共产党人发动革命，夺取了俄国的政权。新政府立即与德国举行和谈。此后，德国可以将东线部队调往西线作战，协约国面临的局势似乎更为艰难。

在战争中，英国拥有世界上最强大的舰队。英国试图利用这支舰队阻断德国的粮食和物资的供给。德国的海军也很强大，但实力仍比不上英国舰队。所以德国的大型舰只大部分时间都不得不停留在自己的海域里，而派出称为 U-潜艇的潜水艇击沉向英国运送物资的协约国和中立国的船只。1915 年 5 月 7 日，一艘 U-潜艇未加警告便在爱尔兰海岸附近击沉英国客轮卢西塔尼亚号，1198 名乘客死难，其中有 128 名美国人。美国政府提出抗议，德国暂时停止攻击中立国船只或客轮。

U-潜艇

The British and German navies finally met in the Battle of Jutland off the coast of Denmark on May 31 and June 1, 1916. Although Britain lost more ships than Germany, it still ruled the seas. Now it seemed to the Germans that the only way to win the war was to build more submarines and again begin sinking neutral ships, so as to starve Britain into surrender. After several more American ships were sank the Americans became angry, and on April 6, 1917, the United States declared war on Germany. A huge American army was sent to France. In the end, about 2 million Americans served in Europe.

In early 1918, Germany launched a series of offensives. The Allied forces fought stubbornly, and both sides suffered heavy losses. In May German troops reached the Marne River. During June, U.S. troops drove the Germans out of Belleau Wood, a wooded area near the Marne. On July 18 the Allied forces launched a counter-attack with forces that included several American divisions. One of the centers of fiercest battle

1916 年 5 月 31 日至 6 月 1 日，英国与德国的海军终于在丹麦水域的日德兰半岛海战中交火。虽然英国损失的军舰多于德国，但英国依然控制着海洋。这时在德国人看来，唯一打赢战争的办法就是建造更多的潜艇，重新开始攻击中立国船只，用饥饿迫使英国投降。又有几艘美国船只被击沉后，美国人愤怒了。美国政府于 1917 年 4 月 6 日向德国宣战。一支美国大军派往法国，最后，在欧洲服役的美国人达到大约 200 万。

1918 年初，德国发动一系列攻势。协约国军顽强抵抗，双方兵力损失惨重。5 月，德国军队推进到马恩河。6 月，美国军队将德军逐出马恩河附近的贝洛林地。7 月 18 日，协约国军队发起反攻，美军的几个师也投入战斗。战斗最激烈的地点之一是蒂耶里堡，美军在这里取得首次决定性胜利。德军被

日德兰半岛海战

was at Chateau-Thierry, where the American troops won their first decisive victory. The German armies were forced back across the Marne. The Second Battle of the Marne marked the turning point of World War I. After winning the battle, the Allies advanced steadily.

On September 26, 1918 the Allied forces launched the last great offensive of World War I. A fierce battle, known as the Battle of the Meuse-Argonne, was fought between the Argonne Forest and the Meuse River. About 60,000 U.S. troops took an active part in the fighting. The battle finally broke down German resistance. After Bulgaria, Turkey and Austria surrendered to the Allies one after another, Germany asked for an agreement to stop fighting.

In the early morning on November 11, 1918, the Germans signed the agreement, accepting the terms demanded by the Allies. Germany agreed to withdraw all it troops from the territories it had taken during the war; to give up large numbers of arms, ships, and other war materials; and to allow the Allied powers to occupy German territory along the Rhine River.

In January 1919, representatives of the victorious powers gathered in Paris to draw up the peace settlement. The meeting was called the Paris Peace Conference. In May, the peace conference approved the treaty

迫退回马恩河北岸。第二次马恩河战役标志着第一次世界大战的转捩点。赢得这次战役后,协约国开始稳步向前推进。

1918 年 9 月 26 日,协约国军队发动了第一次世界大战中最后一次大规模进攻。在阿尔贡森林和默兹河之间发生激烈战斗,这场激战称为默兹-阿尔贡战役。大约 6 万美军也投入了战斗。战斗最终粉碎了德军的抵抗。保加利亚、土耳其和奥地利先后投降协约国之后,德国要求议和。

1918 年 11 月 11 日清晨,德国签署和约,接受了协约国提出的条件。德国同意德军从在战争中夺取的所有领土上撤出;放弃大批武器、军舰和其他战争物资;允许协约国占领莱茵河地区。

1919 年 1 月,各大国代表会集巴黎起草和约。这次会议称为巴

签署停战协定

and presented it to Germany. Germany agreed to it only after the Allies threatened to invade. The treaty was signed in the Palace of Versailles near Paris on June 28, 1919. Under the Treaty of Versailles, Germany gave up territory to France, Poland, Belgium, and Denmark, and lost its overseas colonies to the Allied powers. An Allied military force, paid for by Germany, was to occupy the west bank of the Rhine River for 15 years. Germany was forced to pay a huge sum of money for the destruction and loss caused by the war. The Treaty of Versailles punished Germany more severely than the nation had expected. It created conditions that helped Adolf Hitler gain power in Germany, which led to World War II.

黎和会。5月，和会通过条约，交给德国。德国在协约国入侵的威胁下，接受了条约。条约于1919年6月28日在巴黎附近的凡尔赛宫签署。根据凡尔赛和约，德国向法国、波兰、比利时、丹麦和日本割让了领土，海外殖民地被协约国列强瓜分。一支协约国军队将占领莱茵河东岸15年，军队的开支由德国支付。德国还被迫为战争造成的破坏和损失支付一大笔赔款。凡尔赛和约对德国惩罚之严重出乎德国人的预料。它为阿道夫·希特勒在德国上台铺平了道路，从而导致第二次世界大战。

第一次世界大战阵亡者公墓

🎯 题外话

　　林语堂这样评价凡尔赛和约："凡尔赛和约岂止是不公平，简直是粗鄙和缺乏'涵养'。如果法国人在他们胜利之际有一点道家修养的话，他们就不会将凡尔赛和约强加于人，因而现在他们的头枕在枕头上要安稳得多。""凡尔赛会议如果请老子去做主席，今日就不会有个希特勒。"

2. Postwar Economic Problems

The war left Europe exhausted, never to regain the controlling position in world affairs that it had held before the war. During World War I, more than 10 million men were killed and more than 20 million were wounded. Great Britain's losses were also great. 750,000 British members of the British armed forces were killed in battle. German submarines sank a large number of British ships and more than 14,000 sailors died on the sea. Numerous soldiers and civilians died of wounds, diseases, hunger, and other war-related causes.

The war also created severe economic problems for Britain and shook its position as a world power. World War I cost the British government one thousand million pounds. It raised part of the money to pay for the war through income taxes and other taxes. But most of the money came from borrowing, which created huge debts. In addition, Britain lost many of the markets for its exports while producing war goods. The United States and Japan had taken much of its export business. Germany and Russia, which used to be Britain's best customers before the war, could not afford its goods after the war. With the decline in foreign trade, especially after large numbers of soldiers returning from the war, prices rose and wages became low and many people could not find jobs. Labor unions attempted to protect their members by

战后经济问题

战后的欧洲精疲力竭，再未能恢复到战前在国际事务中强势地位。一千多万人死于战火，两千多万人负伤。英国的损失也十分巨大。英军中 75 万英籍军人死于战场。德国潜艇击沉大量英国船只，14000 名水手死于海战。大批士兵和平民死于伤病、饥饿和其他与战争有关的原因。

战争在英国造成严重的经济问题，动摇了它世界强国的地位。英国政府的战争开支高达 10 亿镑。战争所需费用部分靠征收所得税和其他税种来支付。但大部分资金都来自贷款，结果债台高筑。此外，由于生产军用物资，英国失去出口产品的许多市场。其出口贸易中的相当大份额被美国和日本夺走。德国和俄国在战前曾是英国的最大主顾，战后无力购买英国货。随着对外贸易的衰落，特别是在大批士兵复员后，物价上涨，工资降低，很多人找不到工作。工会屡屡举行罢工，保护会员的利益，但这使国家的经济更加恶化。

organizing frequent strikes, which made the economy of the country worse.

3. The Issue of Ireland

At the beginning of the 20th century, the conflict over the issue of Ireland became serious. During the late 19th century, some Irish people had begun to demand home rule for their country. Under home rule, Ireland would have remained part of Britain but would have had its own parliament for domestic affairs. The British Liberal Party favored the plan. But Protestants in Ulster opposed it because they feared to live under the rule of Catholics. The British Parliament defeated home rule bills in 1886 and 1892. The situation in Ireland became worse and worse after that.

In 1905, an Irish journalist named Arthur Griffith founded a political organization called "Sinn Fein", meaning "We Ourselves" in Gaelic. The organization insisted that the Irish should be allowed to govern themselves. Another organization, called The Irish Republican Brotherhood (IRB), was also fighting actively in the early 20th century for an independent Irish republic. Members of the IRB became known as republicans. In 1914, facing the possibility of fighting two wars — one in Europe and the other in Ireland, the British Parliament finally passed a home rule bill, in spite of oppo-

爱尔兰问题

20 世纪初，在爱尔兰问题上的冲突更加严重。早在 19 世纪末，一些爱尔兰人就已经开始要求自治。在自治条件下，爱尔兰仍是英国的一部分，但将有自己的议会处理爱尔兰内部事务。英国自由党赞成这项计划，但阿尔斯特的新教徒反对，他们担心自己将生活在天主教徒的统治之下。英国议会在 1886 年和 1892 年两次否决自治法案。此后，爱尔兰的局势日益恶化。

1905 年一个叫做亚瑟·格里夫斯的记者建立了一个称为"新芬党"的组织。"新芬"在盖尔语里意为"我们自己"。这个组织坚持争取爱尔兰自治。另一个组织，称为爱尔兰共和兄弟会（IRB）也在 20 世纪初为建立独立的爱尔兰共和国而积极进行斗争。IRB 的成员被称为共和党人。1914 年英国议会面对打两场战争的可能性，一场在欧洲，一场在爱尔兰。不顾阿尔斯特的新教徒反对，英国议会最终通过了自治法案。但一战的爆发使

sition from Ulster Protestants. But the outbreak of World War I prevented the bill from taking effect. Most of the Irish people supported Britain during the war. But the republicans, led by Patrick Pearse, believed that the war gave Ireland a chance to gain independence. They began a rebellion in Dublin on Easter Monday 1916. The rebellion became known as the Easter Rising. British troops defeated the rebels after a week of fierce fighting. The British executed 15 republican leaders after the uprising.

At first, the Easter Rising received little support from the Irish people. But the executions aroused great sympathy for the republicans and Sinn Fein, which was believed to have taken part in the uprising, became more popular. In 1918, Sinn Fein members won 73 of Ireland's 105 seats in the British Parliament. But instead of going to London to take their seats in Parliament, the new members met in Dublin and declared all Ireland an independent republic on January 21, 1919. Following the declaration, bitter fighting broke out between the Irish rebels and British forces.

In 1920, the British Parliament passed the Government of Ireland Act. This act divided Ireland into two states — one consisting of 6 counties of Ulster and the other consisting of 3 counties of Ulster and 23 southern counties. Each state was to remain part of Britain and have some powers of self-government. The 6 Ulster counties, which had a Protestant majority, accepted the act and formed the state of

法案未能实施。在战争期间，大部分爱尔兰人支持英国。但在帕特里克·皮尔斯的领导下共和党人认为战争给爱尔兰一个赢得独立的机会。他们于 1916 年复活节次日在都柏林发动起义。这次起义称为复活节起义。经过一周的激战，英国军队打败了起义者。英国处决了 15 名共和党领袖。

起初，复活节起义在爱尔兰人当中没有得到多少支持。但处决起义者激起了人们对共和党人的巨大同情。据说参加了起义的新芬党也更得人心了。1918 年，新芬党在英国议会里爱尔兰的 105 个席位中获得 73 席。但这些新当选的议员们没有出席议会，却聚会在都柏林，于 1919 年 1 月 21 日宣布爱尔兰为独立的共和国。此后，爱尔兰叛乱分子与英国军队展开激战。

1920 年，英国政府通过爱尔兰政府法案。这个法案将爱尔兰分成两个邦。一个邦包括阿尔斯特地区的 6 个郡，另一个包括阿尔斯特地区的 3 个郡和 23 个南方郡。每个邦都是英国的一部分，但拥有某些自治权。阿尔斯特地区的 6 个郡的大部分人口是新教徒，它们接受了这个法案，成立了爱尔兰北方

Northern Ireland. The Assembly of Ireland rejected the act, and southern Ireland began fighting for complete independence. The Irish Republican Army (IRA), as the rebels were called, attacked British army and government buildings. The British dealt with the rebels with a strong hand and were bitterly hated by the Irish people. Finally, in 1921, Britain and the rebels signed a treaty that allowed southern Ireland to become a dominion. That is, it would be a self-governing member of the British Empire. The new dominion was called the Irish Free State. Most of the people of northern Ireland were Protestants, and they did not want to be part of the Roman Catholic Irish Free State. Northern Ireland remained in the United Kingdom, which was renamed the United Kingdom of Great Britain and Northern Ireland. Ireland did not become an independent republic until 1949.

邦。爱尔兰议会否决了这一法案，爱尔兰南方开始为完全独立开展斗争。被称为爱尔兰共和军（IRA）的叛乱分子攻击英国军队和政府部门。英国人以强硬手段对付叛乱分子，加深了爱尔兰人对他们的仇恨。1921年，英国与叛乱分子最终签署了一个条约，允许爱尔兰南方成立自治领。这意味着爱尔兰成为英帝国里的一个自治成员。新成立的自治领称为爱尔兰自由邦。爱尔兰北部的大多数人口是新教徒，他们不愿意成为罗马天主教爱尔兰自由邦的一部分。爱尔兰北部留在联合王国内，联合王国更名为大不列颠及北爱尔兰联合王国。爱尔兰在1949年才成为独立的共和国。

4. The Decline of the Liberal Party and the Rise of the Labour Party

自由党的衰落和工党的兴起

The Liberal and Conservative parties had replaced the Whig and Tory parties as Britain's two largest political organizations by the middle of the 19th century. During the second half of the century, the Liberals and Conservatives took

在19世纪中叶，自由党和保守党替代了辉格党和托利党成为英国的两个最大的政党。此世纪的后半期，自由党与保守党在英国政府里轮流执政。在最著名的自由党领

control of the British government by turns. Under the most famous Liberal leader Gladstone the Liberals made a lot of social reforms in favour of the working classes. In the early 20th century, the party made more reforms, which laid the foundation for the establishment of Britain's welfare state.

When Lloyd George became prime minister in 1916, the Liberals and Conservatives formed a union to govern the country. But the government consisted largely of Conservatives. Some of the Liberals opposed the union, and the party broke up into two groups. Since then the Liberal Party began to decline and became much smaller. At the same time the Labour Party grew stronger, and replaced the Liberal Party as the main opposition to the Conservative Party. Many voters could see little difference between Conservatives and Liberals. They saw the Labour Party, which declared itself in favour of socialism and represented trade unions, as an alternative to the Conservative Party.

In 1924, James Ramsay MacDonald formed the first Labour government. But he remained in office for only 10 months. He was defeated partly because his government was considered too friendly toward the Soviet Union, and partly because he failed to solve the problem of unemployment. In the 1929 elections, the Labour Party became the largest party for the first time, and MacDonald formed his

袖格莱斯顿执政时期，自由党进行了许多有利于工人阶级的社会改革。20 世纪初，自由党完成更多的改革，为英国的福利国家奠定了基础。

劳合·乔治于 1916 年成为首相，自由党和保守党结成联盟治理国家。但在政府中保守党居多数。一些自由党党员反对这个联盟，结果自由党分裂成两个集团。从那以后自由党开始衰落并萎缩。与此同时工党日益壮大，取代自由党成为保守党的主要反对党。许多选举人看不出保守党与自由党有多大差别。他们将宣称赞成社会主义、代表工会的工党视为可以替换保守党的政党。

劳合·乔治

詹姆斯·拉姆齐·麦克唐纳

second government as prime minister. A few months later, the worldwide Great Depression began and it struck Britain hard. Unemployment rose rapidly. MacDonald was unable to deal effectively with the problem of unemployment, and his government resigned in August 1931. MacDonald agreed to head a national government made up of Labour, Conservative, and Liberal Party members to deal with the economic crisis. A large majority of the Labour members of Parliament disagreed with him and expelled him from the Labour Party. The Labour Party did not take power again until 1945.

1924 年，詹姆斯·拉姆齐·麦克唐纳组建头一届工党政府。但他当政仅 10 个月就被迫辞职。他之所以下台部分因为他的政府被认为与苏联关系过于密切，部分因为他未能解决失业问题。在 1929 年的选举中，工党首次成为议会最大党，麦克唐纳再次出任首相组阁。几个月后开始了世界范围的经济大萧条，英国遭受沉重打击。失业率迅速上升。麦克唐纳未能有效解决失业问题，他的政府于 1931 年 8 月辞职。他同意组建一个包括工党、保守党和自由党的联合政府以处理经济危机。议会里的大多数工党议员与他意见相左，将他开除出党。工党直至 1945 年才重新上台执政。

5. Chamberlain and the Munich Agreement

张伯伦与慕尼黑协定

Neville Chamberlain was a Conservative, who served as prime minister of Britain from 1937 to 1940. Chamberlain was closely associated with the policy of appeasement toward Nazi Germany. This policy was based on the

内维尔·张伯伦是保守党领袖，于 1937~1940 年出任英国首相。张伯伦与对纳粹德国的绥靖政策紧密相关。这一政策是基于这样一种想法：如果德国独裁者阿道

belief that war could be prevented if some of the demands of the German dictator Adolf Hitler were satisfied.

Adolf Hitler was the leader of the Nazi Party, a group of men who wanted to conquer the world. He took control of Germany in 1933. Soon after that he began building a big army and air force, but few leaders in Britain, France or elsewhere, saw the danger and did anything to stop him. In March 1938, Germany took over Austria by force. A few months later Hitler said he wanted to take Sudetenland region of Czechoslovakia, because most people living there were Germans. At the time, France was an ally of Czechoslovakia, and Great Britain was an ally of France. Hitler threatened to send his army into Czechoslovakia, and Mussolini, the dictator of Italy, suggested a meeting in the German city of Munich. Chamberlain and Premier Edouard Daladier of France flew to Munich to have a talk with Hitler.

Both France and Great Britain were afraid of Germany and were not willing to go to war to save Czechoslovakia. Chamberlain and Daladier agreed that Hitler could take Sudetenland region, and in return, Hitler promised that Germany would demand no more territory in Europe. The government of Czechoslovakia was not given any voice in the matter, but Czechoslovakia was too weak to fight Germany alone and had to give in. The Munich Agreement was signed in September 1938.

When Chamberlain returned home, he met

夫·希特勒的某些要求得到满足，战争就可以避免。

阿道夫·希特勒是纳粹党魁。而纳粹党是一群想征服世界的人。希特勒于 1933 年控制了德国。不久后，他开始建立庞大的陆军和空军，但是英国、法国或其他国家很少有领导人看到危险并采取措施制止他。1938 年 3 月，德国用武力占领奥地利。几个月后，希特勒声称他想要夺取捷克斯洛伐克的苏台德地区，因为当地大多数居民是日尔曼人。当时，法国是捷克斯洛伐克的盟国，而英国又是法国的盟国。希特勒威胁要派军入侵捷克斯洛伐克，意大利的独裁者墨索里尼建议在德国城市慕尼黑举行会议。张伯伦和法国总理爱德华·达拉第飞往慕尼黑与希特勒会谈。

法英两国都害怕德国，不愿为救援捷克斯洛伐克而卷入战争。张伯伦和达拉第同意希特勒占领苏台

内维尔·张伯伦

sharp attacks in the House of Commons. Winston Churchill, a Conservative, called the Munich Agreement "a disaster".

The Munich Agreement has become a classic example of appeasement — giving in rather than fight when threatened. Like most appeasements, it did not succeed. Five months later, Hitler seized the rest of Czechoslovakia. On September 1, Germany invaded Poland. Two days later, Chamberlain led Britain into the war against Germany. Chamberlain was forced to resign in May 1940 and was succeeded by Sir Winston Churchill.

德，作为交换，希特勒许诺德国不再提出更多的欧洲领土要求。捷克斯洛伐克政府在此事上被剥夺了发言权，但捷克斯洛伐克过于弱小，无法独自与德国对抗，不得不让步。慕尼黑协定于 1938 年签署。

张伯伦回国后在下院遭到尖刻的批评。保守党的温斯顿·丘吉尔称慕尼黑协定为 "一场灾难"。

慕尼黑协定已成为绥靖政策的经典例子——受到威胁时退让而不是战斗。与大多数绥靖政策一样，它没有成功。5 个月之后，希特勒占领了捷克斯洛伐克的其余地区。9 月 1 日，德国入侵波兰。两天后，张伯伦代表英国向德国宣战。1940 年 5 月，张伯伦被迫辞职，温斯顿·丘吉尔继任。

慕尼黑会议，从左至右：张伯伦、达拉第、希特勒和墨索里尼

🎯 题外话

张伯伦成了 "绥靖主义" 的代名词，但并不见得公正。英国内阁是集体负责制，绥靖并不是张伯伦个人的政策。当时对希特勒抱有幻想的人肯定不在少数。

有人认为不应全盘否定英法的绥靖政策，因为它毕竟为英法争取了一年的时间来进行战备。但这种说法不能成立。首先，这种政策的后果是使国民对和平心存幻想，并不利于全面调动积极性。再说，在这一年的时间里，德国并没有睡大觉，它战备的速度和效率要远远大于英法。而且，它吞并了整个捷克斯洛伐克，从而大大增强了自己的军事和工业实力。

6. Edward VIII

Edward VIII (1894-1972) became famous in history because he was the only king of Britain who gave up the throne. Edward was educated at the Royal Naval College and Oxford University. He served in the army in World War I and after the war he visited many countries, promoting world peace, foreign trade, and the unity of the British Empire. He became popular because of his democratic spirit, charm, and skill of dealing with people without offending them. At home, he was concerned about the living conditions of the poor people and working classes.

Edward was the oldest son of King George V and Queen Mary of the House of Windsor. He succeeded his father and became King Edward VIII of Britain on January 20, 1936.

Before long it rumoured that Edward had a love affair with Wallis Warfield Simpson, a divorced American woman. Prime Minister Stanley Baldwin advised Edward to remove all cause for the rumours. Soon after that the king told Baldwin that he intended to marry Mrs. Simpson even if it meant he would have to give up the throne. The intended marriage was proposed, but the government, the Church of England, and many British people were opposed to accepting Mrs. Simpson as queen. On December 11, 1936, therefore, the king formally

爱德华八世

爱德华八世（1894-1972）在历史上留名是因为他是自愿放弃王位的唯一的一个英国国王。爱德华曾在皇家海军学院和牛津大学上学，第一次世界大战中在军队服役，战后到许多国家访问，致力于促进和平、外贸和英帝国的团结。他作风民主，富于魅力，善于交际，因而深得人心。在国内，他关心穷人和工人阶级的生活状况。

爱德华是温莎王朝国王乔治五世和玛丽王后的长子。父亲去世后，他于 1936 年 1 月 20 日继位为英国国王爱德华八世。

不久后，有传闻说爱德华与一个美国离婚女人辛普森夫人有恋爱关系。首相斯坦利·鲍德温劝说爱德华澄清所有谣传。其后不久，国王通知鲍德温，他打算娶辛普森夫人为妻，即使这意味着不得不放弃王位。这桩婚事提出后，政府、国教以及许多英国人都反对接受辛普森夫人为王后。于是，1936 年 12 月 11 日，国王正式宣布将王位让给弟弟约克公爵。约克公爵继位，成为乔治六世。爱德华接受了温莎公爵的称号，离开英国，于 1937 年 6 月在法国与辛普森夫人成婚。爱德华和妻子大部分时间住在美国

declared that he gave up the throne to his brother, the duke of York, who became King George VI. Edward received the title duke of Windsor and then left England and married Mrs. Simpson in France in June 1937. Edward and his wife lived mostly in the United States and France because the British government would not treat his wife as a royal duchess.

During World War II, Edward volunteered for a military position and was made a liaison officer. In 1940, George VI made him governor of the Bahamas, which were then a British colony. He served there until 1945. After the war, Edward lived mostly in France.

和法国，因为英国政府不愿将他的妻子当做公爵夫人给予礼遇。

第二次世界大战期间，爱德华志愿参军，被任命为联络官。1940年，乔治六世任命他为巴哈马总督。巴哈马当时是英国殖民地。他在那里任职到1945年。战后，他大部分时间住在法国。

爱德华与辛普森夫人

7. World War II

第二次世界大战

World War II was the biggest and most destructive war that has ever been fought. Some 1,700 million people, about three-fourths of the world's population, from 61 nations were involved in the war, which was fought on the land, on the sea, and in the skies of Europe, East and Southeast Asia, North Africa, and the

第二次世界大战是历史上规模最大、破坏力最强的战争之一。约占世界总人口四分之三、来自61个国家的17亿人卷入战争。战火遍及欧洲、东亚、东南亚、北非以及太平洋岛屿的海洋、陆地和天空。大约7000万人在军队服役，

islands of the Pacific Ocean. About 70 million people served in the armed forces and about 17 million of them lost their lives. The war caused more destruction, cost more resources, and probably had more far-reaching consequences than any other war in history.

The causes of World War II can be found in the political and economic problems left unsolved by World War I. First, many nations were dissatisfied with the treaties that ended the war. The defeated nations thought the treaties unfair, because they imposed too harsh punishment on them, forcing them to give up territory and resources and pay large sums of money. Some winning nations also disliked the treaties, because the treaties did not let them gain as much as they had expected. Secondly, World War I seriously damaged the economies of European countries. Both the winners and the losers came out of the war in poverty. Before their economies could return to the normal, an economic crisis, called the Great Depression, struck them in the early 1930s. Millions of people lost their jobs, and they were poorer and filled with despair. Democratic governments lost support and extreme political movements became stronger because they promised to end the economic problems.

As the political and economic problems became more serious, nationalism grew stronger. Many nationalists viewed foreigners and members of minority groups as inferior. They thought they had good reason to conquer other countries

其中大约有 1700 万人死于战场。战争造成的破坏、浪费的资源及其深远影响，是任何其他战争所无法相比的。

第二次世界大战的原因根植于第一次世界大战后未能解决的政治和经济问题。首先，许多国家对和约不满。战败国认为条约不够公正，对它们的惩罚过于苛刻，不但要它们割让土地和资源，还要它们支付大笔赔款。有些战胜国也不喜欢和约，因为条约并没有充分满足它们的期望。其次，第一次世界大战严重破坏了欧洲的经济。无论战胜国还是战败国，战后都成了穷国。在经济恢复正常之前，一场称为"大萧条"的经济危机在 30 年代初袭击了这些国家。数百万人失业，他们更加贫困，充满绝望情绪。民主政府失去支持，极端政治组织开始壮大，因为它们许诺解决经济问题。

政治和经济问题日趋严重，民族主义情绪随之高涨。许多民族主义者歧视外国人和少数民族。他们认为自己有理由征服其他国家，虐待少数民族。当一个民族受其他民族的欺侮时，民族主义会变得特别强烈。许多德国人对国家在一战中的失败和凡尔赛和约强加于他们的苛刻条件感到屈辱。他们希望看到自己的国家强大起来，能够主张自己的权利。在 30 年代，他们热心

and treat minorities badly. Nationalism grows especially when a people feel they are unfairly treated by other peoples. Many Germans felt humiliated by their country's defeat in World War I and the harsh treatment they received under the Treaty of Versailles. They wished to see their country powerful and able to insist on its rights. During the 1930s, they enthusiastically supported a violently nationalistic organization called the Nazi Party. The Nazi Party declared that Germany had a right to become strong again. Nationalism also gained strength in Italy and Japan.

Nationalistic leaders in several countries took advantage of the political and economic problems to seize power. During the 1920s and 1930s, dictatorships came to power in Italy, Germany, and Japan. In these countries one person or a small group of people had absolute power and used force to stop people from criticizing their rule. The dictators in Germany, Italy, and Japan all had ambition to conquer more territory.

While Germany and Italy took aggressive actions, Great Britain and France were hesitating, afraid of fighting another war so soon after World War I. This attitude actually encouraged the aggressors.

The aggressors soon formed an alliance. In 1936, Germany and Italy agreed to support one another's foreign policy. The alliance was known as the Rome-Berlin Axis. Japan joined the alliance in 1940, and it became the Rome-

支持一个叫做纳粹党的极端民族主义的组织。纳粹党宣称德国有权强大起来。民族主义势力在意大利和日本也增强了。

有几个国家的民族主义组织的领袖利用政治和经济问题来夺取政权。在20和30年代，意大利、德国和日本都建立了独裁政权。在这些国家里，个人或一小撮人掌握绝对权力，使用暴力禁止人们对他们的批评。德国、意大利和日本的独裁者都有扩张领土的野心。

当德国和意大利采取侵略行动时，英法两国犹豫不决，害怕一战刚刚结束，就打另一场战争。这一态度实际上鼓励了侵略者。

侵略者们不久便结成联盟。1936年,德国和意大利约定支持彼此的外交政策。联盟称为罗马-柏林轴心。日本于1940年加入联盟,联盟成为罗马-柏林-东京轴心。最终有六个国家加入轴心。战争期间,与轴心国作战的称为同盟国。到战争结束时,同盟国增加到50个国家。

1939年3月，德国撕毁慕尼黑协定，占领了捷克斯洛伐克的其余地区。9月1日，德国入侵波兰。一般认为这一事件是第二次世界大战的开端。英法两国看到绥靖政策已告失败，两天后向德国宣战。1940年4月，德国军队入侵丹麦和挪威。张伯伦于5月10日辞职，当天德国入侵了荷兰和比利

Berlin-Tokyo Axis. Six other nations eventually joined the Axis. During the war, countries fighting the Axis were called the Allies. The Allies included 50 nations by the end of the war.

In March 1939, Germany broke the Munich Agreement and seized the rest of Czechoslovakia. On September 1, Germany invaded Poland. This event is generally considered to be the start of World War II. Great Britain and France saw that appeasement would not work, and two days later they declared war on Germany. In April 1940, German troops invaded Denmark and Norway. Chamberlain resigned on May 10, the same day Germany invaded the Netherlands and Belgium. King George VI then asked Winston Churchill to become prime minister. Churchill told the British people he had nothing to offer them but "blood, toil, tears, and sweat" to win "victory at all costs".

When British and French forces rushed into Belgium to save the country, the Germans cut behind them to the south and reached the English Channel. By May 26, the British and French were pushed into a narrow area around the French seaport of Dunkerque on the English Channel. For a while it seemed as if the British and French troops would all be killed or taken prisoners. The British government at once sent a fleet to rescue the troops. The fleet included destroyers, yachts, ferries, fishing vessels, and motorboats. Under heavy bombardment, the vessels evacuated about 338,000 troops from

时。国王乔治六世要求温斯顿·丘吉尔出任首相。丘吉尔告诉英国人民，他所能奉献的没有别的，只有"热血、辛劳、眼泪和汗水"，要"不惜一切代价赢得胜利"。

当英法军队匆忙进入比利时援救这个国家时，德军在南面切断了他们的后路，一直推进到英吉利海峡。5 月 26 日，英法军队被迫后撤到濒临英吉利海峡的法国港口敦刻尔克周围的一块狭长地带。一时间，英法军队似乎即将被杀死或被俘。英国政府立即派出一支船队营救被困部队。这支船队包括驱逐舰、游艇、渡船、渔船和摩托艇。这些船只冒着猛烈的炮火，从 5 月 26 日至 6 月 4 日共营救大约338000 名士兵。敦刻尔克大营救保存了英军的大部分兵力。但是，所有了坦克和装备都丢下了。

法国陷落后，只剩下英国与希特勒对抗。美国运送大炮、飞机和物资援助英国，但没有加入战争。希特勒开始盘算征服英国。但在入侵英国之前，德国必须先打垮英国皇家空军。不列颠战役于 1940 年 7 月打响。当年德国飞机不断轰炸英国城市，炸死数千人，但英国人民更坚定了打赢战争的决心。皇家空军在三个月内击落 2000 架敌机，直至希特勒放弃从空中击败英国的计划。

德国进攻法国时，意大利加入

May 26 to June 4. The evacuation of Dunkerque saved most of Britain's army. But the army left behind all its tanks and equipment.

After the fall of France, Great Britain stood alone against Hitler. The United States sent guns, planes and supplies to help the British, but was not in the war. Now Hitler wanted to conquer Great Britain. Before the Germans could invade England, however, they had to defeat Britain's Royal Air Force. The Battle of Britain began in July 1940. All through that year German planes bombed the cities of England, killing thousands of people, but the British people became more determined than ever to win the war. The Royal Air Force shot down 2,000 German planes in three months, until Hitler had to give up his attempts to defeat Britain from the air.

When Germany attacked France, Italy entered the war on Germany's side. In August 1940 Italian army went to North Africa to invade British Somaliland (now northern Somalia) and Egypt. The Axis wanted to control Egypt so as to cut Britain off from oil fields in the Middle East and from the Suez Canal. Britain struck back at the Italians in December 1940, sweeping them out of Egypt. Early in 1941, Hitler sent tank units led by General Erwin Rommel to help the Italians in northern Africa. During the spring, Rommel recaptured the territory the Italians had lost and drove into Egypt

皇家空军喷火式战斗机

德方作战。1940 年 8 月，意大利军队进入北非，入侵英属索马里兰（即现在的索马里）和埃及。轴心国企图控制埃及以切断英国与中东油田和苏伊士运河的联系。1940 年 12 月英军向意军发起反攻，将意军逐出埃及。1941 年初，希特勒派遣隆美尔将军率领的坦克部队援助北非的意大利军。当年春天，隆美尔夺回意大利军的失地，然后开入埃及，直抵离运河不远的阿拉曼。但他的军队被蒙哥马利将军率领的英军击败。阿拉曼战役是北非战争的一个转折点。

1941 年 6 月 22 日，德军突然入侵苏联，尽管事先与苏联签署了友好条约。德国起初战事进展顺利。他们俘获、击毙了数十万苏军部队，逼近莫斯科和列宁格勒。此时俄国的严冬开始了，德军的推进受阻，苏军收复了一些失地。

二战于 1939 年在欧洲爆发时，美国保持中立。是日本最终使

until he reached El Alamein, not far away from the Suez Canal. But his troops were defeated by the British army under General Bernard Law Montgomery. The Battle of El Alamein proved to be the turning point of the war in North Africa.

On June 22, 1941, the Germans suddenly invaded the Soviet Union, even though they had made a treaty of friendship with that country. At first the Germans did very well. They captured and killed hundreds of thousands of Soviet troops, and came very close to Moscow and Leningrad. Then the extremely cold Russian winter began, the German advance was stopped, and the Russians were able to win back some of the territory they had lost.

After World War II began in Europe in 1939, the United States had remained neutral. It was Japan that finally brought the United States into World War II. The United States opposed Japan's expansion in Southeast Asia. The Japanese military leaders believed that only the United States Navy had the power to check Japan's expansion. They decided to damage the U.S. Pacific Fleet with one forceful blow. On December 7, 1941, Japanese planes attacked without warning United States military bases at Pearl Harbor in Hawaii and damaged much of the Pacific Fleet and destroyed many planes.

The United States, Canada, and Great Britain declared war on Japan on

美国卷入大战。美国反对日本在东南亚的扩张。日本军队统帅们认为只有美国海军有力量阻止日本的扩张。他们决定出重拳一举摧毁美国的太平洋舰队。1941 年 12 月 7 日，日本飞机偷袭了夏威夷的珍珠港美军基地，重创了太平洋舰队，摧毁了许多飞机。

美国、加拿大和英国于 1941 年 12 月 8 日向日本宣战。次日，中国向轴心国宣战。德国和意大利于 12 月 11 日向美国宣战。第二次世界大战演变成一场全球冲突。

1942 年，德国再次开始进攻俄国。他们向俄国纵深推进，远达斯大林格勒（现在的伏尔加格勒）。在北非，德军已逼近苏伊士运河时才受阻。在大西洋，德国潜艇击沉了大量同盟国的船只，补给缺乏的英国几乎用光了战争物资和粮食。

这时战局发生了转变。在斯大林格勒，俄国军队阻止了德军的推

罗斯福向日本宣战

December 8, 1941. The next day, China declared war on the Axis. Germany and Italy declared war on the United States on December 11. World War II had become a global conflict.

In 1942, the Germans started to advance again in Russia. They got as far as Stalingrad (now Volgograd). In North Africa the German forces went very close to the Suez Canal before they were stopped. In the Atlantic Ocean, German submarines sank so many Allied ships that the British nearly ran out of war supplies and food.

蒙哥马利与参谋们

Then the tide turned. At Stalingrad the Russians stopped the German army and started a counterattack in mid-November 1942, and in February 1943, the last German troops in Stalingrad surrendered. The Battle of Stalingrad marked a turning point in World War II. It halted Germany's eastward advance. About 300,000 German troops were killed or captured.

In North Africa Montgomery struck the Axis forces at El Alamein in October 1942. He won a great victory and began driving the German and Italian forces into Tunisia. Soon after that the Allies invaded French colonies in northern Africa. Vichy French forces in northern Africa fought back for a few days and then joined the Allied side. After a battle in Tunisia the last Axis forces in northern Africa surrendered in May 1943. By clearing the Axis forces from northern Africa, the Allies obtained bases from which to invade southern Europe.

进, 并于 1942 年 11 月中旬发起反攻。1943 年 2 月, 斯大林格勒的最后一支德军投降。斯大林格勒战役是二战转折的标志。它阻止了德国在东线的攻势。大约 30 万德军战死或被俘。

在北非, 蒙哥马利于 1942 年 10 月在阿拉曼向轴心国发起进攻。他取得了重大胜利, 开始将德意军队驱逐到突尼斯。不久后, 盟军攻入北非的法国殖民地。维希政府在北非的法国军队抵抗数日后, 加入盟军一方。北非的轴心国残余部队在突尼斯打过一仗后, 于 1943 年 5 月投降。肃清了北非的轴心国军队后, 盟军获得了进攻南欧的立足点。

7 月, 盟军在西西里岛登陆。经过一个月的激战, 夺取了该岛。9 月, 美英军队攻入意大利。意大

In July, Allied forces landed on the island of Sicily. After a month's bitter fighting they captured it. In September, the Americans and British invaded Italy. Italy surrendered immediately but the Germans in Italy continued to fight until they surrendered in May 1945.

Meanwhile thousands of American troops were arriving in England, and American and British planes began bombing German cities and factories. The Russians were winning back all the territories they had lost to Germany.

On June 6, 1944 (known as D-Day), about 2,700 ships carried 176,000 Allied troops crossed the English Channel. They landed on the coast of Normandy in northern France. Other soldiers were dropped by parachute behind German lines to capture bridges and railroad tracks to prevent the Germans from bringing fresh troops to stop the landing. D-Day took the Germans by surprise. But they fought back fiercely. After much hard fighting the Allies cleared the Germans out of most of northwestern France during August, and advanced eastward toward Paris. The French people in Paris rose up against the occupying German forces. American and Free French forces liberated Paris on August 25.

The Russians launched a counterattack after their victory in the Battle of Stalingrad. Their troops moved slowly forward during the summer and autumn

利立即投降，但意大利的德军则继续作战，直至 1945 年 5 月才投降。

同时，成千上万的美军抵达英国，美英两国的飞机开始轰炸德国的城市和工厂。俄国人正在收复所有被德国占领的领土。

1944 年 6 月 6 日（称为 D 日），大约 2700 艘船载着盟军 176000 人渡过英吉利海峡。他们在法国北部的诺曼底海岸登陆。还有一些士兵空降到敌军战线后方占领桥梁和铁路，以防止德国运送后续部队阻止盟军登陆。D 日行动使德国人措手不及。但他们展开了凶猛的反击。一番艰苦的战斗之后盟军在 8 月清除了法国西北部所有的德国人，然后向东进军巴黎。巴黎人民起义反抗德国占领军。美军和

诺曼底登陆

of 1943, and finally drove the Germans out of the Soviet Union by August 1944. In September, Soviet troops forced Bulgaria, Romania and Finland to surrender. In October the Russians and the forces of Tito liberated Belgrade. The Germans withdrew from the Balkans.

In 1944, Germany began to use missiles called V-1 and V-2 against Britain. The missiles caused great damage in London and other English towns. But fortunately the Germans did not have many of these new weapons and they were too late to produce more of them.

At the beginning of 1945, the Russians advanced through Poland, took Czechoslovakia, Budapest, the capital of Hungary, and Vienna, the capital of Austria. Soviet troops then entered eastern Germany.

After liberating the whole France and Belgium, the allied forces cleared the Germans out of the Netherlands and moved into northern Germany. They crossed the Rhine River into the heart of Germany in March 1945, and the next month they met on the Elbe River the Russian Army, which was coming from the other direction. By April 25, 1945, Soviet troops had surrounded Berlin and as they took the city, Hitler killed himself. On May 8, 1945, a day called V-E Day, or Victory in Europe Day, the German government signed a statement of unconditional surrender. World War II had ended in Europe.

自由法国军队于 8 月 25 日解放巴黎。

在斯大林格勒战役中取得胜利后，俄国人发起反攻。他们的军队在 1943 年夏季和秋季缓慢向前推进，到 1944 年 8 月终于将德国人逐出苏联领土。9 月，苏军迫使保加利亚、罗马尼亚和芬兰投降。10 月，苏军和铁托的军队解放了贝尔格莱德。德军退出巴尔干。

1944 年，德国开始使用 V-1 和 V-2 导弹袭击英国。导弹在伦敦和其他城市造成巨大破坏。所幸德国人的新式武器数量不多，而且已来不及大量生产了。

1945 年初，俄国人已穿越波兰，占领捷克斯洛伐克、匈牙利首都布达佩斯、奥地利首都维也纳。苏军然后进入德国东部。

盟军解放整个法国和比利时后，扫除了荷兰的德军，然后突入德国北部。他们渡过莱茵河，于 1945 年 3 月进入德国中部地区。4 月，他们在易北河上与自东而来的俄军会师。1945 年 4 月 25 日，苏军包围柏林，在夺取这座城市时，希特勒自杀。1945 年 5 月 8 日，德国政府签署无条件投降声明。这一天被称为 V-E 日，即欧洲胜利日。第二次世界大战在欧洲到此结束。

8. Winston Churchill

Sir Winston Churchill (1874-1965) is generally regarded as the greatest British leader of the 20th century and one of the greatest statesmen in world history. By his courage, decisiveness and political experience, he led his country through World War II, one of the hardest struggles in British history. Churchill was also known for his eloquent speeches, his works on British history and politics, and even his paintings. As a writer he showed an excellent command of the English language. In 1953, he won the Nobel Prize for literature.

Churchill's full name was Winston Leonard Spencer Churchill. He was a descendent of John Churchill, the first duke of Marlborough, one of England's greatest military commanders in the 17th century. At the age of 12, Winston went to Harrow School, a famous school for boys. But he was the worst student in his class. He stammered when he talked, and did poorly in his schoolwork. His classmates did not like him because he was very stubborn. Later, however, he began to love the English language very much.

His father noticed that Winston would spend many hours playing with toy soldiers. He thought it might be better for the boy who is not clever to become a soldier. In 1893, at the age of 18, Winston entered the Royal Military College at Sandhurst. He had failed the entrance exami-

温斯顿·丘吉尔

温斯顿·丘吉尔（1874-1965）被普遍认为是 20 世纪英国最伟大的领袖人物，世界历史上最伟大的政治家之一。由于他的勇气、果断及政治经验，他领导英国经受住了英国历史上最困难的时期，即第二次世界大战。丘吉尔还以他雄辩的演说，他的英国历史和政治著作，乃至他的绘画著称于世。作为作家，他在英语的运用上表现出突出的才能。1953 年，他获得诺贝尔文学奖。

他的全名是温斯顿·利奥纳德·斯宾塞·丘吉尔。他是 17 世纪最伟大的军事统帅之一约翰·丘吉尔，马尔伯勒公爵第一的后裔。温斯顿 12 岁在哈罗学校学习，这是一所为男童开办的著名公学。但他是班里最差的学生。他说话时口吃，学习成绩不佳。同班同学不喜欢他，因为他脾气倔强。然而，他后来却开始喜欢上了英语。

他父亲注意到，他常花费几个小时的时间摆弄玩具士兵。他父亲认为这个孩子不够聪明，也许最好去当兵。1893 年，温斯顿 18 岁时考进桑德赫斯特的皇家军事学院。此前他已经考过两次试，但均未能通过。但是他不久成了班里最

nations twice before passing them. But he soon became one of the top students in his class. In 1895, Churchill was appointed a second lieutenant in the 4th Hussars, a proud cavalry regiment.

When he was 21, Churchill was on leave from the army, and went as a reporter with the Spanish to Cuba where the people had revolted against their Spanish rulers. In Cuba he wrote colorful articles on the revolt for a London newspaper. After that he went to northwestern India and reported battles fought between the British and the natives. While writing Churchill took part in bloody fighting. In 1898, when a British force in Egypt was to invade the Sudan, Churchill went there as a newspaper reporter. He took part in the last great cavalry charge of the British army. Then Churchill returned to England and wrote a book about the battle in the Sudan.

When the Boer War in South Africa broke out between the Boers (Dutch settlers) and the British in October 1899 Churchill was hired by a London newspaper to report the war. Soon after he arrived in South Africa, he was captured by the Boers and imprisoned. He climbed over the prison wall one night, and slipped by the sentries and then traveling on freight trains, he went across 480 kilometers of enemy territory to safety. He became a famous hero overnight. He then joined the war and at the same time wrote about it.

好的学生之一。1895 年，丘吉尔在一个荣誉骑兵团，即第四轻骑兵团任少尉。

21 岁时，丘吉尔请假离开军队，以新闻记者的身份与西班牙人一起去古巴，因为当地人民起义反对西班牙的统治者。在古巴，他为伦敦报纸写了有关起义的有趣的报道。接着，他去了印度西北部，报道英国人和土著的战斗。在写作的同时，丘吉尔还参加了血腥的激战。1898 年，埃及的英军即将入侵苏丹，丘吉尔以报社记者的身份前往非洲。他参加了英军的最后一次骑兵进攻。返回英国后，他写了一部关于苏丹战斗的书。

青年时代的丘吉尔

After he returned to London in the summer of 1900, his newspaper articles were reprinted in two books.

After the Boer War, Churchill decided to enter politics. He was elected to Parliament as a member of the Conservative party. He soon began to criticize many Conservative policies openly and sharply. In 1904, Churchill broke with his party completely. In 1906, he changed parties and became a Liberal. During the next few years Churchill was given three important government positions. He was first appointed undersecretary of state for the colonies in 1906, then president of the Board of Trade in 1908, his first cabinet post. In 1910 he became home secretary, responsible for police and the prison system. He held this post until 1911, making a series of liberal reforms of Britain's prison system.

Churchill got married in 1908. His wife Clementine Hozier was the daughter of a retired army officer. Years later, Churchill wrote: "My most brilliant achievement was my ability to persuade my wife to marry me." They had five children, one of whom died as a young child. Churchill was a devoted father to his children.

In 1911, Prime Minister Herbert H. Asquith appointed Churchill first lord of the admiralty. Churchill threw himself into this task, developing heavier guns, faster battleships, and naval aviation. When Britain entered World War I in 1914, the fleet was ready.

In 1915, Churchill urged an attack on the Dardanelles Strait controlled by Turkey, to open

1899 年 10 月南非的布尔战争爆发，丘吉尔受雇于一家伦敦报社报道战争。他到达南非后不久便被布尔人俘获，关押起来。一天夜里，他爬过监狱的围墙，躲过站岗的哨兵，搭乘铁路货车穿过 480 公里敌占区，回到安全地区。他一夜之间成为英雄。然后，他加入战斗，同时写战争报道。1900 年夏天，他返回伦敦，他将战地报道编成两本书出版。

布尔战争后，丘吉尔决定从政。他当选保守党议员，但不久便开始公开而尖锐地抨击保守党的许多政策。1904 年，他脱离保守党，两年后，他转而加入自由党。此后几年，丘吉尔受任政府的三个重要职务。1906 年，他出任殖民副大臣，1908 年任商务大臣，首次进入内阁。1910~1911 年间任内政大臣，负责警察和监狱系统，对英国的监狱做了多项自由主义的改革。

丘吉尔于 1908 年结婚。他的妻子克莱门婷·霍齐尔是一个退役军官的女儿。多年后，丘吉尔写道：“我最辉煌的成就是能够说服妻子嫁给我。”他们有 5 个孩子，一个夭折。丘吉尔是个关爱孩子的父亲。

1911 年，阿斯奎斯首相任命丘吉尔为海军大臣。丘吉尔将全部精力投入工作，研制生产了重型大

a route to the Black Sea and send military supplies to the Russian armies. But this attack turned out to be a disaster, and the Allies suffered great losses. Churchill was blamed. He resigned from the admiralty. For a few months he was in low spirits. He began to paint, a hobby that brought him pleasure for the rest of his life. Later in the same year Churchill joined the British army and fought for a while in France.

When David Lloyd George became prime minister in December 1916, he appointed Churchill minister of munitions. Under Churchill's direction Britain began to produce tanks in large numbers.

After World War I ended in 1918, Churchill was appointed secretary of war and then colonial secretary. However, in 1922, when the Conservatives returned to power, he lost his election to the House of Commons. He then tried three times to enter the House of Commons again, but was unsuccessful.

Churchill finally won election in 1924, after he joined the Conservative Party again. He was later named chancellor of the exchequer under Prime Minister Stanley Baldwin. He held the office for the next five years. The Conservatives lost the 1929 election, and Churchill left office. He did not hold a Cabinet position again until 1939. He kept his seat in Parliament throughout this period.

During the years between World Wars I and II, Churchill spent much of his spare time painting and writing. He showed his talent for paint-

炮，高速战舰以及海军军用飞机。1914 年，在英国参加第一次世界大战时，舰队已做好准备。

1915 年，丘吉尔力主攻打土耳其控制的达达尼尔海峡，打开通往黑海的航道，向俄国军队运送军用物资。但这次进攻以失败告终，协约国损失惨重。丘吉尔为此受到指责。他辞去海军职务。几个月内，他情绪低落。他开始绘画，将这种给他带来快乐的爱好保持终生。当年晚些时候，丘吉尔加入英军，有一段时间在法国参加战斗。

劳合·乔治于 1916 年出任首相，任命丘吉尔为军需部长。在丘吉尔的指导下，英国开始大量生产坦克。

第一次世界大战于 1918 年结束后，丘吉尔先后被任命为国防大臣和殖民大臣。1922 年，保守党重新执政后，他未能当选议员。他曾三次试图进入下院，但没有成功。

丘吉尔重新加入保守党后，终于在 1924 年选入议会。不久后出任鲍德温内阁的财政大臣，任职 5 年。保守党在 1929 年的选举中失利，丘吉尔离职。直到 1939 年他才再次获得内阁职务。但他在这一时期，一直保有议会席位。

在一战与二战之间，丘吉尔的业余时间大部分用于绘画和写作。他显示出绘画才能，而且乐于绘

ing and took pleasure from it, but considered writing more important. He wrote *World Crisis*, a record of the history of World War I, and *Marlborough, His Life and Times*, a study of his ancestor.

After 1932, Churchill tried to call the attention of his nation and the world to the danger of Nazi Germany. But few people listened to him. His warnings made him more and more unpopular. Some people even called him a warmonger.

In 1938, British Prime Minister Neville Chamberlain signed the Munich Agreement, which allowed Hitler to take part of Czechoslovakia. Churchill strongly criticized Chamberlain's policies to avoid war with Germany by giving in to Hitler. When Hitler broke his promise and began to invade Poland in 1939, Great Britain and France had to declare war on Germany. Chamberlain at once named Churchill first lord of the admiralty. In May 1940, Chamberlain was forced to resign and Churchill, at the age of 66, became prime minister of Great Britain. Churchill told the British people he had nothing to offer them but "blood, toil, tears and sweat" to win "victory at all costs".

Britain was in great danger at the time. The Germans had already captured Poland, Denmark, and Norway. In May, they overran Luxembourg and invaded Belgium, the Netherlands, and France. France fell

丘吉尔爵士

画，但认为写作更为重要。他的著作有《世界危机》，是一战的历史记录；《马尔伯勒的生平与时代》，是对他的祖先的一部研究著作。

1932 年以后，丘吉尔试图使英国和世界关注纳粹德国的危险。但很少有人听从他的意见。他的警告使他越来越不得人心。有些人甚至称他为战争贩子。

1938 年，英国首相张伯伦签署慕尼黑协定，允许希特勒侵占捷克斯洛伐克的部分地区。丘吉尔猛烈抨击张伯伦通过让步以防止与德国交战的政策。当希特勒撕毁协定，于 1939 年入侵波兰时，英法两国不得不向德国宣战。张伯伦立即任命丘吉尔为海军大臣。1940 年 5 月，张伯伦被迫辞职，温斯顿·丘吉尔继任英国首相，时年 66 岁。丘吉尔告诉英国人民，他所能奉献的没有别的，只有"热血、辛劳、眼泪和汗水"，要"不惜一切代价赢得胜利"。

英国当时处于巨大危险中。德国人已占领了波兰、丹麦和挪威。5 月，他们踏过卢森堡，侵入比利时、荷兰和法国。法国于 6 月陷落，英法军队被驱赶到濒临英吉利海峡的法国港口

in June when the Allied army was driven to a narrow area around the French seaport of Dunkerque and had to retreat across the Channel to England. Churchill then showed himself to be a great and inspiring leader. He made many stirring speeches. He told his people that even though all of Europe might fall, "... we shall not flag or fail. We shall go on to the end ... we shall fight in the seas and oceans ... we shall fight on the beaches, we shall fight on the landing-grounds, we shall fight in the fields and in the streets, we shall fight in the hills; we shall never surrender..."

After the fall of France, Britain stood alone. The German air force began to bomb British ports and cities. When the Battle of Britain began, the Royal Air Force suffered heavy losses, but managed to turn back the powerful German air force. During the German bombing raids on London, Churchill defied air-raid alarms and went into the streets as the bombs fell. He inspected defenses and visited victims of the air raids. He inspired his people with powerful speeches. Everywhere he went he held up two fingers in a "V for victory" gesture. To the people of the Allied nations, this gesture became an inspiring symbol of faith in their final victory.

In 1941 Germany invaded the Soviet Union, and although Churchill had always opposed the Communist rule, he offered to help the Communist country. He declared in speech, "Any man or state who fights on against Nazidom will have our aid. Any man or state who marches with

敦刻尔克周围的一块狭长地带,必须渡过英吉利海峡撤回英国。此时丘吉尔表现出其伟大领袖和鼓动家的才能。他多次发表激动人心的演说。他对同胞们说,即使整个欧洲都落入敌手,"我们也不会气馁,不会屈服。我们将坚持到底……我们要在海洋上作战……我们要在滩头上作战,在登陆地点作战,我们将在田野里、街巷中和山区作战;我们永不投降……"

法国陷落后,英国陷于孤立。德国空军开始轰炸英国的港口和城市。不列颠战役开始时,皇家空军损失惨重,但成功击退了强大的德国空军。在德国空袭伦敦期间,丘吉尔不顾空袭警报,在轰炸时走上街头,视察防御工事,抚慰遭到空袭的百姓。他用有力的讲话来鼓舞人民。每到一处,他都举起两根手指做"V"字手势,以表达必胜的决心。对于盟国人民,这一手势成为必胜信念的象征。

1941年,德国入侵苏联,虽然丘吉尔一贯反对共产主义统治,他仍然提出要援助这个共产党国家。他在演讲里宣告,"任何坚持与纳粹政权作战的人或国家都将得到我们的援助。任何与希特勒并肩同行的人或国家都是我们的仇敌……这就是我们的政策,我们的宣言。因而,我们将尽一切可能帮助俄国和俄国人民。"

Hitler is our foe...That is our policy and that is our declaration. It follows therefore that we shall give whatever help we can to Russia and the Russian people."

Churchill also influenced the Americans to help the British. In August 1941 President Franklin D. Roosevelt met Churchill aboard ship off the coast of Newfoundland. They drew up the Atlantic Charter, declaring the United States and Britain would support each other. Churchill and Roosevelt always remained friendly to each other, though they had some different points of view. Churchill felt proud of the British Empire, but Roosevelt was suspicious of British colonial policies. Churchill distrusted the Soviet Union, but Roosevelt did not.

During World War II, Churchill attended most of the famous international conferences. In August 1942, Churchill went to Moscow to meet with Joseph Stalin. In January 1943, Churchill and Roosevelt met in Casablanca, Morocco, and announced that the Allies would accept only unconditional surrender from Germany, Italy, and Japan. In November of the same year Churchill, Stalin, and Roosevelt had their first meeting in Teheran, Iran. The Big Three, as they were called, decided the British-American would

丘吉尔也影响了美国人，使他们帮助英国。1941 年 8 月，罗斯福总统在纽芬兰附近海面上的一艘军舰上会见了丘吉尔。他们制定了《大西洋宪章》，宣布美国和英国将相互支持。丘吉尔和罗斯福一直保持友好关系，虽然两人的某些观点不同。丘吉尔为英帝国感到自豪，而罗斯福则怀疑英国的殖民政策是否正当。丘吉尔不信任苏联，罗斯福则不然。

二战中，丘吉尔参加了大多数著名的国际会议。1942 年 8 月，丘吉尔前往莫斯科会见了斯大林。1943 年 1 月，丘吉尔和罗斯福在摩洛哥的卡萨布兰卡会晤，宣布盟国只接受德国、意大利和日本的无条件投降。同年 11 月，丘吉尔、斯大林和罗斯福首次聚会于伊朗的德黑兰。三巨头决定次年春天英美

三巨头在雅尔塔

invade France the following spring. In February 1945, when the end of the war in Europe was in sight, the Big Three met in Yalta in the Soviet Union. They made plans to occupy defeated Germany. Churchill distrusted Stalin. He feared the Soviet Union might keep the territories in eastern Europe that its troops occupied.

Germany surrendered on May 7, 1945, and in July, Churchill met with Truman (Roosevelt had died) and Stalin in Potsdam, Germany, to discuss how to rule Germany. But Churchill lost his post as prime minister in the middle of meeting. An election had been held in Britain. The Labour Party gained a majority in Parliament because it promised social and economic reforms that the Conservatives had refused to make. Besides, many people blamed the Conservatives for having failed to get prepared earlier for World War II. Clement R. Attlee succeeded Churchill as prime minister. Churchill was deeply disappointed. He had been very popular as a leader during the war, and had not expected to be defeated.

After the Labour victory, Churchill took his place as leader of the opposition in the House of Commons. He urged Parliament to plan for national defense, and warned the western world against the dangers of the growing Communist threat. Many people in the United States and Britain considered him a warmonger. Meanwhile he began to write memoirs, *The Second World War*.

联军将入侵法国。1945 年 2 月，欧战结束在望，三巨头在苏联的雅尔塔会晤，制订占领德国的计划。丘吉尔不信任斯大林。他担心苏联会不肯撤出其军队占领的东欧国家的领土。

1945 年 5 月 7 日，德国投降。7 月，在德国的波茨坦，丘吉尔会晤杜鲁门（罗斯福已去世）和斯大林，讨论如何统治德国。但在会议期间，丘吉尔失去首相职位。英国举行了选举，工党获得议会多数，因为工党许诺进行社会和经济改革，而保守党却不肯。另外，许多人指责保守党未能提前为二战做准备。艾德礼接替丘吉尔为首相。丘吉尔大失所望。作为战时领导人，他声望很高，没想到会竞选失利。

工党获胜后，丘吉尔担任议会反对党领袖。他督促议会制定国防计划，警告西方世界对日益增长的共产主义威胁提高警惕。美国和英国的许多人认为他是战争贩子。此时，他开始撰写回忆录《第二次世界大战》。

1951 年，保守党赢得选举，丘吉尔再次出任首相。他极力促进英美的团结，以减少核战争的危险。1953 年，女王伊丽莎白二世授予他嘉德勋位，英国的最高骑士勋位。此后，他被称为温斯顿·丘吉尔勋爵。同年，他由于自己的历

In 1951 the Conservative Party won the elections and Churchill again became prime minister. He worked hard to encourage unity of Britain and America and reduce the danger of nuclear war. In 1953 Queen Elizabeth II made him a knight of the Order of the Garter, Britain's highest order of knighthood, and he became Sir Winston Churchill. In the same year he won the Nobel Prize for literature for his historical and biographical works and for his oratory. In April 1955 he resigned as prime minister but remained a member of the House of Commons. In his retirement, Churchill worked on completing *A History of the English-Speaking Peoples*, a work begun in the late 1930s but postponed during World War II. He devoted much of his leisure in his later years to his favorite pastime of painting, ultimately producing more than 500 canvases. In 1963 the U.S. Congress made Churchill an honorary citizen of the United States.

Churchill died peacefully at his town house in London, two months after his 90th birthday.

史和传记著作及演讲获得诺贝尔文学奖。1955年4月，他辞去首相职，但保留了议会下院的席位。退休后，丘吉尔继续完成著作《英语民族历史》。这部著作开始于30年代末，但由于二战而搁置。他晚年的闲暇用于绘画，自己喜爱的消遣。他的油画总计达500幅。1963年美国国会授予丘吉尔美国荣誉公民的称号。

丘吉尔在度过90岁寿辰后两个月，在伦敦的住宅中安然长逝。

题外话

- 在第二次世界大战中，丘吉尔的很多决策都很明智而果断。当法国显然无法抵御德国的强大攻势时，法国曾要求丘吉尔派遣战斗机帮助法国，但丘吉尔断定英国的战斗机不足以拯救法国的败局。他做出了一个困难然而明智的决定，拒绝了法国的请求，将有限的空军力量用于英国本土的防御，结果使英国坚持下来，成为西欧抗德的最后一个堡垒。1940年6月，丘吉尔前往法国，建议英法组成联合政府，组建统一的军事力量。但此建议被法国所拒绝。当月法国投降德国。丘吉尔预见到法国的海军力量有可能被轴心国所利用，便要求法国海军并入英国舰队，或解散法国海军。法国海军拒绝了这项建议，丘吉尔当机立断，在英国所能控制的港口击沉或破坏法国舰只，或将它们俘获，以增强英国海军。在英国面临德国入侵的威胁时，丘吉尔竟将英国唯一装备齐全的装甲师派往埃及，保卫有战略意义的苏伊士运河。他认为，如果英国不能在海上和空中阻止德国的入侵，一个装甲师的力量挽救不了英国。装甲师只有在埃及才能派上用场。事实也证实了他的决策的正确性。

- 在三巨头会见的照片中，罗斯福（罗斯福去世后则是杜鲁门）居中，将丘吉尔与斯大林隔开。三人的位置反映了三人之间的关系。丘吉尔仇视共产党政权，对斯大林霸占东欧的野心深怀疑虑。罗斯福则较温和，对斯大林的信任多于仇视。

9. Bertrand Russell

Bertrand Russell (1872-1970) was one of the greatest philosophers of the 20th century. He has also been regarded as the most important logician since the ancient Greek philosopher Aristotle.

Russell's full name was Bertrand Arthur William Russell. He was a member of an old and noble family. In 1931, on the death of his older brother, he inherited the family title and became Earl Russell.

Russell was educated at Trinity College, University of Cambridge. After graduation in 1894, he was made a fellow of Trinity College. He studied logical and mathematical questions, and made his most important contributions in formal logic and the theory of knowledge. Russell collaborated for eight years with the British philosopher and mathematician Alfred North Whitehead to produce the monumental work *Principia Mathematica*. It became a masterpiece of rational thought.

However, Russell's influence was not limited to these fields. He developed a prose style of extraordinary clarity, wit, and passion. He received the 1950 Nobel Prize for literature.

From an early age Russell developed a strong sense of social consciousness. Later in his life, he became an influential and controversial figure on social, political, and educational

伯特兰·罗素

伯特兰·罗素 (1872-1970) 是 20 世纪最伟大的哲学家之一。他也被视为自古希腊哲学家亚里士多德以来最重要的逻辑学家。

罗素的全名是伯特兰·亚瑟·威廉·罗素。他是一个古老贵族家庭的后裔。1931 年，他的长兄死后，他继承了家族的爵位，成为罗素伯爵。

罗素在剑桥大学三一学院受教育。1894 年毕业后，他受聘为三一学院研究员。他研究逻辑和数学问题，在形式逻辑和知识论领域做出重大贡献。罗素与英国哲学家兼数学家怀特海合作 8 年，写出划时代巨著《数学纲要》。这部著作是理性思维的杰作。

然而，罗素的影响并不仅仅限于哲学和数学领域。他的写作风格极其明晰，机智，而又充满激情。他获得了 1950 年的诺贝尔文学奖。

罗素少年时所受的教育使他毕生关注社会问题。后来他成为在社会、政治与教育问题上有重大影响，而又引起争议的人物。他是个直言不讳的和平主义者，对性、婚姻和教育方法鼓吹极端自由主义的态度。他在第一次世界大战中批评交战双方，因此被捕入狱，并被解

issues. He was an outspoken pacifist and advocated extremely liberal attitudes toward sex, marriage, and methods of education. He criticized both sides in World War I, and for this he was imprisoned and deprived of his teaching post at Cambridge. After the war he visited the Soviet Union, and in a book he wrote after the visit he expressed his disappointment with the form of socialism practiced there. He felt that the methods used to achieve a Communist system were intolerable and that the results obtained were not worth the price paid. Russell taught at Beijing University in China during 1921 and 1922. In his work *The Problem of China*, he praised Chinese culture, and pointed out both the virtues and defects of the Chinese people. Later in the United States, however, he was barred from teaching at the College of the City of New York by the state supreme court because he attacked religion in such works as *What I Believe* and expressed his idea of sexual freedom in *Manners and Morals*.

During World War II, Russell abandoned pacifism to support the Allied cause, but he strongly opposed nuclear weapons. In 1949 he was awarded the Order of Merit by King George VI, and in the following year he received the 1950 Nobel Prize for Literature. He led a move-

除在剑桥大学的教职。战后他访问了苏联，在访问后写的一本书里对苏联搞的社会主义表示失望。他觉得为实现共产主义目标所采取的手段令人难以容忍，所取得的成就也得不偿失。1921 年和 1922 年，罗素在中国的北京大学讲学，在其后发表的《中国问题》一书中，他赞扬了中国文化，同时指出中国人的优缺点。但后来在美国讲学期间，他被纽约州立法院禁止在纽约市大学讲学，因为他在《我的信仰》等著作中攻击宗教，在《风俗与道德》一书中宣扬性自由。

伯特兰·罗素

ment in the late 1950s advocating unilateral nuclear disarmament by Britain, and at the age of 89 he was imprisoned after an antinuclear demonstration.

Russell's other important works include *A History of Western Philosophy, German Social Democracy, Roads to Freedom, Why I Am Not a Christian, Marriage and Morals*, and his autobiography.

第二次世界大战期间，罗素放弃了和平主义，支持盟国的行动，强烈反对核武器。1949 年国王乔治六世授予他荣誉勋章，次年，他获得 1950 年诺贝尔文学奖。50 年代，他鼓吹英国的单边核裁军，在 89 岁高龄由于反核示威而被监禁。

罗素的其他重要著作有《西方哲学史》、《德国社会民主》、《通向自由之路》、《我为什么不是基督徒》、《婚姻与道德》以及他的自传等。

🔘 题外话

罗素是 20 世纪知识分子中最伟大的一个。读一读他那本厚厚的自传，会发现他所记述的，主要不是他的哲学思想，而是他的社会活动。罗素有点像古代中国那些悲天悯人、经世致用、积极干政的在野儒生。幸运的是，他生活在 20 世纪的英国，基本上可以合法而安全地干政，不必最终堕落为奴才，或悲壮地走向刑场。罗素最突出的特点是强烈的责任感和极大的道德勇气。在世界充满民族仇恨时，他公然主张和平主义，反对民族主义和爱国主义；当西方的政客、军人、传教士和商人们对中国文化和中国人充满了偏见时，他挺身而出，为中国文化和中国人民辩护；在维多利亚式的虔诚和贞洁的观念仍主宰英国时，他坦诚表达自己对宗教的不可知论观点，并鼓吹性自由；当冷战正酣，军备竞赛达到高潮时，他却公开主张单方面核裁军。患软骨病的人实在应该从他的作品和人格中汲取钙质。

10. Withdrawal from the Empire

脱身英帝国

In the 20th century, Britain found it more and more costly and difficult to maintain its vast empire. In 1931 Britain created the Commonwealth of Nations, a loose organization of nations with historic ties to Britain. The colonies of Canada, Australia, New Zealand, and South

在 20 世纪，英国发现维持其庞大的帝国代价越来越高昂，难度也越来越大。1931 年英国建立英联邦，这是一个历史上与英国关系密切的国家的松散组织。加拿大、澳大利亚、新西兰和南非成为英联

Africa became independent nations within the Commonwealth.

After World War II, nationalism became strong rapidly in many areas of the British Empire where the majority of the population were not British immigrants. Britain could no longer keep control of its colonies.

As a result, India, where a movement for independence had become very strong, was granted independence in 1947. Meanwhile Hindus and Muslims — the two largest religious groups in India — had become more and more hostile toward each other. The continued peace-keeping efforts had been too costly for the British government. The Labour government, which opposed colonialism, decided to give up its control of India as quickly as possible. The last governor-general of India, Louis Mountbatten, made his last effort to settle the religious conflict by dividing the country between largely Hindu India and Muslim Pakistan. The British withdrawal in 1948 resulted in more religious conflicts and a terrible civil war. The civil war resulted in the deaths of between 250,000 and 500,000 people, among them the nationalist leader Mohandas Gandhi, who was assassinated by a Hindu extremist opposed to the division of India.

Following the independence of Indian and Pakistan Ceylon (now Sri Lanka) and Burma (Myanmar) won their independence in 1948. Ceylon became a member of the Commonwealth but Burma left the Commonwealth. In

邦中的独立国家。

二战后,在英帝国的许多非英国移民占主要人口的地区,民族主义势力迅速壮大。英国无法再控制这些殖民地。

结果,争取独立的运动已声势浩大的印度于 1947 年获准独立。同时,印度两个大教派,即印度教徒和穆斯林越来越仇视对方。持续不断的维和努力所需要经费已成为英国政府难以承受的重负。反对殖民主义的工党政府决定尽快放弃对印度的控制。印度的最后一任总督路易斯·蒙巴顿做了最后一次努力来解决宗教冲突。他将这个国家大致分为印度教徒的印度和穆斯林的巴基斯坦。英国于 1948 年撤出,结果导致更加严重的宗教冲突和一场可怕的内战。25 万至 50 万人在内战中丧命,其中包括民族主义领袖甘地。甘地被反对印度分裂的印度教极端主义分子刺杀。

印度和巴基斯坦独立后,锡兰(现在的斯里兰卡)和缅甸于 1948 年赢得独立。锡兰成为英联邦成员,但缅甸则脱离英联邦。1949 年,爱尔兰自由邦宣布成立独立的爱尔兰共和国,也脱离了英联邦。英国在非洲的殖民地黄金海岸于 1957 年宣布独立,称为加纳。1960 年以后的几年里,随着国际压力的增强(特别是在联合国)和独立观念在殖民地和英国人民中的传

1949, the Irish Free State declared itself the independent Republic of Ireland and also left the Commonwealth. The British colony in Africa the Gold Coast became independent (as Ghana) in 1957. In a few years after 1960, Britain's remaining colonies in Africa, Asia, and the Caribbean got their independence one after another as international pressure became greater (especially at the United Nations) and as the idea of independence spread both in the colonies and among the British people. In 1961 South Africa withdrew from the Common-wealth because Britain had criticized its racial policies. It remained outside the Commonwealth until 1994. Other African colonies, including Nigeria, Uganda and Kenya, followed Ghana to become independent states and joined the Commonwealth of Nations. They developed into republics and adopted British forms of government and law. In 1980 Britain recognized the independence of Rhodesia, whose name was changed to Zimbabwe.

However, Britain had a problem in dealing with Egypt. The British had occupied Egypt since 1882, but a nationalist movement forced Britain to grant Egypt independence in 1922. But British troops kept control of the Suez Canal.

In April 1954, Gamal Abdel Nasser became prime minister. In October, Great Britain agreed to remove all its troops from Egypt by June 18, 1956. But in 1956, the Egyptian government seized control of the Suez Canal Company from its British and French owners and

播，英国在非洲、亚洲和加勒比地区剩下的殖民地也相继宣布独立。1961年南非因英国批评其种族政策而退出英联邦。直到1994年才重新加入。其他非洲国家，包括尼日利亚、乌干达和肯尼亚，跟随加纳宣布独立并加入英联邦。他们发展成为共和国，采用英国的政府和法律形式。1980年，英国承认罗得西亚独立，其名称改为津巴布韦。

然而，英国与埃及的关系出现了问题。英国自从1882年就占领了埃及，但一场民族主义运动迫使英国于1922年承认埃及独立。但英国军队仍占据着苏伊士运河。

1954年4月，加麦尔·阿卜杜勒·纳赛尔出任埃及总理。10月，英国同意于1956年6月18日从埃及撤出所有军队。但在1956年，埃及政府从英国和法国业主手中夺取了苏伊士运河公司，将其国有化，以此为阿斯旺高坝工程筹集资金。

英法两国被激怒了，急于夺回苏伊士运河的控制权。1956年，以色列入侵埃及，迅速占领大部分西奈半岛，与此同时英法两国攻入塞得港，开始占领运河区。然而，一周之内，联合国在苏联和美国的敦促下要求停火，迫使英国、法国和以色列撤出占领区。虽然苏伊士运河公司的财产损失得到了补偿，

1973 年的英联邦首脑会议

末任香港总督彭定康撤离香港

nationalized it to obtain money for the Aswan High Dam project.

Britain and France were angry and eager to take back their control of Suez Canal. In October 1956, Israel invaded Egypt and quickly occupied most of the Sinai Peninsula, while Britain and France invaded Port Said and began occupying the canal area. Within a week, however, the United Nations, urged by both the Soviet Union and the United States, demanded a cease-fire, forcing Britain, France, and Israel to withdraw from the lands they had occupied. Although Suez Canal Company was compensated for the loss of its property, the Suez crisis showed that Britain had lost all its influence in the region and it was no longer a great power.

The last important British colony, Hong Kong, was returned to China in 1997. By then, almost nothing remained of the empire. The British monarch, however, is still recognized as head of the Commonwealth, a body of nations that are held together by shared traditions, institutions, and experiences as well as by economic self-interest.

11. The Welfare State

When the Labour Party came to power in 1945, the government with Attlee as prime minister began to carry out a series of social programmes. The programme of nationalization put

苏伊士危机表明英国已失去在这一地区的所有影响，它已不再是一个强大国家。

英国的最后一个重要的殖民地香港于 1997 年归还了中国。此时英帝国几乎什么也没剩下。但英国的君主仍被承认为英联邦的首脑。这些国家由于共同的经济利益，共同的传统、制度和经历，仍留在这个国家组织里。

题外话

"英联邦"里的形容词"英"(British)字，1946 年后在正式名称里被删除。

福利国家

1945 年工党上台后，以艾德礼为首相的政府着手实行一系列的社会计划。国有化计划将最重要的行业，包括英格兰银行、煤炭、电

under public control the most important industries, including the Bank of England, the coal, electricity, gas industries, and iron and steel industry. The government also took control of the railroads and airlines. Social welfare programmes established in 1948 were most far-reaching. They provided nationwide social security services for sickness, unemployment, retirement, maternity, disability, old age, and death. Social welfare programmes were based on the National Insurance Act of 1946. The National Health Service, set up in 1948, provided free medical service for all British citizens. As people said at the time, the social security system provided welfare for the people "from the cradle to the grave". Thus Britain became the first welfare state in the world. In the following decades, it was greatly admired by other European countries.

In 1951 the Labour Party lost its majority in Parliament, and the Conservative Party regained control. The Conservatives returned the iron and steel industry to private ownership, but left the major parts of the welfare state unchanged.

力、煤气和钢铁工业收归国有。政府也控制了铁路和航空业。1948 年确立的社会福利建设计划意义更为深远。这些计划在全国范围内为病人、失业者、退休者、孕妇、残疾人、老年人和逝世者提供社会保障服务。社会福利计划的依据是 1946 年通过的"国民保险法"。1948 年建立的国民医疗保健制度，为所有英国公民提供免费医疗服务。如当时人们所说的，"社会保障制度为人民提供了'从摇篮到坟墓'的福利"。英国因而成为世界上头一个福利国家。此后的几十年里，英国受到其他欧洲国家的高度赞扬。

1951 年，工党在议会失去多数，保守党重新执政。保守党将钢铁工业归还私有企业经营，但保留了福利国家的大部分制度，未加改动。

克莱门特·理查·艾德礼

约翰·凯恩斯

题 外 话

- "福利国家"使英国成为基本消灭了贫困,社会实现高度平等的发达国家。英国的福利国家思想在很大程度上受到英国经济学家约翰·凯恩斯学说的影响。凯恩斯的著作《就业、利息和货币通论》否定了从亚当·斯密开始的自由放任的传统经济理论,提出要用国家干预的方法刺激消费,促进生产,达到充分就业,从而消灭贫困。他认为在经济不景气期间,政府应采用增加开支、削减赋税的方法促进投资、非政府消费行为以及充分就业,以达到刺激经济复苏的目的。
- 在国有化和福利制度政策上,保守党与工党基本上达成了共识。保守党在社会改革上总比较为激进的政党慢半拍,但改革一旦成功,保守党便开始发挥作用,它维持改革的成果,并使之完善。只是到了 1979 年保守党才开始重新评估各项福利和国有化措施的利害得失。

12. Returning to Europe

重返欧洲

After World War II, Britain withdrew from its empire, but it had difficulty in returning to Europe. Other nations of Western Europe began to unite by joining together in various economical and political organizations. Britain was reluctant to join them. Throughout history, Britain had been reluctant to get involved in European affairs — unless it had to. It had considered itself to be the centre of an empire, or the Commonwealth, or at least a country that belonged to the English-speaking world, rather than a European country. If it joined the organizations, it might have to give up some of its independence, and weaken its relationship with the Commonwealth.

In the 1950s, Britain refused to join the European Coal and Steel Community and the European Atomic Energy Community. Most important, it did not join the European Economic

二战后,英国从英帝国中脱身出来后,却难以重返欧洲。其他欧洲国家开始通过建立各种经济和政治组织联合起来。英国不愿与它们联合。在整个历史上,除非迫不得已,英国一直不愿卷入欧洲事务。它将自己视为一个帝国的中心,或英联邦的中心,或至少是一个英语世界的国家,而不是一个欧洲国家。如果加入这些组织,它将不得不放弃某些独立性,削弱其与联邦国家的关系。

50 年代,英国拒绝加入欧洲煤钢联营和欧洲原子能联营。最重要的是,它没有参加欧洲经济共同体(EEC,亦称欧洲共同市场),因为它担心会丧失对本国经济政策的控制。欧洲经济共同体显示出成功迹象后,英国与 6 个其他国家组成

Community (EEC, also called the European Common Market), because it was afraid of losing some of control over its economic policics. After the EEC showed signs of success, Britain set up the European Free Trade Association (EFTA) with six other nations. But with the growing success of the EEC (called the European Community after 1967) Britain realized that it had been a mistake not to join the EC. After years of difficult negotiations, Britain finally joined the EC in 1973.

However, many people were still opposed to joining the EC, mainly because they felt Britain contributed too much to the EC budget. The Labour government called a national referendum on the issue in June 1975. In spite of strong opposition from some groups, the British people voted for continued membership.

In 1980s many EC members decided to take various measures to move towards closer European unity. But British Prime Minister Margaret Thatcher opposed this. When John Major became prime minister, he adopted a moderate approach toward the idea of European unity.

In February 1992, representatives of the 12 member countries of the EC signed the Treaty on European Union (EU) in Maastricht, the Netherlands. This pact, also known as the Maastricht Treaty, changed EC into EU to extend cooperation among the community's members to many more areas. The pact required the member nations should replace national currencies with a single European currency by 1999.

欧洲自由贸易联盟（EFTA）。但随着欧洲经济共同体（1976年后称为"欧共体"）的成就日增，英国意识到它没有参加欧共体是个错误。经过多年艰苦的谈判，英国终于在1973年加入欧共体。

但是，仍有许多人反对加入欧共体，主要因为他们觉得英国对欧共体预算的贡献过大。1975年6月工党政府就此问题举行全民公决。尽管有某些团体强烈反对，英国人民投票赞成继续留在欧共体内。

80年代，许多欧共体成员决定采取各种措施加强欧洲一体化。但英国首相玛格丽特·撒切尔表示反对。约翰·梅杰出任首相后，采取温和的行动向欧洲一体化的理念靠拢。

1992年2月，欧共体12个成员国的代表在荷兰的马斯特里赫特签署了欧洲联盟条约(EU)。这个条约亦称马斯特里赫特条约，将欧共体改变成欧洲联盟，将成员国的合作扩大到更多的领域。条约要求成员国在1999年用单一的欧洲货币代替本国货币。英国不赞同条约的某些条款，被许可不遵守它们。这些条款包括不加入经济和货币联盟，不参加统一社会和就业政策。

Britain refused to approve some elements of the treaty and was allowed to choose not to accept those elements. These included not joining Economic and Monetary Union and not taking part in unifying social and employment policy.

13. Economic Problems

经济问题

A Conservative government returned to power in 1951 under Winston Churchill. The Conservatives accepted most of the changes the Labour Party had made. By 1955, economy had improved. Jobs were easier to find and workers were better paid. The British economy continued to expand until the early 1960s. But by the mid-1960s Britain's economic growth began to slow down. Britain's industries had developed too slowly to be competitive. Factories and machines were old, but labour costs were high. Britain was importing far more goods than it was exporting. The nation had to borrow more and more money from other countries and international agencies. To make the situation worse, workers staged hundreds of strikes. Britain tried to join in the European Economic Community

　　1951 年，温斯顿·丘吉尔领导下的保守党政府上台执政。保守党接受了工党已完成的大部分变革。1955 年，经济有所改善。工作较容易找到，工人工资也提高了。英国经济持续增长直至 60 年代初。然而到了 60 年代中，经济增长开始放缓。英国工业发展一直缓慢，因而缺乏竞争力。工厂和机器已经老化，而劳力成本过高。英国进口大于出口。国家不得不向外国和国际机构连连举债。工人举行的数百次罢工使局势恶化。英国试图加入欧洲经济共同体以改善出口贸易，但法国不愿接受它，直至 1973 年才得以加入。

　　工党于 1974 年赢得选举，因

to improve its export trade, but France would not accept it until 1973.

The Labour Party won the election of 1974 by promising not to interfere with the unions. The unions won wage increases. Workers now had more money to spend, while the amount of goods they could buy on the market remained the same. As a result, prices for products began to rise, and inflation followed. Wages and prices soon increased out of control. Only a supply of oil drilled from the North Sea off the coast of Scotland saved Britain from being unable to pay its foreign debts. Even with the new supply of oil, the government could not afford to keep its promise of raising wages for union members in nationalized industries. It had to raise taxes on income and on consumer goods. As a result of high taxes, people had little money left to invest in businesses. When the Labour Party tried to keep down further rise of wages, another round of strikes took place.

为它许诺不干涉工会事务。结果工会提高工资的斗争取得胜利。工人现在有更多的钱花，但市场上可购货物的总量却没有增加。结果物价开始上涨，紧接着发生了通货膨胀。工资与物价轮番上涨，不久便失去控制。幸而苏格兰附近北海海域钻探出来的石油挽救了英国，使之不致没有能力偿还外债。即使有了新近获得的石油供应，政府仍无法实现其诺言，提高国有化企业工会会员们的工资。政府不得不提高所得税和消费税的税率。由于高额税率，人民没有多少剩余资金来投资企业。工党政府试图抑制工资的进一步增长，结果开始了新一轮的罢工。

题外话

不少经济学家，特别是货币学派，对凯恩斯的学说提出挑战。他们怀疑凯恩斯主义的政策是否真正能够达到充分就业和稳定经济的目的。他们将 70 年代美国和其他国家经历的 "滞胀"（高通胀和高失业率）归罪于凯恩斯主义的政策。他们的批评降低了凯恩斯主义在决策者当中的影响。

14. The Conflicts in Northern Ireland

北爱冲突

The continuing conflicts between Catholics and Protestants in Northern Ireland became a

60 年代末和70 年代，北爱尔兰天主教徒和新教徒间持续不断的

serious problem for Britain during the late 1960s and the 1970s. Catholics fought to create a single Ireland; Protestants fought to maintain union with Britain. In 1969, Britain began sending troops to Northern Ireland to try to keep peace. In 1972, the British government suspended Northern Ireland's government and rule the region directly from London. It tried to set up a stable government in which Catholics and Protestants shared power, but the effort was not successful. The trouble continued and on January 30, 1972, a day later known as "Bloody Sunday," British troops killed 13 Catholic civil rights protesters. In that year 467 people, including 321 civilians, were killed. Irish Republican Army (IRA), a secret military group that has used violence to win Northern Ireland's freedom from British rule, and some Protestant military groups used terrorism and killed many civilians in both England and Dublin. In late 1970s, about 100 people were killed each year and many times the number injured. The violence became less in the 1980s, but still 50 to 100 political murders and assassinations occurred each year.

In 1979 the IRA murdered the uncle of Queen Elizabeth II, British naval hero Lord Louis Mountbatten, and on the same day attacked a group of British soldiers, killing 18 of them. Lord Mountbatten's murder was generally condemned. In 1980 and 1981, a number of imprisoned IRA members went on hunger strikes and ten of them starved themselves to death. Their deaths aroused public's sympathy for IRA

冲突成为英国的严重问题。天主教徒为创建统一的爱尔兰而战；新教徒则为继续留在联合王国而战。1969 年，英国开始派军队到北爱尔兰维持和平。1972 年，英国政府中止北爱政府的职能，由伦敦直接统治北爱。英国政府试图建立一个稳定政府，由天主教徒和新教徒分享政权，但这一努力未能成功。两派纠纷不断发生，结果在 1972 年 1 月 30 日（后来被称做"血腥的星期天"），英国军队杀死 13 名争取民权的示威者。当年有 467 人，包括 321 名平民，死于冲突。曾用暴力争取北爱脱离英国的秘密军事组织爱尔兰共和军 (IRA) 和某些新教军事组织使用恐怖手段杀死英格兰和都柏林的许多平民。70 年代末，每年都有大约 100 人被杀，数倍于此的人受伤。80 年代，暴力活动有所减少，但每年仍有 50~100 起政治性谋杀和行刺发生。

1979 年，爱尔兰共和军暗杀伊丽莎白二世的叔父、英国海军英雄路易斯·蒙巴顿勋爵，并在当天攻击英军士兵，杀死 18 人。暗杀蒙巴顿勋爵受到广泛谴责。1980 和 1981 年，被囚禁的爱尔兰共和军成员绝食抗议，10 人饿死。他们的死再次激起公众对爱尔兰共和军的同情，并使爱尔兰共和军的政治组织新芬党争得民心。新芬党开始

again, and made Sinn Fein, the political wing of IRA, popular. The party began winning parliamentary and local council seats.

In 1985, the United Kingdom and the Republic of Ireland signed the Anglo-Irish Agreement, under which the two governments agreed to consult regularly on major aspects of Northern Irish policy. But during the late 1980s and early 1990s, terrorist bombings by the IRA and Protestant military groups became more frequent in Northern Ireland and Britain.

The Downing Street Declaration, issued in 1993 by British Prime Minister John Major and Irish Prime Minister Albert Reynolds, guaranteed self-determination for the people of Northern Ireland. The British government promised to recognize a unified Ireland if a majority of Northern Ireland's people agreed, and Ireland promised to abandon its constitutional claim to Northern Ireland in the event of a political settlement.

In late 1994, the IRA and the Protestant groups declared a cease-fire, and detailed peace negotiations began. But disagreement in the British Parliament hindered government progress on the peace process, and in early 1996 the IRA bombings began again.

In 1997, after Tony Blair took office, the British government dropped its demands that the IRA completely disarm before allowing Sinn Fein to take part in the talks. New negotiations began in September 1997. Sinn Fein joined the negotiations.

The Belfast Agreement (also known as the

在议会和地方议事机构赢得席位。

1985 年，联合王国和爱尔兰共和国签署英爱条约，两国政府商定就北爱尔兰政策的主要方面保持经常磋商。但是 80 年代末和 90 年代初，爱尔兰共和军和新教军事组织在北爱和大不列颠的恐怖炸弹袭击更加频繁。

1993 年，英国首相约翰·梅杰和爱尔兰总理艾尔伯特·雷诺兹发表唐宁街宣言，保障北爱尔兰人民自决。英国政府许诺，如果北爱尔兰人民大多数赞同，它将承认统一的爱尔兰，而爱尔兰政府许诺，在政治解决北爱问题之后，爱尔兰宪法不再主张对北爱的领土要求。

1994 年末，爱尔兰共和军和新教军事组织宣布停火，内容详尽的谈判开始了。但英国议会中的分歧阻碍了政府的和谈进程。1996 年，爱尔兰共和军重新开始炸弹袭击。

1997 年，托尼·布莱尔执政，英国政府不再坚持要求在允许新芬党参与和谈之前爱尔兰共和军完全解除武装。新一轮谈判于 1997 年 9 月举行。新芬党参加了谈判。

贝尔法斯特协定（亦称"受难日协定"）于 1998 年 4 月签署。根据协议的条款，将举行选举成立新政府，北爱尔兰的所有政党都将允许参加选举。5 月，爱尔兰和北爱尔兰举行全民公决，94% 的爱尔

Good Friday Agreement) was signed in April 1998. Under the terms of this agreement, a new government would be set up from elections in which all political parties in Northern Ireland would be allowed to participate. Referendums were held in Ireland and Northern Ireland in May and the agreement received the approval of 94 percent of voters in Ireland and 71 percent in Northern Ireland. The agreement required all participating paramilitary groups to declare an end to violence. In return, a program was drawn up for the release, in phases, of all convicted prisoners who belonged to groups that had declared cease-fires.

But the IRA did not give up their weapons until much later.

兰投票人和 71% 的北爱尔兰投票人赞成协议。协议要求所有参加议会选举的非法军事组织宣布停止暴力活动。作为交换，制定了一项计划，将分阶段释放所有属于已宣布停火组织的服刑囚犯。

但爱尔兰共和军很久以后才放下武器。

题外话

实际上，不仅仅在爱尔兰和北爱尔兰，苏格兰和威尔士也有人主张脱离英国而独立。还有不少人认为苏格兰和威尔士应有它们各自的立法机构。但也有很多人主张维持现状。1979 年英国政府允许苏格兰和威尔士人投票决定是否应建立自己的立法机构。结果，两地未能通过建立立法机构的建议。

15. Margaret Thatcher

玛格丽特·撒切尔

Margaret Thatcher (1925-) became the first woman prime minister of the United Kingdom after the Conservative Party defeated the Labour Party in parliamentary elections in 1979. She held the post for the next 11 and a half years from 1979 to 1990, longer than any other person in the 20th century.

Thatcher was strongly opposed to the socialist policies of the Labour Party. During her terms of office, she worked to reduce government control over the British economy. The

在 1979 年的议会选举中，保守党击败工党后，玛格丽特·撒切尔（1925- ）成为英国历史上首位女首相。从 1979 年至 1990 年她执政 11 年半，比 20 世纪任何其他首相执政时间都长。

撒切尔坚决反对工党的社会主义政策。在执政时期，她致力于减少政府对英国经济的控制。政府许多企业的所有权出售给个人和私营企业。政府还将成千上万所公有住

government sold its interests in many industries to private citizens and businesses. It also sold thousands of public-owned houses to their tenants. Thatcher based her policy on the theory of monetarism. This theory involved strictly controlling the money supply to reduce inflation, lowering tax rates to encourage investment, and reducing government control of industry and businesses. It seemed at first that her policies led to an even more rapid decline. By 1981 both interest rates and unemployment reached the highest level after the war, and a growing number of British firms faced bankruptcy. Many people, and even members of her own party, began to criticize the government policies. But Thatcher stood firm. Her firmness in carrying out her policies later earned her the nickname of "Iron Lady".

A world economic recovery helped to improve the British economy and reduce inflation. The profits from industries sold to investors and the large sums of money gained from the sale abroad of North Sea oil gave a powerful support to the government. In 1982, Thatcher won praise for her decisive handling of a conflict with Argentina. Since 1833, Britain has ruled the Falkland Islands, which lie about 515 kilometers east of the southern coast of Argentina. But Argentina has long claimed ownership of the islands. In April 1982, Argentine troops invaded and occupied the Falklands. Britain then responded by sending troops, ships, and planes to the islands. Air, sea, and land battles broke

宅出售给房客。撒切尔政策的基础是货币主义理论。这一理论主张严格控制货币供应量以降低通胀，降低税率以鼓励投资，减少政府对工商业的控制。起初，她的政策似乎导致更为急剧的衰退。到了 1981 年，利率和失业率双双达到战后最高水平。越来越多的英国企业濒临破产。许多人，甚至保守党的人，开始批评政府的政策。但撒切尔毫不动摇。她执行政策时的坚定后来为她赢得"铁娘子"的绰号。

世界经济的复苏改善了英国的经济，降低了通货膨胀。出售给投资者的工业获得的利润和出口北海原油获得的大量资金给政府以强大的支持。1982 年，撒切尔果断处理与阿根廷的冲突，赢得好评。自从 1833 年开始，英国就统治着位于阿根廷南岸以东 515 公里的福克兰群岛。但阿根廷长期主张该岛的所有权。1982 年 4 月，阿根廷军队入侵并占领福克兰群岛。英国立即做出反应，派遣军队、军舰和飞机前往福克兰。阿根廷和英国在空中、海上和陆地上的战斗全面展开。结果，阿根廷军队战败，于 6 月投降。福克兰群岛战争后，撒切尔声望大增，在 1983 年的选举中大获全胜。同年，政府在与工会的斗争中也取得胜利，大大削弱了工会的力量。

80 年代中期，英国的经济开

out between Argentina and Britain. The Argentine forces were defeated and surrendered in June. Thatcher became very popular after the Falkland Islands War and she won a great victory in a second election in 1983. In the same year, the government also won a victory in the struggle with the trade unions, and greatly reduced their power.

By the mid-1980s British economy began to improve. Monetarist policy had brought down interest rates and encouraged investment. Inflation was checked, and the remaining British industries slowly became competitive in the international market.

But Thatcher was unable to end the conflict in Northern Ireland. An IRA terrorist bombing at the Conservative Party conference in 1984 nearly killed Thatcher and several senior members of her government. Nonetheless, she succeeded in 1987 in winning a third general election.

Thatcher did not finish her third term. She disagreed sharply with a number of Cabinet ministers over economic and foreign policies, and as a result, in November 1990 she failed for the first time to receive the required number in the Conservative Party's annual election for party leader. John Major was chosen to succeed her on November 27. Thatcher resigned as prime minister the following day and was replaced by Major. She remained in the House of Commons until 1992. In that year, Thatcher was made a baroness for her service as prime minister. She also became a member of the House of Lords.

始得到改善。货币主义政策降低了利率，鼓励了投资。通货膨胀受到抑制，没有破产的英国工业慢慢恢复了在国际市场上的竞争力。

但撒切尔未能结束北爱尔兰的冲突。在 1984 年保守党的会议上，爱尔兰共和军的恐怖炸弹袭击险些炸死撒切尔和几位政府高级官员。然而，她在 1987 年的第三次选举中再度获胜。

撒切尔未能执政到第三任期结束。她在经济和外交政策上与几位内阁大臣产生严重分歧。结果，在 1990 年 11 月保守党领袖的年度选举中，她首次未能获得必要的票数。11 月 27 日，约翰·梅杰当选继任她的职务。次日，撒切尔辞去首相职务，梅杰代替了她。她保留下院议席直至 1992 年。同年，撒切尔由于她担任首相期间的贡献受封为女男爵，而且成为上院议员。

玛格丽特·撒切尔

16. Britain in the 1990s

90 年代的英国

In 1990, John Major succeeded Thatcher as Conservative Party leader and prime minister. He had been serving as Chancellor of the Exchequer, which involves managing the country's economy. Under Major's government, the United Kingdom supported the United States in its effort to drive Iraq from Kuwait in the Persian Gulf War of 1991. In 1992, the Conservatives won election again, and Major remained prime minister. But the British people soon lost confidence in the Conservatives. In July 1995, in an attempt to strengthen his position in his party, Major resigned as leader of the Conservatives, forcing an election for a new leader. Major won again.

In March 1996 a crisis began in the country's beef industry. British experts announced that a brain disease in humans might be linked to eating beef from cows with a similar disease, called mad cow disease. Shortly after the announcement, the European Union banned British beef exports. Major's government was severely criticized for its handling of the crisis. The Conservative popularity

1990 年，约翰·梅杰接替撒切尔出任保守党领袖和首相。他一直担任财政大臣，处理国家经济问题。梅杰任职期间，英国支持美国在 1991 年的海湾战争中将伊拉克逐出科威特。1992 年，保守党再次赢得选举，梅杰继续担任首相。但是英国人民不久便对保守党丧失信任。1995 年 7 月，为加强自己在党内的地位，梅杰辞去保守党领袖职，迫使保守党选举新领袖。梅杰再次当选。

1996 年 3 月，英国养牛业出现危机。英国专家宣布，人类患的一种脑病可能与食用牛肉有关，而这种牛肉来自患有相似疾病的肉牛。此病称为疯牛病。消息一出，欧洲联盟立即禁止英国牛肉出口。

梅杰

further decreased when some high government officials were involved in a series of personal scandals. The divorce of Prince Charles and Princess Diana in 1996 also hurt the Conservatives, who were strong supporters of the monarchy.

Meanwhile, Labour's popularity grew. Tony Blair, leader of the British Labour Party reorganized the party after the loss of the 1992 elections, and made some changes in its policies. The party moved toward the political center and kept its distance from labour and the trade unions that had long influenced its policy. In 1997 the Labour Party won a great victory in British national elections, and Blair became prime minister, the youngest one since the 19th century.

After taking office, Blair continued to carry out the programs to stimulate economic growth established by the Conservatives. He made the Bank of England independent of government. At the same time, he made efforts to improve relations with the European Union, established separate parliaments for Scotland and Wales, giving them more regional control and political independence, and made reforms in welfare and health care. In November 1999 Blair made a move to modernize the government. He stripped many of the hereditary peers in the House of Lords of their right to sit and vote in Parliament. The House of Lords Act eliminated all but 92 of the more than 750 seats held by hereditary members of Parliament's upper house.

政府处理危机的措施受到严厉批评。此后某些政府高级官员卷入一系列个人丑闻，使保守党的声威进一步下降。查尔斯亲王与戴安娜王妃的离婚也伤害了保守党，因为它是王室的坚定支持者。

与此同时，工党的声望日隆。1992 年选举失利后，工党领袖托尼·布莱尔重组了工党，在政策上进行了一些改动。工党朝着政治中心移动，与长期影响其政策的工人运动和工会组织保持距离。1997 年，工党在大选中大获全胜，布莱尔出任首相，是 19 世纪以来最年轻的一个。

就任后，布莱尔继续实行保守党制定的刺激经济增长的计划。他使英格兰银行脱离政府。同时，他努力改善与欧盟的关系，为苏格兰和威尔士建立独立的议会，给它们以更多的地方控制权和政治独立，并在福利和医疗保健方面做了进一步的改革。1999 年 11 月，采取一项措施使政府现代化。他剥夺了上院许多世袭贵族的席位和投票权。上院法案撤消了议会上院世袭议员的 750 多个席位中的多数，只保留了 92 席。

在 2001 年 6 月的大选中，工党再次获胜，布莱尔再次出任首相。

In the national elections of June 2001 the Labour Party won its second victory, and Blair won a second term as prime minister.

布莱尔

17. Elizabeth II

Elizabeth II (born in 1926) is the present queen of the United Kingdom of Great Britain and Northern Ireland. As a constitutional monarch, Queen Elizabeth is formally head of state in the United Kingdom. Her chief public role is to attend ceremonial state occasions and to represent the United Kingdom in visits throughout the world.

Elizabeth was the elder daughter of Albert, duke of York, and his wife, Lady Elizabeth Bowes-Lyon. As the child of the second son of King George V, the young Elizabeth had little hope of becoming the monarch. However, an event that took place in 1936, when she was ten

伊丽莎白二世

伊丽莎白二世(1926 年出生)是当今大不列颠及北爱尔兰联合王国的女王。作为一位立宪制下的君主,伊丽莎白女王在形式上是联合王国的国家元首。她的主要职责是出席国家礼仪活动,并代表联合王国出访世界各国。

伊丽莎白是约克公爵艾尔伯特与妻子伊丽莎白·鲍斯－莱昂的长女。由于她是国王乔治五世次子的孩子,童年时几乎没有继承王位的可能。然而,1936 年她十岁时发生的一件事,大大改变了她的生活进程。她的叔父,国王爱德华八世

years old, greatly changed the course of her life. Her uncle, King Edward VIII, gave up the throne to marry Wallis Warfield Simpson, a divorced American woman. As a result, her father succeeded to the throne and became King George VI. This made her the heir to the throne, since George VI had no sons and she was the older of his two daughters.

Princess Elizabeth and her sister, Princess Margaret, were educated at home by governesses. During World War II they spent much of their time safely at Balmoral Castle in Scotland and Windsor Castle, the British royal family's main residence outside London, when London was bombed by the German air force. In March 1945, Elizabeth served in a military branch called the Auxiliary Territorial Service. She had training to become a mechanic to repair military vehicles for the war effort. But Elizabeth served only until May, when the war in Europe ended.

In 1947, Elizabeth married Philip Mountbatten, a British naval lieutenant and member of the Greek and Danish royal families. Their marriage took place in Westminster Abbey on November 20. Her husband then became Prince Philip, Duke of Edinburgh. The next year their son, Prince Charles, was born. The queen's other children were Princess Anne, born in 1950; Prince Andrew, born in 1960, and created duke of York in 1986; and Prince Edward, born in 1964. At present Prince Charles is heir to the throne. Charles's oldest son, Prince William

为了与一个美国离婚女人辛普森夫人结婚，放弃了王位。结果伊丽莎白的父亲继承王位，成为乔治六世。这使伊丽莎白成为王位继承人，因为乔治六世没有儿子，只有两个女儿，而伊丽莎白是长女。

伊丽莎白公主和妹妹玛格蕾特公主在家中受教育。第二次世界大战期间，当伦敦遭受德国飞机的轰炸时，姊妹二人在苏格兰的巴尔莫勒尔堡和伦敦城外英国皇家宅邸温莎堡避险。1945年3月，伊丽莎白参加本土辅助部队，接受机械师训练，为作战部队修理军用车辆。但她的服役只持续到5月，欧洲战争结束时为止。

1947年，伊丽莎白嫁给了英国海军上尉、希腊和丹麦皇家成员菲利普·蒙巴顿。两人的婚礼于11月20日在威斯敏斯特教堂举行。伊丽莎白的丈夫受封为菲利普亲王，爱丁堡公爵。第二年，他们的儿子查尔斯王子出生。女王的其他孩子有安妮公主，1950年出生；安德鲁王子，1960年出生，1986年受封约克公爵；爱德华王子，1964年出生。目前查尔斯王子是王位继承人。查尔斯的长子，威廉王子在继承人中排在父亲之后，名列第二。

1951年夏，乔治六世病重，公主伊丽莎白和丈夫开始参与国务。10月，她与丈夫一同出访加

(born in 1982), is next in line after his father as the heir.

In the summer of 1951 King George VI became seriously ill, and Princess Elizabeth and her husband began to do more public duties. In October she and her husband set out on a tour of Canada and Washington, D.C. After Christmas in England she and the duke set out in January 1952 for a tour of Australia and New Zealand, but on their way there, news reached them that the king died on February 6. Elizabeth, now queen, at once flew back to England. The coronation of Queen Elizabeth II was held on June 2, 1953, in Westminster Abbey, London.

Beginning in November 1953 the queen and the duke of Edinburgh made a tour of the member nations of the Commonwealth, and in six months they traveled round the world. In 1957, after visits to various European nations, she and the duke visited Canada and the United States. She made a tour of the Indian subcontinent in 1961, and visited South America in 1968 and the Persian Gulf countries in 1979. In 1977, for celebrating the 25th anniversary of her becoming queen, a banquet was held in London and the leaders of the 36 members of the Commonwealth attended it. For the occasion the queen also traveled all over Britain and Northern Ireland, and toured overseas in the South Pacific and Australia, in Canada, and in the Caribbean.

Since Elizabeth became queen, great

拿大和美国首都华盛顿。在英国度过圣诞节后，二人于 1952 年 1 月出访澳大利亚和新西兰，但在途中获悉国王于 2 月 6 日去世。伊丽莎白此时已身为女王，立刻返回英国。女王伊丽莎白二世的加冕礼于 1953 年 6 月 2 日在伦敦的威斯敏斯特教堂举行。

从 1953 年 11 月开始，女王和爱丁堡公爵出访英联邦国家，在半年里周游了世界。1957 年，二人访问过欧洲诸国后，继而访问了加拿大和美国。女王又于 1961 年访问了印度次大陆各国，1968 年访问了南美洲，1979 年访问了波斯湾诸国。1977 年，为庆祝女王加冕 25 周年，伦敦举行了宴会，英联邦 36 国的首脑出席了宴会。为此周年纪念，女王还访问了大不列颠各地和北爱尔兰，并出访南太平洋和澳大利亚、加拿大及加勒比海地区。

伊丽莎白女王即位后，英国人民的生活、英国的实力与声望发生了重大变化。到了 20 世纪 80 年代初，近 40 个英国前殖民地已经获准独立。从 50 年代中期开始，英国就不断地为北爱尔兰的流血冲突所困扰。英国还经历了二战后的经济困难。许多工业国有化了。在 1973 年，英国成为欧洲经济共同体的成员。在整个这段时期，伊丽莎白扮演的重要角色是英联邦国家

changes have taken place in the lives of her people and in the power and prestige of her nation. By the early 1980s, nearly 40 former British colonies had been granted their independence. Beginning in the mid-1950s, her nation was constantly troubled by the bloodshed in Northern Ireland. It also suffered economic difficulties after World War II. Many industries were nationalized, and in 1973 Great Britain became a member of the European Economic Community. Throughout this period Elizabeth's primary role was as a symbol of unity and continuity within the Commonwealth of Nations.

The queen has tried to modernize the monarchy, that is, to make it friendlier and less traditional. She allowed the public to have much more information about the lives of the royal family since the 1980s. She sometimes puts ceremony aside and meets informally with subjects. She hosts luncheons at Buckingham Palace, the official town residence of the British monarch, and her guests may be people of many different walks of life. In 1992 the Queen and Prince Charles agreed to pay income taxes on their personal income, the first time the monarchy has done so. In 1993 Buckingham Palace was opened to tourists to help pay for the repairs at Windsor Castle, which was partly damaged by fire the previous year. The queen is known to favour a simple court life. From 1991 to 1998 the total cost of running the monarchy dropped from 55 million pounds sterling to 47 million pounds sterling. But the reputation of

的团结和持续的象征。

女王努力使王室现代化，使之更接近大众，显得不那么守旧。自20世纪80年代开始，她允许公众获得更多的有关王室的信息。她有时放下架子，无拘无束地会见臣民。她在英国王室在伦敦的宅邸白金汉宫举行午餐会，招待来自各行各业的人士。1992年，女王和查尔斯王子同意缴纳个人所得税，对于王室来说，这是前所未有的。同年，温莎堡遭火灾，部分被焚毁，次年白金汉宫对游客开放，以筹款对温莎堡进行修复。女王更喜欢过简朴的宫廷生活，这是众所周知的。从1991年到1998年，王室的全部开支从5500万英镑削减到4700万英镑。但王室的声望由于女王的两个儿子查尔斯和安德鲁王子的离婚而受损。在戴安娜王妃于1997年8月在巴黎的车祸中罹难后，英国公众开始批评王室，认为它脱离了当代的英国社会生活。

伊丽莎白二世对政府的工作十分关注。她每周都要会见首相，讨论政务。首相也会发现她出的主意很有价值，因为她在多年中毕竟积累了不少的经验。在私生活里，她是个热心的骑马爱好者。她饲养赛马，经常观看比赛。她的收入和财产使她成为世界上最富有的女人之一。

the royal family was damaged when two of her sons, Prince Charles and Prince Andrew, separated from their wives in 1992. After Diana, Princess of Wales, tragically died in a car crash in Paris, France, in August 1997, the British public criticized the royal family, and thought it to be out of touch with contemporary British life.

Elizabeth II is known to take a serious interest in government business. She has a weekly meeting with the prime minister to discuss public affairs. The prime minister may find her advice useful because of her many years of experience. Privately she has become a keen horsewoman; she keeps racehorses, frequently attends races. Her income and property have made her one of the world's richest women.

题外话

伊丽莎白二世是在位时间最长的君主之一。她毕竟与六届政府和十一位首相（从丘吉尔到布莱尔）打过交道，积累了不少政治经验，也有相当高的威望。但近几十年来，英国王室仍遭到越来越多的批评，被视为难以适应21世纪的老古董。人们问道，女王是否与普通百姓有足够的接触？王室是否耗费了纳税人过多的钱财？王室的十几个成员是否必须由国家供养？1997年，与查尔斯王子离异的戴安娜王妃死于巴黎的一场车祸，公众的沉痛悼念她的去世，使英国王室感到尴尬。在戴安娜的崇拜者们的心目中，这位王妃是一个战士，她勇敢地走入被他人不屑一顾的人群中，与他们的苦难做斗争。她对艾滋病人的抚慰至今人们记忆犹新。其实，真正主张废除王室的人恐怕不多。因为王室象征着英国的悠久传统。再说，查尔斯之后，继承王位的将是聪颖、英俊而略显羞涩的威廉王子。人们所希望的是王室能够更加接近平民。

伊丽莎白（左）和妹妹玛格蕾特在二战期间为战事服务

APPENDIX

English and British Monarchs Since William I
威廉一世以来的英格兰及英国君主

Normans		诺曼王朝	
William I	(1066-1087)	威 廉 一 世	(1066-1087)
William II	(1087-1100)	威 廉 二 世	(1087-1100)
Henry I	(1100-1135)	亨 利 一 世	(1100-1135)
Stephen	(1135-1154)	斯 蒂 芬	(1135-1154)

Plantagenet family		金雀花王朝	
Henry II	(1154-1189)	亨 利 二 世	(1154-1189)
Richard I	(1189-1199)	理 查 一 世	(1189-1199)
John	(1199-1216)	约 翰	(1199-1216)
Henry III	(1216-1272)	亨 利 三 世	(1216-1272)
Edward I	(1272-1307)	爱德华一世	(1272-1307)
Edward II	(1307-1327)	爱德华二世	(1307-1327)
Edward III	(1327-1377)	爱德华三世	(1327-1377)
Richard II	(1377-1399)	理 查 二 世	(1377-1399)

House of Lancaster		兰开斯特王朝	
Henry IV	(1399-1413)	亨 利 四 世	(1399-1413)
Henry V	(1413-1422)	亨 利 五 世	(1413-1422)
Henry VI	(1422-1461)	亨 利 六 世	(1422-1461)

House of York	**约克王朝**
Edward IV (1461-1470)	爱德华四世 (1461-1470)

House of Lancaster	**兰开斯特王朝**
Henry VI (1470-1471)	亨利六世 (1470-1471)

House of York	**约克王朝**
Edward IV (1471-1483)	爱德华四世 (1471-1483)
Edward V (1483)	爱德华五世 (1483)
Richard III (1483-1485)	理查三世 (1483-1485)

House of Tudor	**都铎王朝**
Henry VII (1485-1509)	亨利七世 (1485-1509)
Henry VIII (1509-1547)	亨利八世 (1509-1547)
Edward VI (1547-1553)	爱德华六世 (1547-1553)
Lady Jane Grey (1553)	简·格雷郡主 (1553)
Mary I (1553-1558)	玛丽一世 (1553-1558)
Elizabeth I (1558-1603)	伊丽莎白一世 (1558-1603)

House of Stuart	**斯图亚特王朝**
James I (1603-1625)	詹姆斯一世 (1603-1625)
Charles I (1625-1649)	查理一世 (1625-1649)

Commonwealth	**共和国**
Long Parliament (1649-1653)	长期议会 (1649-1653)
Oliver Cromwell (1653-1658)	奥立佛·克伦威尔 (1653-1658)
Richard Cromwell (1658-1659)	理查·克伦威尔 (1658-1659)

House of Stuart	**斯图亚特王朝**
Charles II (1660-1685)	查理二世 (1660-1685)
James II (1685-1688)	詹姆斯二世 (1685-1688)
William III (1689-1702) and Mary II (1689-1694)	威廉三世 (1689-1702) 与玛丽二世 (1689-1694)

| Anne | (1702-1714) | 安　妮 | (1702-1714) |

House of Hanover　　　　汉诺威王朝

George I	(1714-1727)	乔治一世	(1714-1727)
George II	(1727-1760)	乔治二世	(1727-1760)
George III	(1760-1820)	乔治三世	(1760-1820)
George IV	(1820-1830)	乔治四世	(1820-1830)
William IV	(1830-1837)	威廉四世	(1830-1837)
Victoria	(1837-1901)	维多利亚	(1837-1901)

House of Sax-Coburg-Gotha　　萨克斯–科堡–哥达王朝

(Edward VII was the son of Queen Victoria and Albert of Saxe-Coburg-Gotha.)

（注：爱德华七世是维多利亚女王和艾尔伯特亲王的儿子，而艾尔伯特来自德国的萨克斯—科堡—哥达家族，故名。）

| Edward VII | (1901-1910) | 爱德华七世 | (1901-1910) |
| George V | (1910-1917) | 乔治五世 | (1910-1917) |

House of Winsor　　　　温莎王朝

(During World War I George V renounced all the German titles belonging to him and his family and changed the name of the royal house to Windsor.)

（注：第一次世界大战中，由于英国和德国为敌国，乔治五世将萨克斯—科堡—哥达王朝这一与德国有关的称号改为温莎王朝。）

George V	(1917-1936)	乔治五世	(1917-1936)
Edward VIII	(1936)	爱德华八世	(1936)
George VI	(1936-1952)	乔治六世	(1936-1952)
Elizabeth II	(1952-)	伊丽莎白二世	(1952-)

邮购目录

书　　　　名	开 本	定 价
风情英语①——看欧美风情学英语	32K	20.00
风情英语②——看世界名胜学英语	32K	20.00
童话英文①——看童话故事学英语	32K	18.00
童话英文②——看格林童话学英语	32K	20.00
智慧英文①——看寓言故事学英语	32K	20.00
智慧英文②——看趣味故事学英语	32K	20.00
智慧英文③——看励志故事学英语	32K	17.00
智慧英文④——看伊索寓言学英语	32K	19.00
笑爆英语①——看笑话学英语	32K	22.00
笑爆英语②——看幽默故事学英语	32K	17.00
笑爆英语③——英语幽默与笑话	32K	18.00
笑爆英语④——英语幽默与口语表达训练	32K	20.00
趣味故事乐园03——看幽默故事学英语	32K	16.00
趣味故事乐园09——看脑筋急转弯学英语	32K	17.00
趣味故事乐园10——看动物故事学英语	32K	16.00
趣味故事乐园11——唱　歌　学　英　语	32K	22.00
趣味故事乐园12——看名人名言学英语	32K	19.00
趣味故事乐园13——看哲理故事学英语	32K	18.00
趣味故事乐园14——看爱情故事学英语	32K	18.00
趣味故事乐园16——看成功故事学英语	32K	19.00
趣味故事乐园17——看名人故事学英语	32K	19.00
英语成语源来如此	32K	25.00
英语词汇源来如此	32K	20.00
你不可不知道的英语学习背景知识——古希腊罗马神话与西方民间传说	16K	20.00
你不可不知道的英语学习背景知识——英美民间故事与民俗	16K	25.00
你不可不知道的英语学习背景知识——基督教与圣经	16K	33.00
你不可不知道的英语学习背景知识——美国历史重大事件及著名人物	16K	36.00
你不可不知道的英语学习背景知识——英国历史重大事件及著名人物	16K	33.00
教宝宝正确学英语	32K	15.00
英语幽默与笑话	32K	16.00
英语幽默与口语表达训练	32K	18.00
怎样起英文名字	32K	15.00
贺卡英语	32K	16.00
经典英文歌曲	16K	24.00
流行英文金曲	32K	19.80
有问必答——与中学英语语法对话(初中版)	32K	14.00
有问必答——与中学英语语法对话(高中版)	32K	17.00
有问必答——中考英语阅读高分技巧	32K	15.00
有问必答——高考英语阅读高分技巧	32K	15.00
有问必答——中考英语完形填空高分技巧	32K	14.00
有问必答——高考英语完形填空高分技巧	32K	15.00
中考英语作文高分技巧	32K	15.00
高考英语作文高分技巧	32K	16.00
中学英语常用词语辨析	32K	20.00

欢迎大家选购以上图书，邮资免付。　　邮编：100097

地址：北京市海淀区世纪城远大园4-12-1806室　　左小玉